India After Nehru
From Lal Bahadur Shastri to Narendra Modi

Reinforcing the Foundations of Misery

Rajnikant Puranik

ATLANTIC

PUBLISHERS & DISTRIBUTORS (P) LTD

Published by
ATLANTIC
PUBLISHERS & DISTRIBUTORS (P) LTD
7/22, Ansari Road, Darya Ganj, New Delhi-110002
Phones : +91-11-40775252, 23273880, 23275880, 23280451
Fax : +91-11-23285873
Web : www.atlanticbooks.com
E-mail : orders@atlanticbooks.com

Branch Office
5, Nallathambi Street, Wallajah Road, Chennai-600002
Phones : +91-44-64611085, 32413319
E-mail : chennai@atlanticbooks.com

Printed in India at Nice Printing Press, A-33/3A, Site-IV, Industrial Area, Sahibabad, Ghaziabad, U.P.

Dedicated to

The fond memory of my late parents

Shrimati Shakuntala

and

Shri Laxminarayan Puranik

Loyalty to country ALWAYS.
Loyalty to government, when it deserves it.

—Mark Twain

The duty of a patriot is to protect his country from its government.

—Thomas Paine

Patriotism means to stand by the country. It does not mean to stand by the president or any other public official, save exactly to the degree in which he himself stands by the country. It is patriotic to support him insofar as he efficiently serves the country. It is unpatriotic not to oppose him to the exact extent that by inefficiency or otherwise he fails in his duty to stand by the country. In either event, it is unpatriotic not to tell the truth, whether about the president or anyone else.

—Theodore Roosevelt

To cure the British disease with socialism
was like trying to cure leukaemia with leeches.

—Margaret Thatcher

Socialism in general has a record of failure so blatant that only an intellectual could ignore or evade it.

—Thomas Sowell

Preface

Many countries, including those in South-East Asia, which were nowhere near India or were much behind India at the time India got independence, have marched far ahead of India. When you look at their roads, their metros, their city-buses, their well laid-out cities, their infrastructure, their cleanliness, etc. you wonder why India has remained a country of crumbling roads, overcrowded locals, overhanging scary ugly mess of electrical, TV and Internet cables blotting the skyline; a country of absent pavements or encroached pavements, or pavements that stink from the use they are not meant for, being mere patches of broken down pavers, punctuated by uncovered, or partially covered, or precariously or deceptively covered manholes, awaiting their catch; a nation of stinking slums and impoverished villages, open drains and sewers, rotting garbage, dirty and uncomfortable conditions that people live or work in—all testimony to criminal absence of the very basics of being civilised.

Most of the Indian towns, cities and metros are dirty, foul smelling and hideous. They look like a defacement of spaces and a blot on the landscape. Cities in the West, South-East Asia, China and elsewhere get better and cleaner, year after year, while ours get worse, more congested, more difficult to live in and more squalid.

How's it that we got so left behind! What is it that we did, or did not do, after independence, that everything is so shabby and pathetic? Why is an overwhelming majority in India condemned to continue in abysmal misery?

And all this unmitigated misery despite the overwhelming advantage of India as a nation with first-rate people, plentiful natural resources, relatively better position in all fields—infrastructure, trained manpower, bureaucracy, army—at the time of independence, compared with all other nations who have since overtaken us, despite our grand civilisational heritage, rich culture and languages, and unmatched ethical and spiritual traditions.

A question, therefore, arises: Can a country attain greatness even if its leaders are Lilliputs; and vice versa, can the country's leaders be considered great even if the country goes to dogs, or remains wretchedly poor and achieves only a fraction of what it could have?

Unfortunately for the millions of Indians, particularly its poor, Jawaharlal Nehru, despite his best intentions, ended up as being ineffective, unwittingly laying the foundations of India's misery (detailed in *Foundations of Misery*, *India 1947-64: Blunders of the Nehruvian Era*).

Sadly, Nehru's dynasty reinforced those blighted foundations. The book covers the post-Nehru period of that calamitous reinforcement, not comprehensively, but selectively—picking up only those aspects considered critical if India has to rise from the depths to which it has been consigned. Consciously avoiding verbosity and many details, the coverage is deliberately as brief as possible, to make the book more readable.

Starting from the post-Nehru period of Lal Bahadur Shastri, the book covers the period of Indira Gandhi, Morarji Desai, Rajiv Gandhi, Narasimha Rao, Vajpayee and others; the last decade of Sonia-Rahul-Manmohan Singh; and the current relevant aspects related to the Dynasty, the BJP, the AAP, and right up to Narendra Modi.

We all Indian citizens hope that Narendra Modi would usher in a new era that would help India emerge from its misery and propel it forward into the ranks of the prosperous First-World—where India would have been by 1980 itself, had proper policies been followed.

Rajnikant Puranik

Contents

Excerpts

(EXCERPTS FROM THIS BOOK)

What is THE critical factor for assessing a country or a political party?

Its economic philosophy, its economic vision and its economic policies.

~~~

Are one or more of these the factors that make a country poor or prosperous: climate, geography, location, abundance of natural resources, race, history, "type of people", "character of people"?

NO. *None of these.*

What matters is the economic system chosen. All those countries, irrespective of these factors (climate, geography, race, "character",...), who adopted "competitive capitalism" have prospered and are part of the First World, like the US, Canada, the UK, West Europe, Japan, Taiwan, South Korea, Singapore, Australia, New Zealand. China prospered post-Mao after it junked Maoism and adopted a form of *Free Enterprise Economy*. It is worth noting that not a single socialist or communist country has ever prospered.

Raja Vyapari taya Praja Bhikhari.

—*Indian Proverb*

- - -

Mr Jawaharlal Nehru returned from Cambridge with notions of how an all-governing interventionist state can force people into
~~~

happiness and prosperity through socialism.... He sticks to this bias in spite of the demonstration of world experience against it.... I hate the present folly and arrogance as much as I hated the foreign arrogance of those [British] days.

—*C. Rajagopalachari (Rajaji)*

- - -

Sardar Patel, Rajagopalachari and Rajendra Prasad were opposed to socialism. If only they had led India after independence, rather than Nehru, India would have been a prosperous First-World country long ago, and it would hopefully have been saved from the debilitating feudal Dynastic democracy, that is at the root of all miseries.

~~~

It was the mercantile-industrial capitalism that led to democracy. Democracy did not evolve out of monarchy, oligarchy, feudalism, socialism or communism. The latter have only curbed freedom. Competitive capitalism/free enterprise Economy and democracy go together.

- - -

It's not as if there is a menu of systems, and one can choose which to adopt—socialism or communism or their different flavours, Gandhiism, capitalism, and so on.

Free enterprise and capitalism were not something that were first theorised, then planned, and then implemented or rammed down. They evolved as a sequence of civilisational growth, were taken cognizance of, and then theorised after the fact. Facts and practice led to the theory, and then the theory enhanced the practice. Thereafter, it was a beneficial evolving cycle, each helping enhance the other. Democracy, in turn, evolved out of free enterprise and capitalism; and again there was a cyclical effect between the two, each helping enhance the other.

In comparison, there is nothing natural, organic or evolutionary about socialism, communism or Gandhism. They are all highly deficient artificial constructs incapable of practical success because the human civilisational evolution is just too
~~~

complex, and there are far too many variables and too many unknowns for any artificial construct to contend with.

~~~

The term "Hindu rate of growth" is highly inappropriate and unfair, besides being derogatory. Post-independence low rate of growth was thanks to Nehru-Indira-Rajiv's policies. It should rather be called the "*Socialistic* or *Nehruvian* or *Secular* or *NIDP* [Nehru-Indira-Dynasty Policies] Rate of Growth". The rate of growth during the pre-independence colonial period, was even less. In fact, it had even turned negative during several long periods! Why was the rate of growth then not called the "Colonial rate of growth" or the "Christian rate of growth" in a pejorative sense?

~~~

Had India embraced *Competitive Capitalism* and *Free Enterprise Economy* after independence, rather than the successful-in-no-country poverty-perpetuating socialistic claptrap, India would have been a prosperous, first-rate, First-World country like Singapore, South Korea, Australia by 1980.

Unfortunately for the millions of poor, hungry and wretched of India, the Nehru-Indira Dynasty condemned them into the black-hole of copycat socialistic quagmire and callous-colonial-kleptocratic babudom.

- - -

Part-reversal of those world's-worst-economic-practices by the wise non-Dynasts like Narasimha Rao and Vajpayee dramatically turned hopelessness into hope. However, with the return of the Dynasts as UPA-I and II and their rollback to the bad-old-ways, Rao-Vajpayee kindled sunshine of hope again turned into gray cynical hopelessness.

- - -

Much was expected from the new kid on the block full of young fresh faces—AAP. But the party's economic policies seem to have been hijacked by the predominance of pink-to-red-hot jholawallahs.

What then is the difference between the AAP and the Congress plus similar other parties? Only that AAP is sanctimonious, holier-than-thou and is so far not corrupt. But that's because it's a new party, not yet corrupted by power. Would it remain so? Only time can tell—not their loud protestations and self-certifications. But telling white lies, being abusive, defaming others without evidence, and spreading misinformation to gain unfair advantage (in getting votes and power) is also a form of corruption. Corruption is not only about accepting money. If my conscience does not prick in telling destructive lies and being abusive, would it prick when I graduate to also accepting money?

However, AAP deserves credit and kudos for practically demonstrating that even a new political party can win elections without the hitherto-considered-must-negatives (money-power, muscle-power, enticements, casteist or communal propaganda,...), if they can convince people they indeed have something positive to offer. It is also creditable that they have managed to attract many good candidates, with excellent background and clean records, for Lok Sabha elections.

~~~

Corruption is certainly an important issue, but if it is a serious political party which wants to take India out of its depth, it can't be the only issue or even the main issue. The foremost issues have to be economic policies; good governance; implementing wide-ranging economic, administrative, police, judicial and electoral reforms; external security and foreign policy; and internal security, including tackling the red-corridor and the northeast. Reforms themselves would take care of the major avenues of corruption.

~~~

In the context of AAP, MMS (Manmohan Singh), A.K. Antony, and the like, it is well to remember that honesty is a basic requirement, a pre-requisite for a job, it is not a qualification, nor a measure of competence. Can you employ a driver who is honest, but is rash and not quite skilled at the wheels? Further, personal honesty is not enough, professional honesty is the real test. Professional honesty demands you ensure the conduct of those under you is also honest and above board. Personal honesty is easier as it concerns only yourself; while professionally honesty is difficult—it requires guts and competence to manage, evaluate, judge and control those under you, and ability to withstand pressure, if any, from your peers and seniors.

~~~

What about BJP? Would it prove to be better than all the others? BJP of the BJP-Old-Guard-At-Delhi is not much different, though perhaps relatively better. However, Narendra Modi does bring a breath of fresh air and a ray of hope. Modi is honest and has an excellent track record. What would really happen, one can't predict, but for the sake of the nation, one does ardently hope he would deliver and do to India what he has done for Gujarat, and much more. One only hopes the Swadeshi-Jagran-Manch-types won't come in the way.

- - -

One also hopes Modi would bring such communal harmony and peace in India, like he has done during the last 11 years in Gujarat through good governance that the communal cards of the parties like the Congress, the SP and others would go defunct. Among the reasons, these parties are so rabidly anti-Modi is their genuine fear that by doing a Gujarat (post-2002) on India (that is, making all of India as communally peaceful as Gujarat has been since 2003) he may indeed make communalism a non-issue denying them their vote-banks. Establishment-friendly leftist-"secularist" intellectuals and a section of the media are also ferociously anti-Modi afraid their positions and privileges and interests would be adversely affected.

~~~

The DDC [Dynasty-driven Congress] can't countenance others. They think they have an inalienable right to misgovern India.... And they feel they are not finished with India yet—there is still a great scope to take it further to dogs.

~~~
~~~

Madam Prime Minister, can you tell this august House why Indians are successful everywhere in the world except under the rule of your government?

—a revealing parliamentary question to Indira Gandhi addressed by Piloo Mody of Swatantra Party

~~~

One Oleg Kalugin of KGB, who became the head of the Counter Intelligence in 1973, remembered India as *a model of KGB infiltration of a Third World government*. The most shocking comment of Kalugin about India was that *it was as if the entire country was for sale*! He even recalled an occasion where the demand of an Indian minister for $50,000, in exchange for information, was refused by the Soviets, *as they claimed they already had more than enough information*!!

—based on "The Mitrokhin Archive II : The KGB and the World"

~~~

The current Indira regime, founded on 25 June 1975, was born through lies, nurtured by lies, and flourishes by lies. The essential ingredient of its being is the lie.

—Opinion, a Mumbai magazine, on the Emergency of 1975-77

~~~

It was a State off-limits, a government that hijacked the whole edifice of the state, a ruling party and leader who in effect treated the state as their personal estate.... It was one big swoop overtaking the whole country, spreading a psychosis of fear and terror with the new upstarts storming away through whatever came their way, pulling it all down and calling boo to it all. And it happened in this country after 28 years of democratic functioning.

—Rajni Kothari, on the Emergency of 1975-77

Indira Gandhi gave the election slogan "*Garibi Hatao*! (*Remove Poverty*!)" What could be more hypocritical? Was it some other political party ruling since independence that had
~~~

caused "*Garibi* (poverty)"? *Garibi* was thanks to her father's disastrous policies; and she indulged in more of the same.

There is a weirdly funny sense of *déjà vu* when in the current election campaign Rahul Gandhi talks of "*Removing Corruption*!" Who has been responsible for the mega corruptions in the last decade?

Many of the economic reforms required now in 2014 comprise turning the clock back to 1969—the pre-Indira period, since Indira asserted herself 1969 onwards and inflicted heavy dose of debilitating socialistic policies.

~~~

The focus of our socialism is...to attain these ends, we believe the State must control the commanding heights of the economy....

—claimed "economic liberaliser" Rajiv Gandhi in his speech at the Qinghua University

If he [Rajiv] was not the author of the order to 'teach the Sikhs a lesson', he did nothing to countermand it.

—Khushwant Singh on 1984 anti-Sikh attacks

When a tree falls, the earth shakes under it....

—Rajiv Gandhi on 1984 anti-Sikh attacks

Rajiv Gandhi was apparently so unconcerned that he did not even think it necessary to express regret on the attacks or sympathy with the victims in the Parliament. As in the Bofors later, all probes and enquiries were aborted and the guilty were not brought to book. Some of the alleged perpetrators were rewarded with better posts, promotions or ministries.

- - -

...Rajiv Gandhi had 400 MPs, a Supreme Court verdict, and a liberal Muslim (Arif Mohammed Khan) willing to bat for him. That he still flunked it may be attributed either to a lack of a sense of history or a lack of a robust commitment to liberal principles—or perhaps both.

—Ramchandra Guha on Shah Banu Case

- - -
~~~

...But he [Rajiv Gandhi] watched the massive cover-up in India and Sweden and did nothing. Many Indian institutions were tarred, innocent people were punished while the guilty got away. The evidence against Ottavio Quattrocchi was conclusive... bribes paid by Bofors landed in Quattrocchi's account which he subsequently cleaned out because India said there was no evidence linking him to the Bofors deal.... Whenever the public prosecutor Ekblom and I heard of any Indian visits to Stockholm, we would speak to the media expressing our desire to meet them. Can you imagine a situation where no one from India met the real investigators of the gun deal?...

—Sten Lindstrom, the then head of Swedish police, on Bofors

If thousands of freedom fighters won us freedom; if the Nehru-Indira Dynasty plunged India into poverty and economic disaster; then it was Narasimha Rao who ushered in economic freedom—the Second Freedom.

Why rule for the sake of ruling if there is nothing specific to achieve.

—Narasimha Rao

~~~

Manmohan Singh is an honest man in a pecuniary sense, but not in the high political-moral sense, as someone who wants to correct wrongs in governance by taking on dishonest people or practices.

—Comment by a former senior secretary quoted by Vinod Jose in The Caravan magazine of 1 October 2011

- - -

...But the image of the scrupulously honorable, humble and intellectual technocrat has slowly given way to a completely different one: a dithering, ineffectual bureaucrat presiding over a deeply corrupt government....

—Simon Denyer in The Washington Post of 5 September 2012

~~~

The biggest menace threatening India is not poverty or backwardness or corruption or lack of governance or socialism-babudom, but feudal dynastic-democracy, because that is at the root of the former deficiencies, and is the foundation of India's misery. The principal hazards of dynasty politics are: it discounts merit and prevents competent from rising; it thwarts internal democracy in political parties, so vital for a healthy democracy; dynastic politics, nepotism, institutionalised corruption and non-accountability go together; it has a vested interest in continuance at the expense of the nation.

As per the article "World's Only RDC" in *India Today*'s issue of 12 August 2013, Japan, which had almost the same GDP as India in the early 1950s, grew so fast that by 1980, India's GDP was a mere 17% of Japan's. Japan grew at massive 18% annually during the 15-year period starting 1965 and took its GDP from 91 billion dollars to a mammoth 1.1 trillion dollars by 1980. In 1982, India's per capita income was 39% higher than China's; but, by 2012, it had become mere 24% of China's—during the period China's per capita income grew 30 times, while India's grew mere five times. South Korea's per capita income is currently 1400% that of India, although at the time of our independence it was on par! While India is variously terms as a DC (Developing Country) or LDC (Less Developed Country) or UDC (Under Developed Country), the article finds India uniquely as a RDC—*Refusing-to-Develop-Country*.

~~~

Faced with a plethora of negatives and with little positives to show for the overlong dynasty-rule, the unabashed defenders and apologists of the establishment and the dynasty come up with innovative "it could have been worse" counterfactuals: But for the dynasty, India could have fallen apart, it could have been a military dictatorship, it could have gone the way of Pakistan,... What if someone posed an alternate counterfactual: Had India been led by other than the dynasty after independence, it would have been a much more united, strong, rich, prosperous, first-rate country, with hunger and poverty a distant memory, and
~~~

would have joined the First-World countries like the US, the UK, Singapore and Australia by 1980!

~~~

Among the very basics expected from any government is safety for its citizens, particularly the vulnerable sections like the minorities, dalits, women and children. This is fundamental. Other things come later. Communalism and casteism would have become non-issues within a decade of independence had there been good governance and strict enforcement of the "rule of law", coupled with mass-education and mass-campaigns. However, the terms were turned into weapons to commend or condemn parties and people, and to create vote-banks. If a party claims to be secular, the touchstone of its credentials ought to be "governance", and not its words and self-certifications. Like one measures GDP or poverty-index, one needs to also measure Governance Index (GI)—it is GI which would actually reflect Secularism Index (SI).

- - -

It is important to realise that managing a country as large and as complex as India requires deep knowledge of India's different regions and people, its politics, its administration, its economy, its culture, its history, its strengths, its weaknesses and its international relations; intelligence to absorb them, experience to manage, competence to deal with complexities, and wisdom to take right decisions. Do the dynasty scions measure up? Certainly not.

- - -

In the interest of the nation, an iron law should be laid down: First prove your leadership competence in a public or private or political organisation or an NGO; then as a minister in a state or at the Centre or as a Chief Minister of a State for at least five years; and then only a candidate should be allowed to put himself or herself up as a Prime Minister.

- - -

We study, analyse and implement risk-mitigation in all walks of life: finance, banking, management, software, health,
~~~

transport, real-estate, security and so on. Practically, no segment is left untouched by it. However, when it comes to the biggest risk of all—that of the position of the Prime Minister—we seem to be casual, rather criminally callous.

How else to explain the projection of Rahul Gandhi as a candidate for prime ministership? What are his credentials? Has he practically proved himself in any field? And, his talks—grossly immature!

~~~

Looking to the miserable state of India, one would have expected a powerful medium like television, with its vast reach, to highlight problems and issues. But no. The Indian TV channels are happy broadcasting inanities. News for Indian news channels are only some odd things happening at New Delhi or Mumbai. It is as if India of the other metros, over a thousand cities and towns and over six hundred thousand villages does not exist. News is mostly what some political bloke said or what BCCI or IPL did. And, what sort of discussions they have? Gossips based on guesses. 9 pm news and discussions on most news channels seems like post-dinner prattle and time-pass. Most TV debates are as pointless and predictable as the Saas-Bahu serials.

~~~

A typical intellectual is a staid, leftist, "secular" intellectual who does not have anything much different to say from the hundreds others like him. It's like the RSS-types or the communists: all speak the same stale language. A typical Indian intellectual is a conformist who has learnt what types of opinions to vent and what sort of stand to take to be accepted as an "intellectual". He is not a rebel, he knows which side the bread is buttered.

In India, you just have to get familiar with the "leftist, anti-American, pro-Arab, anti-Israel, 'secularist', Hindu-baiting, Muslim-apologist, Nehruvian, JNU-type" refrain and jargon to qualify as an intellectual. It's that easy. No serious knowledge or expertise or research work or analytical ability or originality or depth or integrity is required. Besides, it is safe. Others won't heckle you.

- - -

Then there are the RSS-types. Despite diverse geographic regions and dozens of languages in India, you have to credit them for managing to speak in one language. They have their own elaborate mythology, both on India's past going back thousands of years, and on the contemporary India. What happened to India with a golden past? Why is Kaliyug India weak, poor and wretched? Character! Lack of character! We need to first build character. Our mission: character-building across India. No questions asked. Such a brilliant non-mind-straining diagnosis-remedy pair—uncomplicated, straight-forward and simple, and easy to absorb and repeat and spread! Blasphemy, if someone were to counter-question: "Why Australia of the characterless convicts progressed to be a first-rate, First-World country?"

~~~

INDIA'S BAFFLING MENTAL SLAVERY

You come across building names like Blooming Heights, Delphi, Glen Gate, Kensington, Somerset...; street names like Orchard Avenue, Ridge Street... Advertisements in property pull-out pages of newspapers have firang faces gazing out. Have we run out of Indian names and faces? Or, are Indian names and faces not hip!

- - -

Actors, directors and sundries of Hindi movies, rather than talking in Hindi about their Hindi films, always make it a point to converse only in their atrocious English. No Hindi in Hindi-movie award functions! Only English—broken or otherwise. Even the titles of Hindi movies are mostly in English: *A Wednesday, Blood Money*, *Dirty Picture*, *Don 2*,... Also the titles, credits and castings at the beginning and at the end of Hindi movies.

- - -

Sample the names of the various points at Matheran hill station: Hart Point, Mount Barry, Malet Road, King George Point,...all English names. Strangely, no point is named after
~~~

the persons who made Matheran a popular hill-station by constructing a railway line in 1909 on such a difficult, steep, hilly terrain and running a toy train on it, all with their own investment! Why? Because, those persons happened to be Indians—Adamjee Peerbhoy and his son, Abdul Hussain. What a shame!

~~~

It was only when Bulganin and Khrushchev of the USSR visited India in late 1955 that India changed the names Kingsway to Rajpath and Queensway to Janpath in New Delhi, lest the guests feel shocked at our slavishness! However, Khrushchev did not fail to notice the statue of King George V opposite India Gate when driving down Rajpath, and wondered why the relic still stood. Strangely, it was only in 1968 that the statue was removed, and that too upon public outcry!

~~~

Bengal Club in Kolkata did not allow Indians till a decade after independence! Breach Candy Club in Mumbai continued with its sign "*Dogs and Indians not allowed*" well after independence!! Khushwant Singh wrote that he was turned away from Madras Club because he was wearing sandals. In another context, he wrote that their group was invited to Delhi Gymkhana for a cocktail only to check whether they were properly anglicised and fitted-in!

~~~

Our TV and print media keeps referring to the area of Raisina Hill, Rajpath, and so on as Lutyens' Delhi, after the British architect, Edwin Lutyens, and there have even been grand receptions for his descendents in Delhi from the President down; little realising that Lutyens had utter contempt for India and the Indians, and wrote very insultingly about them like: "...but the low intellect of the natives spoils much and I do not think it possible for the Indians and whites to mix freely and naturally.... They [about an Indian minion] ought to be reduced to slavery and not given the rights of man and beaten like brute beasts and shot like man eaters...."

~~~

What did the "famed" British judicial system do to Reginald Edward Harry Dyer, the *butcher of Amritsar,* who massacred over a thousand and injured many more at Jallianwala Bagh in 1919, and who gave a "crawling order" whereby all Indians using a certain prominent street in Amritsar had to crawl 200 yards on all fours, lying flat on their bellies. Nothing. He was tried by the Hunter Commission, but got away without any punishment—he was only censured. As if that was not enough, upon his return to Britain he was presented a sword of honour and a purse for being "the saviour of Punjab"! In the film *Gandhi* of David Attenborough, the director shows the trial of Dyer to impress the audience the world over the grandness of the British judicial system; without revealing that Dyer received no punishment, and was rewarded back home!

- - -

You hear educated people talk appreciatively of the author Rudyard Kipling. But, what that character, without any conscience, had done? Claiming that Dyer (of Jallianwala massacre) was the man who had saved India, he had started a benefit fund for Dyer, raising over £26,000! A class of Indians is so shameless, slavish, and lacking in self-respect that it wanted to convert the house where Kipling lived in India into a museum!

1
Harvesting Misery—Unabated!

One is reminded of a quotable comment of Konrad Adenauer, the first chancellor of West Germany, that is, Federal Republic of Germany (FRG), who took his nation from the ruins of World War II to the most prosperous nation in Europe: "History is the sum total of the things that could have been avoided." It also holds true for India. How one wishes the quagmire the policies of the Nehru-Indira Dynasty threw India in had been avoided. Even more, one wishes India had altogether avoided the feudal dynastic-democracy that proved to be its undoing.

Chapter 1 of *Foundations of Misery* incorporates detailed recent statistics on varied parameters to bring out the misery that is India. The same is not repeated here. However, statistics are faceless and do not bring home the actual, pathetic status of the masses. As Joseph Stalin had commented, "The death of one man is a tragedy, the death of millions is a statistic." When you empathetically imagine or actually see one innocent, helpless child crying of hunger, going to sleep on empty or half-empty stomach, growing up stunted for lack of adequate food and nutrition, ever liable to diseases, living in dirt and squalor and stink all around for no fault of his or her, that the tragedy strikes you, and when you know it to be the fate of millions that you feel depressed, angry and unforgiving: unforgiving of those who chose to be your leaders—nobody forced them into it—and miserably failed in their basic responsibilities, not on account of any external or internal factors, but primarily on account of their own incompetence, yet continued in their netagiri year after year, without making way for the capable ones.

Had India embraced competitive capitalism after independence, rather than the successful-in-no-country poverty-perpetuating socialistic claptrap, India would have been a prosperous, first-rate, First-World country like Singapore, South Korea, Australia by 1980. Abnormally for India, rather than progressing, we are sliding downhill in many spheres!

Corruption, for example. Rather than the expected gradual decrease to its final disappearance, we have been witnessing ever more increase in corruption both in its scope and its scale: even as the cancer is spreading to more and more areas, its scale is growing phenomenally—scamsters have graduated from what once used to be shocking misappropriation of lacs to a few crores to post-graduation with several hundred crores, to now doctorate and post-doctorate with thousands of crores.

Across the globe, in all progressive countries, metros, cities, towns and villages are getting cleaner and better and more liveable, while ours are going from bad to worse to unliveable! Transportation within metros and cities is becoming more and more a huge pain. Slums are becoming bigger and filthier. You will come across Mumbaikars wistfully describing Mumbai of the fifties, sixties and seventies, while expressing disgust at Mumbai of today. The same applies for most cities—we have become worse, not better!

Our external security has been bleeding us thanks to no border agreements with our two major neighbours.

With the huge expansion of the red corridor, worsening problems in the northeast and J&K, and growing jehadi terrorism, our internal security has been getting more and more precarious.

Rather than an enhancement in the quality and content of our democracy and strengthening of our democratic institutions, what we have been witnessing is a steady erosion since the fifties. While the outward form has been kept, the content has been hijacked through dynastification. Ironically, Nehru who raved mad against rajas, maharajas and feudalism laid the foundation of dynacracy—the dynastic democracy. He ensured his dynasty substituted the dynasty of the feudal maharajas after independence. Following in his footsteps, his daughter and descendents reinforced the foundation. Learning from their example, now you have scores of dynasties at the state level. From a stage soon after independence where Gandhi never promoted his own progeny and Sardar Patel forbade his son and relatives to even meet him in Delhi, where have we come?

There is increased criminalisation of the politics. Democratic institutions were partly compromised by Nehru, hugely subverted by Indira Gandhi, and have since only gone downhill with their descendents.

Arrogant, self-serving colonial babudom, rather than giving way to people-oriented empathetic bureaucracy after independence, has transformed itself into a venal arm of the establishment. No wonder it is now rated as the worst bureaucracy in Asia.

We are told we had truly great leaders like Jawaharlal Nehru, Indira Gandhi and Rajiv Gandhi who lead us respectively for 17, 16 and 7 years after independence—a total of 40 long years! And, all the three were awarded *Bharat Ratnas* for leading India "capably". It is claimed they also laid the foundation for a "strong" India. But the puzzle is: How is it that such great leaders could do no better than make India one of the poorest countries on earth?

Look at anything—nothing makes you feel good. The only good thing is, one is told: it could have been worse! We are told that the economy is now much better thanks to the Narasimha Rao-led period; that it was much worse before; and had pre-Narasimha Rao status continued, the scenario would have been much more horrifying!

This part, Part-II, deals with the reinforcement of the defective Nehruvian foundations in the post-Nehru period, thanks to Indira Gandhi and her dynasty, resulting in "misery unabated".

Incorrigibly, rather than learning lessons from their abysmal performance during the last decade and the pathetic status till 1991, and rather than taking India forward like Narasimha Rao and Vajpayee did, you find Sonia-Rahul-led Congress espousing policies that would take India back to the bad old Nehru-Indira-Rajiv days. The Congress Manifesto of 2014-19 had further handouts and doles lined up and incorporated further regressive steps like "reservation in the private sector".

Apart from the curse of the dynasties, both in the States and the Centre, India has the unique distinction of being gifted with powerful and influential groups and cabals like the LIDS: Leftist Intellectual Deformists ventilating their Socialistic/Nehruvian, Staid, Stale, Self-Serving, 'Secular' claptrap. These parasitic cabals have spawned the sarkari establishments, the academe, the art houses, and the NGOs—even universities abroad. They have also infested the other opinion-making arms like the media. It would be grossly unfair not to credit the LIDS along with the Dynasty for taking India to dogs, and for still persisting and resisting attempts to pull India out of the black hole they have jointly thrown India into, by perverting sensible discourse and spreading misinformation. They can't imagine being dislodged from their cozy positions and are one with the Dynasty in concocting rationale for their joint continuance.

Will the young Indians see through the game?

2

Shastri: Political Idealism Post Nehru

Quite irrespective of the fact that the balance sheet of the Nehru-period was deep in red, it cannot be denied that Nehru was patriotic, honest and meant well: it is another matter that his erroneous understanding of economics, foreign affairs, external security and many more things led to policies that proved disastrous for the country.

Lal Bahadur Shastri, who followed Nehru, came to be immensely respected for his simple living and high thinking. He was exceptionally patriotic and principled, and people had faith he would do well for the nation. Shastri had spent many years in jail fighting for India's independence.

As Home Minister during 1961-63, he appointed a *Committee on Prevention of Corruption* under K. Santhanam. It was Shastri who, concerned with growing corruption, converted the SPE (Special Police Establishment under the Home Ministry) into the CBI (*Central Bureau of Investigation*). Shastri also deliberated on the appointment of a *Lokpal*, proposed by Santhanam. Shastri never shielded the high and mighty if they were found to have indulged in corrupt practices. Within a few days of submission of the Das Commission Report, Shastri took action against Pratap Singh Kairon, Chief Minister of Punjab—someone whom Nehru had defended.

As Prime Minister (PM), although his tenure was short (June 1964-January 1966), he succeeded in bringing focus on agriculture, something neglected by Nehru. He implemented a series of measures that ultimately led to the *Green Revolution*—a revolutionary achievement he unfortunately did not live to see. It thankfully ended the humiliating India-with-a-begging-bowl days under Nehru. The main credit for the Green Revolution should go to Lal Bahadur Shastri, C. Subramaniam, the then Minister for Food & Agriculture, M.S. Swaminathan, Varghese Kurien and also to Nobel Laureate, Norman Borlaug. The ground work for the Green Revolution was laid between 1964 and 1967 under the political guidance of C. Subramaniam, when for the initial years Shastri was the PM. Indira Gandhi helped further it when she took up the actual reins of power upon Congress split in 1969, although she came to power in 1966.

He gave the slogan *Jai Jawan Jai Kisan* that fired up the Indian public and brought focus on the two neglected areas under Nehru: Agriculture and External Security. Shastri was also instrumental in the *White Revolution*. Impressed by what he saw at Anand under Dr Verghese Kurien and Tribhuvandas Patel, he set up National Dairy Development Board (NDDB) in 1965.

Unlike Nehru, Shastri was a quick decision taker. During the 1965 Indo-Pak War, he didn't dilly-dally on the advice of the top-brass of the military and promptly ordered a strike across the Punjab border, which helped India gain an upper hand. Lt. General Harbaksh Singh, the General-Officer-Commanding-in-Chief of the Western Army Command from 1964 to 1969 decorated with Vir Chakra and Padma Vibhushan for his outstanding leadership during the war, had told that the army could never forget that "tallest decision from the shortest man".

This was in sharp contrast to Nehru who had refused in 1962 to call in the air force to relieve pressure on the ground troops. During the period leading up to the 1962 Indo-China War and during the conduct of the war itself, it was the Nehru-Menon duo which was calling the shots, over-ruling and insulting [this, by Menon] the top-brass of the military, and building and executing their own preposterous strategy, which ultimately led to pathetic consequences.

Win in the 1965-war, thanks also to Shastri, helped Indian army regain their prestige, and created a feel-good atmosphere among the Indian public, after the crushing humiliation in the India-China war under Nehru.

Shastri, like Sardar Patel, had little when he died. Although Shastri had been a Cabinet Minister for many years and then the PM, he was poor when he died. All he owned at the end was an old car: that too he had bought in instalments from the government, and for which he still owed money.

More than values, Shastri's early death resulted in loss of opportunity for pragmatic economic policies that he was focussing on. Had he lived, India would have fared significantly well on all fronts, particularly on the economic front, and would have tackled poverty head on.

He was the PM for less than two years—19 months. Yet, within this short period, he gave India hope. He proved in practice through his deeds that an unassuming commoner like him was far more capable of doing good for the nation than the high-profile, hubris-driven Nehru or the dynasts that followed later; and that "After Nehru Who?" was just a charade to publicise the indispensability of Nehru.

Shastri died in January 1966 at Tashkent where he had gone for Indo-Pak talks with the President of Pakistan, General Ayub Khan. Though he reportedly died of heart attack, his death was shrouded in mystery. Apparently, no post-mortem was conducted to ascertain the real cause of death either in the USSR or in India—and that was abnormal. It has been alleged that he died of poisoning, as his body, when brought to India, had turned blue—although that might have been so from embalming. His last meal in the night was sent from the home of T.N. Kaul, the Indian ambassador. Shastri's family suspected foul play.

Request for access to papers relating to Shastri's death under the RTI (Right to Information Act) have been turned down—that raises further suspicion. There appears to be an undisclosed policy not to disclose anything that might in any small or big way impact the dynasty. Papers related to Subhas Bose disappearance remain secret, as also Henderson-Brooks report on 1962 India-China war (please read *Foundations of Misery: Blunders of the Nehruvian Era*).

Incidentally, Ayub Khan, happy with his interaction with Shastri at Tashkent, had stated after Shastri's death that had Shastri lived perhaps Indo-Pak differences would have been resolved.

True to the dynastic tradition, Indira Gandhi acted small and mean on the cremation-related matters of Shastri. Nehru had done so for Dr Rajendra Prasad and others (please see *Foundations of Misery: Blunders of the Nehruvian Era*), and Sonia Gandhi did so for Narasimha Rao. The dynasty's policy is to deny prominence to anyone other than the members of its clan. If cremation was done in Delhi, many more would visit the samadhi in the times to come, and those laid to rest there would be respected and remembered. However, if it was done elsewhere, there was no such risk. Indira Gandhi wanted the cremation to be in Allahabad, Shastri's home town. By that logic, Nehru's funeral too should have been held at Allahabad, which was Nehru's home town. However, in the face of threat of fast unto death by Lalita Shastri, widow of Lal Bahadur Shastri, Indira relented. Indira also didn't want the popular slogan given by Shastri, "*Jai Jawan Jai Kisan*", to be engraved on his Samadhi as desired by Lalita Shastri, but later agreed. It is indeed a matter of shame for the Indian public and its other leaders and media that the dynasty takes such liberties, yet gets away with it!

THE ANAND EPISODE

Here are two contrasting episodes of Nehru and Shastri related to Anand based on the anecdotes in *I Too Had a Dream*, an autobiography of Dr Verghese Kurien of Anand Dairy fame, as told to Gouri Salvi, the author, and published by Roli Books. It is a book full of interesting anecdotes, and is worth reading.

It was Sardar Patel who had backed Kaira's farmers—Kaira is the district in which Anand is situated—and had encouraged the dairy farmers to organise milk cooperatives. Sardar assigned to Morarji Desai the task of coordinating the effort. The main ground work for setting up the milk cooperative was done by Tribhuvandas Patel, who actually deserves the main credit for the success of the Anand Model, along with Kurien.

Looking to the encouraging results of the Anand Model, many dignitaries started paying visit. Nehru came to inaugurate the Dairy on 31 October 1955. 31 October is the birthday of Sardar Patel. There were no hotels or guest houses in Anand in those days, so Nehru and Indira stayed with Kurien. Detailed and elaborate instructions on food and other requirements of Nehru preceded him, including the kind of rose required for his buttonhole.

Nehru came, inaugurated, praised Kurien and other persons involved, and then left. He did not go to the villages or meet the dairy farmers or the workers or showed any interest or inclination to do so—this from a person who reportedly loved his people and wanted his ashes to be sprinkled all over India!

In sharp contrast, Lal Bahadur Shastri, the then PM, who came to Anand on 31 October 1964 for the inauguration of the Cattle-Feed Compounding Factory, sent advance instructions that he would come a day in advance and would stay with a farmer in a village overnight, and that there should be absolutely no special arrangements for him. So that no intimidating security presence be there, Shastri's going to the specific village was kept a secret. The concerned farmer had been told that two foreign guests curious to know village life would come, and that apart from keeping his place clean, he need not do anything special. When told at the last minute who the guests were, he was taken aback, pleading that his family had cooked no special food. Shastri stayed with him, shared his food, went for a walk in the village, talked to the farmers and their families, got first-hand information on their living conditions and on the cooperative, and how it worked. He visited the huts of dalits in the village, sat with them, and talked to them. He also visited the Muslim families in the village. He was busy interacting with the villagers till 2 am in the morning!

Retiring late in the night and waking up early the next day, he visited the cooperative society and interacted with its elected representatives. Shastri later discussed with Kurien how the Anand Model could be replicated across India. This finally led to the foundation of NDDB—National Dairy Development Board.

The sharp contrast between Nehru and Shastri is telling!

3
3G–Indira Gandhi

LOSS OF VALUES

After Shastri's death, values departed from the Indian political life, and politics and governance became increasingly amoral. Indira Gandhi served as PM for about 11 years between 1966 and 1977, and then again for about five years between 1980 and 1984, a total of about 16 years. Despite struggling for many years in India and abroad, Indira could not complete her graduation. It is another matter that many universities/institutes are named after Nehru, Indira and Rajiv despite all of them having been gross academic under-achievers notwithstanding the liberal facilities they enjoyed and expenses on their education abroad.

With Indira Gandhi, politics became personalized. Cronyism dominated. Indian National Congress under Indira Gandhi was no longer the party which had fought for independence. In fact, "Indira Congress" is an appropriate nomenclature for the Congress since Indira Gandhi, so as to remove its association with the pre-independence Congress and its values. The Congress since Indira has no business to claim the heritage. Indira Congress became a party of sycophants. Sycophancy indeed commenced with Nehru, but it reached its ugly nadir with Indira Gandhi.

Institutions began to erode. CBI was set up by Lal Bahadur Shastri to fight corruption. But CBI came into real prominence under Indira, not to fight corruption, but to harass her opponents —she converted it into an instrument of vendetta and tyranny. Her descendents are upholding those 'great' traditions.

Economic strangulation thanks to Indira's further descent into poverty-and-misery perpetuating socialism-babudom, coupled with shameless loss of values, ultimately led to Emergency.

EMERGENCY

Midnight, 25-26 June 1975 was the blackest hour for Indian democracy. On that hour, not for any larger or national consideration, but driven solely by preservation of personal position and the Dynasty rule, Indira Gandhi replaced democracy and freedom for the next 21 months between 25-26 June 1975 and 23 March 1977 with the darkest period in the history of Indian democracy—the Emergency—converting India into a tin-pot dictatorship. The Emergency officially ended on 23 March 1977, although the elections were announced on 23 January 1977. She jailed political opponents, silenced media-critics, censored news, and extinguished fundamental rights. Extremely strict press censorship was imposed—criticism of the government or of the Emergency was not permitted. She promoted herself and her unscrupulous, irresponsible son, Sanjay. A personality cult around her and her son was shamelessly built. Corrupt practices both in terms of money and in exercise of power became the norm. Like in a dictatorship, no compunction was shown in deploying any means to demolish anyone who stood in their way.

A High Court judge in Allahabad found Indira Gandhi guilty of electoral malpractices in 1975. An appeal against the judgement could have been made to the Supreme Court. However, pending the Supreme Court's decision, Indira Gandhi would have had to vacate prime minister's chair, and let another Congress person take the PM's chair in the interim. Even this little temporary arrangement she was not ready for. Nehru-Gandhis felt they were born to rule, and the thought of vacating their ruling-position, even temporarily, was abhorrent to them. What was the solution? Declare internal Emergency and retain power. The excuse given was the disruption of peace thanks to the veteran Gandhian Jayaprakash Narayan's movement against corruption and misgovernance, and of a 'foreign hand' wanting to destabilise India. There was actually no threat to India whatsoever. It was the freedom of public opinion and of media that was a threat to Indira, and that had to be muzzled through the Emergency.

Wrote *Opinion*, a Mumbai magazine: "The current Indira regime, founded on 25 June 1975, was born through lies, nurtured by lies, and flourishes by lies. The essential ingredient of its being is the lie."

Indira Gandhi was not new to the Emergency's dictatorial methods. She entertained a dictatorial mindset and arrogance since long. Writes Kuldip Nayar in *Beyond the Lines*: "Her [Indira Gandhi] record as minister for information and broadcasting was considered to have been at best mediocre. There were many who had been slighted by her during Nehru's days in power." She used to resent her father accommodating views of those she didn't like and yielding powers to states. The democratically-elected Communist government of Kerala was dismissed in 1956 during her presidency of the Congress, and at her instance.

The babudom—IAS, IPS, IRS and the police and the babus down the line—caved in to the dictates of the dictatorial and unscrupulous Indira and her irresponsible wayward son, Sanjay, rather than upholding the institutions they were responsible for. IAS, the so-called steel frame—may have been steel frame for the British to suppress the natives—showed their true colours: willingness to lick the boots of the powerful so long as their position, perks and pelf remained protected.

As for the Main Stream Media (MSM), L.K. Advani summed it up best: "When they were asked to bend, they preferred to crawl." Sadly, the current MSM is not much better—most still suck up to the Dynasty and the Establishment. A few editors had even gone to meet Indira Gandhi to congratulate her for imposing the Emergency. Indira, in her usual arrogance, asked them as to what had happened to the big names in journalism because not a dog had barked! About a lakh were arrested and detained indefinitely without trial during the Emergency, while many more were ruthlessly treated and mercilessly harassed.

The article "Never Forget the Emergency!" by M.G. Devasahayam dated 26 June 2010 in rediff.com says: "The dark era was far more devious than just denial of personal liberty, arrest and torture of several thousand individuals and forced sterilisation by the state. It was about basic violations of democratic norms and crude attempts to legitimise a new type of regime and new criteria of allocation of rights and obligations. It was the abrogation of any sense of boundary or restraint in the exercise of power, and the striking growth of arbitrariness and arrogance with which citizens were turned into subjects." It also quotes civil rights activist Rajni Kothari: "It was a State off-limits, a government that hijacked the whole edifice of the state, a ruling party and leader who in effect treated the state as their personal estate.... It was one big swoop overtaking the whole country, spreading a psychosis of fear and terror with the new upstarts storming away through whatever came their way, pulling it all down and calling boo to it all. And it happened in this country after 28 years of democratic functioning."

The American economist, statistician, writer and Nobel Laureate Milton Friedman in his highly influential and analytical book *Capitalism and Freedom* argued, among other things, that economic freedom (which competitive capitalism provides) was a precondition for political freedom, giving example of many countries. The *Times Literary Supplement* selected it as one of the 'hundred most influential books since the war' and *The Economist* described Milton Friedman as "the most influential economist of the second half of the 20th century...possibly of all of it." The book was first published in 1962. Had it been published after 1977, Friedman could have included so illustrative an example as the Indian Emergency of 1975-77 as an additional proof of his theory. India's slide into leftism and socialism under Nehru, and its turning pink under his daughter and her leftist-socialist-crypto-communist Kashmiri-mafia comprising P.N. Dhar, T.N. Kaul and R.N. Kao had to lead to poverty, want, hunger, deprivation, followed by public unrest and ultimately loss of liberty in the form of Emergency.

That 'Indira Gandhi had love and respect for democracy' which many 'chamchas' [flatterers] advance, was certainly not the reason, although various reasons have been offered on why Indira lifted the Emergency and declared elections. One reason advanced was her fear of a possible assassination attempt on her if she continued with her dictatorship—a plausibility dealt with by L.K. Advani in his blog "Memories of the Emergency" of 19 June 2010, in which he also quoted from an article by Ashis Nandi titled "Invitation to a Beheading : A Psychologist's Guide to Assassinations in the Third World".

DESTRUCTION OF INSTITUTIONS

While it was Shastri who converted the SPE [Special Police Establishment under the Home Ministry] into the CBI [Central Bureau of Investigation] to specifically curb the growing corruption; it was under Indira that the CBI assumed special importance—not to curb corruption, but to chastise her critics and harass her opponents. Congress under Indira converted it into an instrument of tyranny to be used for all purposes other than what it was intended for. The governments that followed Indira faithfully followed her legacy—particularly the UPA-I and UPA-II controlled by her daughter-in-law since 2004.

Like the self-serving sham of '*Garibi Hatao*', Indira Gandhi propagated the principle of '*committed*' bureaucracy, '*committed*' judiciary, '*committed*' parliament, '*committed*' state legislatures, '*committed*' everyone. *Committed* not to the nation or to the constitution or to India's development or to the removal of poverty or to high moral principles or to the service of common man, but '*committed*' to her and her wayward son in ensuring that the dynasty remains in power forever.

Apart from concocting self-serving hollow words like '*Garibi Hatao*' and '*committed*', Indira Congress also made certain words popularised by Nehru the benchmarks by constantly rubbing them in—words like 'secular', 'non-communal', 'casteist', 'pro-dalit', 'pro-disadvantaged', 'progressive policies', 'pro-poor policies', and so on. 'Secular', 'non-communal' and 'non-casteist' claims never got translated into systemic changes and institutional initiatives to root out communalism and casteism from the society. They remained mere empty words to keep the minorities, dalits and poor scared and insecure so as to garner their votes.

To demonstrate what she meant by '*commitment*', as per her definition, she ensured the three senior-most judges of the Supreme Court, Justices Shelat, Hegde and Grover who had ruled that "the basic structure of the constitution could not be altered even by parliament" were superseded and their junior A.N. Ray was appointed the Chief Justice, through her pliant Law Minister H.R. Gokhale.

It has been in the news that prior to the delivery of his judgement disqualifying Indira Gandhi, Justice Sinha was reportedly offered a bribe by a Congress MP and had also been offered elevation to the Supreme Court if he gave a judgement favourable to Indira. Reportedly, words were sent to 'fix' Justice Sinha soon after the Emergency was declared.

Even justices of the Supreme Court like Bhagwati and Chandrachud, after initial reluctance, became '*committed*'! They later expressed regret after the Emergency was lifted—but what use was that when they failed to stand up when required.

ECONOMIC STRANGULATION

Rather than learning from her father's mistakes, Indira pushed India further into the abyss of socialism. It was in the Emergency-period that the retrograde pseudo-socialist laws were passed in the sixth-year of an illegitimate Parliament, including insertion of the word "socialist" in the preamble of the Constitution.

Note the hypocrisy of the election slogan of the Indira Congress '*Garibi Hatao*!', as if it was some other third party that had ruled India and caused *Garibi* (poverty), and not the Congress itself, which had been ruling uninterrupted since Independence! The *Garibi* brought about by her father's policies was further exacerbated by her *more of the same*, and far worse socialistic policies. It was not so much the concern for the poor or the economic content that attracted the Congress of Nehru and Indira to socialism, as its pro-poor image-projection potential for winning elections.

The licensing became Kafkaesque under Indira, and corruption rose dramatically. It was actually gross economic failure, massive unprecedented rise in prices, and increased corruption at all levels that led to the JP movement and agitations against her regime. To save her position, she declared Emergency, and went in for suppressive measures.

Many of the economic reforms required now in 2014 comprise turning the clock back to 1969—the pre-Indira period, since Indira asserted herself 1969 onwards. The state usurped enormous powers during her tenure. 1969 onwards, Indira Gandhi turned pink as part of her political manoeuvring and survival strategy, plunging India deep into the License-Permit-Quota-Control Raj.

NON-WORKING "WORKING" CLASS

Indira Gandhi nationalised banks, insurance companies and many industries, which rendered them into corrupt, inefficient sarkari establishments. The main motive was populism and votes and to get support of the Left.

The current generation would obviously not be personally aware of how badly the statism and licence-permit-quota-raj socialism debased the whole work-culture, so let us take some illustrative examples from the Indira period.

Those used to the current customer-friendly behaviour of the private banks would be shocked to know how rudely the clerks of the nationalised banks began to behave after nationalisation in 1969 and later. Same was the case in other public sector industries and institutions. Customers counted for nothing. Services went for a toss. Government-department-type rude behaviour became the norm. It even rubbed off on private companies! In other words, *sarkari* culture flourished during those bad old times. Here is one of the many, many real shocking cases witnessed in those bad old days.

An old lady, perhaps in her early seventies, came to a nationalised bank branch. She asked for her Savings Bank passbook, which she had given a few months ago for update. The counter clerk told her dismissively to come after a week. She protested she gave the passbook three months ago and had come several times since, and each time she has been told to come later. Irritated, the clerk told her to come in behind his desk from the side door. When she came in, he pointed to a corner where lay a mountain of passbooks. "Search your passbook in them and bring it, I would update," said he indifferently. The poor lady went to the corner, sat on the ground and started looking at the passbooks one by one from the heap. Her eyesight was poor, and it was taking her quite some time to read the name on each passbook. One wondered how many hours it would take her to find her passbook. When another customer, watching with sympathy, asked the concerned clerk how could the poor old lady find her passbook in the heap, the concerned clerk, who was then posting his cheque for cash payment in the ledger, got up and threw the cheque in his face and told the client challengingly, "Why don't you go and help her? Now I would handle your cheque only after you find her passbook!"

Atrocious! Unbelievable! Here is another real case. A person had gone to his nationalised bank branch to deposit cash. The queue was moving really very slow. At last his turn come. He requested the receiving cashier, who had been gossiping with another in his cabin, to please expedite counting of his notes, as he had an urgent business elsewhere. The cashier, aggrieved at this, simply threw his note bundles out over the cabin grill and told him to come only when he is not in any urgency! There was a big commotion. Union leaders stepped in. Manager came in apologetically and requested the cashier to please accept the cash, as the concerned person was an employee of one of the reputed clients of the bank, and was a regular visitor to the bank for transacting business on behalf of the client. Mind you, the manager did not fire him, he only pleaded with the cashier—the manager knew he couldn't force him or even get the work done by an alternate cashier, as the Union would jump in, and the higher management rather than being supportive in taking action against the cashier would advise the manager to be tactful. Despite the manager's pleading, the cashier did not budge till the concerned customer apologised to him!

Such were the terrible days. The Unions were so strong—thanks to the political support of the Congress and the Communists and the like—that there was nothing that bank officers or managers could do. If they intervened they only invited further problems—gherao, lightening strike, and counsel from their seniors in the Regional, Zonal or Head Office to handle matters with tact! That was because they were themselves helpless with the clerks and peons in their own Regional, Zonal or Head Office!!

And, mind you, these clerks never forgot to celebrate 19 November every year—the date of nationalisation, and Indira Gandhi's birthday—for it delivered them from work!

See how times have changed. Now the bankers or their agents come to your office or home to provide you service! Mostly private banks, of course. It is difficult to imagine the horrid times then, even though similar conditions do prevail in many sarkari establishments.

Here is yet another real case of a nationalised bank branch. A middle-aged person—apparently not well off, going by his turn out—came to the counter and said he wanted to open a savings account. The clerk at the counter asked him where he lived. He gave the address. Then the clerk asked him that in coming from his residence to that branch, how many banks had he passed by on the way? He was a little perplexed, but then he made a gesture of recalling and counting, and said four. Asked the clerk: "Why here then? Why didn't you go to the first bank nearest to your residence, or the other three? Why trouble us?" The customer became uncertain wondering whether to leave. Noticing that he had still not left, the clerk reeled out a list of requirements and documents for opening the account. Do you have them, he asked, rather challengingly. The customer replied that he did not right then have all those documents. Come with all those then, said the clerk, and added, "Try that first bank also, or the other three, before coming here." As the customer was leaving deeply embarrassed, the clerk, and his neighbouring colleagues burst out laughing!

Such were the Indira Gandhi times!! Major time of a bank's management went in managing the clerical staff, and somehow getting the work done. Expanding business, better managing the current business, serving clients, and getting new clients were secondary functions. Even if the clerks did not complete their work, or did not do their work properly, there was nothing one could do about it. Even if one started disciplinary proceedings, it would stretch on for months and years, and ultimately the clerk would go scot free—the action itself would have taken further unnecessary toll of the management's time and energy.

The better alternative seemed to be to somehow carry on. Higher management also appreciated that. If you took action, it meant they too would be constrained to take a position, which they did not want. They too were under pressure from management higher to them, and from Union leadership. You were a good manager if the higher management was not troubled in any way. If there was any trouble from any member of the Union, you tackled it. If the fellows did not work, you overworked and made up for it. If the fellows misbehaved, you ignored it or tolerated the insults. That was the acceptable way of doing things. If in the process of this "management" business took a back-seat or clients were not well served, it was fine. After all, you were a 'nationalised' bank, and you needed to fall in line with the sarkari babudom culture.

Everyone from top to bottom knew, but no one was bothered. The babus (IAS) were mighty happy. With nationalisation, yet another huge area came under their power. Babus were used to the abysmal standard of work in the government departments any way—in fact, the work at the nationalised bank might have appeared to them to be far too efficient, and far too honest at the beginning. They set about bringing it down to their standards. Yet another interesting thing of those days was that the bank managements tracked the figures of branch deposits and advances, but never bothered about profits and losses! The latter didn't seem to matter in the socialistic set up!

NON-ENCASHMENT OF OPPORTUNITY

Although people tend to give credit to Indira for creation of Bangladesh, the fact remains that Pakistan brought it upon themselves, thanks to the callousness and the racist and colonialist attitude of the West Pakistani political and military elite. Of course, the leadership of Awami League was also a factor.

True, Indira did show guts to deploy the army—guts her father certainly did not have. But there was little alternative. True, she managed the fallout well, and showed determination and decisiveness. But, when it came to crux, she faltered. No vision, or understanding, or leadership, or statesmanship there. She let go of the big, big bargaining advantage the Indian military win gave her.

We returned 93,000 Pakistani PoWs, we returned the land won by our armed forces on the western front, while we remained burdened with the refugees. And what did Indira Gandhi get from Bhutto in return? Nothing. A mere oral promise at the Shimla Conference in 1972. It was a golden opportunity for India to settle the Kashmir issue with Pakistan, and close all outstanding issues. We lost it.

Her defenders claim it was the sly Bhutto who went back on his promise, and Indira can't be blamed. The question then arises is: Was she, her cabinet and the foreign ministry establishment all innocent about what Bhutto and the Pakistanis had been up to for many, many years. Was she not aware of the Pakistani duplicity in the past, and their conduct both in the Kashmir war of the late forties and the 1965-war? Was she not aware that Pakistani leadership cannot be trusted? And if she and her colleagues still did what they did, it only demonstrates their lack of wisdom and their incompetence in protecting the country's interests. One has to know when to hit the iron. And, in political history, such opportunities do not come again.

We lost many soldiers, spent hundreds of crores of rupees, accumulated lacs of refugees, won the war, but gained nothing! We simply frittered away the strategic advantage the war conferred on us.

Wrote Inder Malhotra in an article "Revisiting Shimla" in *The Indian Express* of 2 July 2012: "P.N. Dhar, who had headed the PM's secretariat from 1970 to 1977, first published a candid and detailed account of the talks between the two PMs well after the Shimla negotiations were declared a 'failure'. He even quoted Bhutto's exact words—'*aap mujh par bharosa keejiye* [please do trust me]'. Almost immediately there was an avalanche of disdainful denials from across the border. Close to the bone, however, was an article by Humayun Gohar. While praising Bhutto's '*diplomatic artistry*', he wrote: "Face it Mr Dhar, even if we accept what you say, Mr Bhutto fooled your prime minister."

".... The nub of the matter at this stage was to have a credible commitment by Bhutto 'gradually' to change [LoC] this line (he at one stage suggested it may be called the 'Line of Peace') into an international border. That is where his plea that he could not commit himself to this in writing and his word should be trusted came in. Indira Gandhi accepted it. Later, when she and Bhutto disclosed their agreement to their respective top advisers, P.N. Dhar demurred and she frowned on him.... However, many still wonder how India's most clear-eyed and hard-headed PM agreed to trust Bhutto's word. Many years later I took this question to her confidant, the legendary spymaster R.N. Kao. To my surprise he answered it frankly and allowed me to quote him. "I am also totally surprised", he said. "Before leaving for Shimla, she had asked me 'Can I trust Bhutto? People tell me that if I shake hands with him, I should immediately count my fingers.'"

Writes Arun Shourie in *Will the Iron Fence Save a Tree Hollowed by Termites*: "...as is even the deeper pain he [Field Marshal K.M. Cariappa] felt when—without binding Pakistan to lasting commitments: on Kashmir, and other issues—political leaders returned the 93,000 Pakistani prisoners and threw away the other gains that our armed forces had secured in 1971."

Indira Gandhi and her confidants, the leftist-socialist-crypto-communist Kashmiri-band comprising P.N. Dhar, T.N. Kaul and R.N. Kao, utterly failed to derive any national advantage and long-term benefit for the country from the victory—they merely used it for domestic advantage for the Congress. The leftist Dhar-Kaul-Kao "Kashmiri Mafia" and Indira, rather than leveraging the brilliant military victory for a lasting strategic gain, used it domestically to further turn disastrously left on economic policies. What was the result? Even more corruption, run-away inflation, price-rise, popular unrest, and finally Emergency! Seventies and eighties, rather than gaining from the victory, became the lost decades.

NATION ON SALE!

Mitrokhin Archives is a collection of Soviet documents relating to USSR's clandestine intelligence operations around the world, including India. One of the books based on these archives and other sources is *The Mitrokhin Archive II : The KGB and the World* written by Christopher Andrew and Vasili Mitrokhin, and published by Penguin/Allen Lane. It was first published in 2005, and covers KGB operations in Latin America, Middle East, Asia, and Africa. Chapters 17 and 18 of this book deal with India.

Vasili Mitrokhin was a KGB archivist for 30 years, and when he defected to the UK in 1992, he carried a huge collection of secret documents with him. FBI called it "the most complete and extensive intelligence ever received from any source".

The book has much to reveal on the funding of the Communist Party of India and the Congress, and about some of their prominent leaders. KGB funded both the CPI and the Congress agents, one of the most senior Congress agents being a minister. Who? That is not revealed by the book. KGB routinely bribed the Left and the Congress politicians. Certain influential journalists and newspapers advancing leftist lines were also in KGB's pay.

One Oleg Kalugin of KGB, who became the head of the Counter Intelligence in 1973, remembered India as *a model of KGB infiltration of a Third World government*. He claimed that KGB had scores of sources across the Indian Government in various wings and ministries such as Intelligence, Counter Intelligence, Police, Defence and External Affairs. He even recalled an occasion where the demand of an Indian minister for $50,000, in exchange for information, was refused by the Soviets, *as they claimed they already had more than enough information*!! The most shocking comment of Kalugin about India was that *it was as if the entire country was for sale*! He also stated that KGB and CIA had penetrated India so much that neither wanted to trust India with any sensitive information for fear that the very next day it would be known to the other side!!

While many countries like the UK, the USA, Italy, and others, about whom too revelations had come out, took them very seriously, set up expert committees to minutely examine all aspects, and took appropriate action; India, true to its character fashioned by the dynasty and its leftist supporters and 'intellectuals', only engaged in denying what had been revealed, and attributed motives to the authors. India made no attempt to examine the matter. Somnath Chatterjee, then Speaker of the Lok Sabha (between 2004 to 2009 during UPA-I government headed by the Congress), and a member of the CPM, the party affected by the revelations, agreed with the Congress claim that the book was 'fiction' and stonewalled a discussion in Parliament. Such is our feudal dynastic democracy, and so ineffective has been the opposition headed by the BJP-Old-Guard.

It was like revelations on Bofors or black money or foreign bank accounts or WikiLeaks. By default, the government always goes into the denial mode. However, if forced by the media or the opposition, it most reluctantly drags its feet to show it is doing something, hoping that after sometime the noise would die down. That nobody is caught or punished is because in practically all cases it is the government and the powerful people behind it who are the actual culprits. Why should a government move against itself?

This is also one of the reasons Indian people must rise against dynastic politics and dynacracy—whether at the central level or at the state level. Dynasties in power, being the affected party, would always prevent access to our own documents and archives, what to speak of foreign ones. That is why changes in government are necessary. You should not have one party and one dynasty ruling. That is very harmful for democracy. Monopoly is bound to lead to malpractices.

It is worth noting that the Mitrokhin Archives were minutely examined by the British Government at various levels over a long period of about seven years (1992 to 1999), so voluminous were the archives. Then, the British Government did due diligence to identify the person most suitable to co-author the volumes with Vasili Mitrokhin. They zeroed-in on Professor Christopher Andrew of the Cambridge University. The first volume, which covered countries in the West, was published in 1999. In the British House of Commons, tribute was paid to Vasili Mitrokhin for his courage and the risk that he took, even though there were many adverse revelations about Britain. This was in sharp contrast to the attitude of the Indian Government which seemed very keen to sweep the inconvenient facts under the carpet, vilify the author, and call the contents of the book mere fiction—without making any enquiry or doing due diligence.

In fact, what was published in the book was very limited, so voluminous were the documents. Therefore, MI6 and the British Foreign Office had made it clear that friendly countries and intelligence agencies were free to request access to the voluminous Mitrokhin papers, at least to sections and dossiers that concern them. But India took no initiative whatsoever to get the documents and conduct an enquiry.

The foreword in the Mitrokhin's book says that a report by the British Intelligence and Security Committee revealed that other Western intelligence agencies found the Mitrokhin material very useful for the leads provided by it, and were extremely grateful for it. Countries like Britain, the US, Germany and Italy have made use of the Mitrokhin material to uncover spies, and set their house and institutions in order. But not India! Rather than using them, we want to run away from them!!

Media too did little to pursue the matter as it affected the establishment, the ruling Congress and the Left. Opposition too failed.

EVALUATING 3G—INDIRA GANDHI

The only two positives of Indira Gandhi were the handling of the Bangladesh affair, excluding post-war negotiations, and taking further the Green and White Revolution initiatives that began under Shastri.

Indira Gandhi's decades can be termed as the '*lost decades*'. She took India further down the precipice of socialistic suicide. Rather than '*Garibi Hatao*' (her election slogan), she spread Garibi further.

While she made no headway with China and the other neighbours, her major foreign policy failure was frittering away the leverage the military provided by winning the Bangladesh war to permanently settle the J&K and boundary issues with Pakistan. Shimla summit was a huge failure for India, and a huge win for Pakistan.

On the internal security front, while the position in Kashmir deteriorated, her politics and that of her son and the Congress led to the creation of a brand new problem—that of Punjab, which took a huge toll of human life and property, and affected the unity of India.

Babudom got further entrenched, thanks to the spreading tentacles of socialism and nationalisation. Corruption came to be institutionalised during her tenure. Brazenly unethical state of affairs resulted in a feeling of hopelessness. All round cynicism prevailed.

'*To hell with democracy and the freedom of others*' she decided, and got the Emergency promulgated, when in the wake of the court verdict her position became untenable—saving self and her dynasty was more important.

There was a deliberate propagation of the myth that India can only be ruled by the Congress and the Nehru-Gandhi dynasty—myths that demeaned India and the Indians. She brazenly engaged in shameless, undemocratic, detrimental-to-the-nation, dynastic acts of first unleashing a gone-case misfit like Sanjay Gandhi on the nation, followed by yet another incompetent, inexperienced and unqualified son—Rajiv Gandhi.

She totally subverted the Congress Party. She did not allow competent leaders to emerge, lest they threaten either her position or that of her sons. Ill-treatment and humiliation of the capable and those with promise became a norm. As Tavleen Singh remarked, "Dynasties thrive by making everyone else seem like dwarfs." Nehru's famous letters to his daughter could not have been more wasted than they were on her. Politics for her was a series of gimmickry.

4
4G–Sanjay Gandhi

Those who talk of induction of young blood must not forget what an arrogant, power-drunk, inexperienced, ill-educated, ill-mannered, uncultured, reckless youth is capable of, and what kind of mess it can put the country in. In the dynasty tradition of academic underachievement, Sanjay Gandhi reportedly never attended any college! Sanjay Gandhi was totally unscrupulous, and many Emergency excesses were thanks to him. Sanjay Gandhi converted the civil servants into a servile breed; the willing tools of tyranny.

On the lifting of the Emergency, wrote Kuldip Nayar on his talks with Sanjay Gandhi in *Beyond the Lines*: "The first question I asked Sanjay was how he thought that they would get away with it: the Emergency, the authoritarian rule, and the rest? He said there was no challenge to them and that they could have carried on with the Emergency for at least 20 to 25 years or more until they felt confident that they had changed people's ways of thinking. In their scheme of things, he said, there would have been no elections and they would have ruled from Delhi, with the help of provincial satraps like Bansi Lal from Haryana and like-minded bureaucrats in other states. It would have been a different kind of governance, with power centralized in Delhi. I recalled that Kamal Nath had during the Emergency given me the manuscript of a book arguing along the same lines and detailing the machinery such a government would establish to rule with the help of police and some selected bureaucrats. In the scheme of Sanjay's rule, there was no Congress leader of eminence and experience. Anyone who wanted to be part of the form of governance he was contemplating had to believe in a state completely devoid of fundamental rights, freedom of speech and expression. The judiciary would have to function accordingly."

The Congress pro-Emergency group led by Sanjay Gandhi even spread the impression that democracy was not suited to India's genius!

Many books have been written on the Emergency, its excesses and Sanjay Gandhi's dubious role, and the scope of this book can't accommodate those details.

BEFORE THE TREE FELL

Though there were other factors too, the creation and the exacerbation of the Punjab problem and the Sikh disaffection was largely thanks to Sanjay Gandhi, his mother and their faithful factotum, Giani Zail Singh. What were they aiming for? Unseat the Akalis, and get back the power in Punjab. Such a heavy price for mere crumbs of power! That was what Indira and her son were all about! They thought they had the divine right to rule (or, rather misrule) India, and any means were fair means to achieve their goal—rather, means did not matter to them.

Zail Singh together with Sanjay Gandhi and with Indira Gandhi's consent picked up a relatively obscure, young and fundamentalist preacher Jarnail Singh Bhindranwale and built him up as an Akali rival, by allowing him to advocate extremist causes that could embarrass the Akali Dal. They didn't reckon they were thereby being Frankensteins unleashing the Bhindranwale monster.

Writes Kuldip Nayar in *Beyond the Lines*: "It was Sanjay Gandhi, known for his extra-constitutional methods, who suggested that some 'Sant' should be put up to challenge the Akali government. Both Sanjay and Zail Singh, particularly the latter, knew how the former Punjab chief minister Pratap Singh Kairon had fought the Akalis. He had built up Sant Fateh Singh against Master Tara Singh, the Akali leader, who had become a hard nut to crack. Zail Singh and Darbara Singh, who was a CWC member and later became Chief Minister, selected two persons for Sanjay's evaluation. As Sanjay's friend, Kamal Nath, a Member of Parliament, recalled: 'The first one we interviewed did not look a 'courageous type'. Bhindranwale, strong in tone and tenor, seemed to fit the bill. We would give him money off and on,' Kamal Nath reminisced, 'but we never thought he would turn into a terrorist.' Little did they realize at that time that they were creating a Frankenstein. Zail Singh too maintained contacts with Bhindranwale, although he denied this after he became President."

But Bhindranwale had his own agenda. After he had done enough damage, and transformed himself into a Frankenstein Monster, Indira proceeded to eliminate him, severely damaging the Golden Temple in the process. For the sake of one person, you yourself once promoted, destroy the whole of holy place!

Golden Temple has a very strong religious and historical significance for the Sikhs. So many times it was destroyed by the invaders like Ahmad Shah Abdali, and was rebuilt. But for free, independent India to act like Ahmad Shah Abdali? True, the intention was not to destroy it, but to eliminate Bhindranwale and the terrorists holed up inside. But, was the damage to the temple unavoidable? Could not some other way have been found? Operation Blue Star was avoidable. Yet, it was launched, killing Bhindranwale and his gang, and also destroying the temple.

India paid too heavy a price for that ill-thought operation. Sikhs got disaffected. Insurgency took roots. While Indira Gandhi failed to solve any of the huge problems facing India, she created this new monster. It was later left to the people like K.P.S. Gill under the wise P.V. Narasimha Rao to control and root out insurgency in Punjab.

Strangely, Khushwant Singh had many good things to say about Sanjay Gandhi. Khushwant Singh's two volume *History of Sikhs* is very well written. It is a *must read*. So also his autobiography, *Truth, Love and a Little Malice*—thoroughly readable. However, politics was not his cup of tea. Or, rather, not his glass of scotch. He must have been taken for a ride by

Sanjay and Indira Gandhi. Or, was Khushwant a simpleton when it came to weighty matters, Sikh history that he wrote being an exception. And, was he enamoured at the opportunity of being close to power, and didn't mind turning a courtier and a flatterer? Overwhelming number of India's post-independence intellectuals have been pro-establishment conformists always able to concoct an "intellectual" reason to back the dynasty.

One wonders if Khushwant Singh later regretted admiring Sanjay, because it was Sanjay who promoted Bhindranwale, who did what he did, leading to Operation Blue Star by his mother, and the damage to the Golden Temple, which not only made Khushwant Singh return his Padma Bhushan, but also led to killing of Indira Gandhi by her Sikh bodyguards, which ultimately resulted in the most shameful episode in the post-independence Indian history—attack on Sikhs in 1984.

In a way, one can trace the hands of Sanjay, Indira and Rajiv in the misfortune that befell Sikhs. It was thanks to Sanjay that Bhindranwale came up, it was thanks to Indira Gandhi that Operation Blue Star happened, and it was thanks to Rajiv Gandhi that little was done to either save the Sikhs in the 1984 attacks or to bring the culprits to justice.

5
4G—Rajiv Gandhi

Upon the death of Indira Gandhi, her son, Rajiv Gandhi, who was not even a minister and had no relevant experience, inherited the throne of prime ministership, thanks to Nehru-Indira who had converted the vibrant Indian democracy into a dynacracy (feudal dynastic democracy), and the Congress into a private estate.

Like a typical scion from the Nehru dynasty, Rajiv was an academic underachiever. Rajiv Gandhi failed to do his graduation despite all the expenses at London. He was at Cambridge till 1965, but left it without a degree, because he did not appear for the examinations. He joined Imperial College, London in 1966, but again left it after a year, without a degree.

Nehru dynasty scions do not need academic qualifications or expertise in any field or ground-level political experience or experience of running a panchayat or a municipality or a district or a state or a ministry to get into the top-most slot of prime minister. They do not need to prove themselves in anything; not even in public speaking or debates, so vital for a politician. They have been poor thinkers and articulators, bereft of any worthwhile vision. They have also been third-rate speakers, without exception. India is condemned to bear the exceptionally high risk of them at the apex, and the invariably disastrous consequences that flow from that. They just parachute down as prime ministers.

WHEN THE TREE FELL

'1984 anti-Sikh attacks' in the wake of Indira Gandhi's assassination is a permanent, inerasable black mark on the Indian state. The period also heralded the rise of the 4G Dynast, Rajiv Gandhi, who remained PM for about 5 years between October 1984 and December 1989.

There are four sets of questions about the 1984 anti-Sikh attacks.

One. Why the attacks started? Who started it? Who encouraged it? Who looked the other way? Why the police and the army did not quell it? The surprising and the inexcusable part was: how could the attacks continue for four days; and that too in the capital of India, having no dearth of police, and with the army on call?

Two. Post attacks, why were the guilty not booked? Why instead the victims were further harassed? Why sham enquiries were conducted?

Three. Why the guilty and those suspected of involvement in the attacks were being protected? Why many of them were given cushy or better positions and promotions?

Four. Why no justice has been done till date—even after 29 long years?

The only plausible explanation is that if the State itself is guilty of its failure to protect, and is determined not to get caught, where is the question of justice, and punishment of the guilty. Especially, when the people at the top positions are involved—on account of either their inexcusable silence and inaction, or on account of their deliberate complicity. This is obvious from the way no stone was left unturned to scuttle all probes, and abort the legal process.

This has a parallel with Bofors. The State ensured the guilty were not caught. Set up JPCs and Enquiry Commissions, hand over probe to the investigative agencies, when you could no more avoid them, and then systematically abort them. There are people who call it 1984 riots. How are they riots. Riots are when two sides attack each other. But, in 1984, only the Sikhs were on the receiving end—and brutally. 1984 anti-Sikh attacks have established such *high watermarks* on many counts that they are unlikely to be ever breached:

One. The scale of the attacks.

Two. The gruesomeness of the attacks.

Three. The complicity of the powerful and those responsible for protection of the people—either through their involvement or their irresponsible silence and inaction.

Four. Exceedingly callous and exceptionally irresponsible manner of response of the State in the immediate aftermath of the attacks, providing little succour to victims.

Five. Shamelessly insensitive justification of the attacks at the highest level—by Rajiv Gandhi: "When a tree falls, the earth shakes under it...."

Six. Brazenness with which the State went about scuttling all probes and attempts to get at the truth and punish the guilty.

Seven. Exoneration of the guilty. Also, rewarding the guilty: accommodation and promotion of the guilty.

Rajiv was apparently so unconcerned that he did not even think it necessary to express regret on the attacks or sympathy with the victims in the parliament.

Was it his lack of concern or was it his guilty conscience that led him to keep silent on the sordid affair? Why didn't he prevent the attacks? Even if it is granted that on the first day he was taken by surprise, what prevented him from acting on the second or the third or even the fourth day? Khushwant Singh had rightly remarked: "If he [Rajiv] was not the author of the order to 'teach the Sikhs a lesson', he did nothing to countermand it."

Incidentally, a Sardar was the President of India then—Giani Zail Singh. Sitting right there in Delhi, with all the power at his command, he did nothing to save the Sikhs of Delhi! This is what the dynasty has done to leaders and babus. Make them totally loyal, subservient and spineless. Giani Zail Singh could not have been President unless Indira Gandhi was satisfied he was faithful to her, besides being obsequious and gutless. He did nothing either to prevent the attacks on Sikhs, or to bring the guilty to book, later. Why? Because, he just wanted to continue as president. The least he could have done was to have resigned in protest. Even much earlier, did he do anything to prevent the Operation Blue Star, and the reduction of the revered Sikh Shrine to rubble? Could he not have prevailed upon Indira Gandhi to use alternate methods, so as not to damage the shrine—and resigned if she persisted!

Strangely, it was Giani Zail Singh who, as president, swore Rajiv Gandhi as Prime Minister, upon the death of Indira Gandhi—violating all parliamentary procedures. Normally, it should have been the senior most cabinet minister who should have been sworn in as the prime minister. Rajiv Gandhi then was not even a minister. Why did Giani Zail Singh do so? Not to uphold the constitution or the parliamentary procedures, but to demonstrate his loyalty to the dynasty! Person sitting in the highest office was reduced to being merely a lackey.

Those who are unaware of the facts should read *When a Tree Shook Delhi* by Manoj Mitta and H.S. Phoolka, published by Roli Books, and *I Accuse...: The Anti-Sikh Violence of 1984* authored by Jarnail Singh and published by Penguin/Viking. Also, *The Ghosts of Mrs. Gandhi*, a recollection of his personal experience during the anti-Sikh violence in Delhi written by Amitav Ghosh and included in his collection *The Imam and the Indian* published by Ravi Dayal/Penguin, is worth reading.

DYNASTIC GAME OF COMMUNAL POLITICS

In what came to be known as the Shah Bano case, the Supreme Court awarded alimony to a divorced Muslim woman, Shah Bano, in April 1985, and called for honouring the constitutional commitment to a Uniform Civil Code. With a two-thirds majority in Parliament, the Congress could have taken the Court's verdict forward. Instead, Rajiv Gandhi had a Bill passed, the Muslim Personal Law Bill, overturning the Supreme Court's verdict.

Rajiv Gandhi thereby bent down to Muslim fanatics, ignoring the just stand taken by his own minister, who also happened to be a Muslim—Arif Mohammad Khan. Khan finally resigned in protest! Was it not expected of a PM to back up what was just and proper, and show support for the poor, old lady, and many like her. If you cannot be just and fair and back up a good cause, even when the Supreme Court is on your side, and you have an overwhelming majority in the parliament, can you ever be just and fair?

But, again the dynasty instinct. Who cares for the poor, old lady; who cares for the suffering Muslim women; who cares for reforms or justice! What matters is your continuance in power and that of your Dynasty, and that requires votes of the minority. Your dynasty instinct tells you that if you support what is backward and unjust, you may be compensated with votes. However, it was not as if Rajiv's government was in any difficulty and he desperately required support. His government had an overwhelming majority and there was absolutely no threat to his power. But, why not secure the future too for the Dynasty—whatever it may cost to the nation and its people and its minority!

And, after having thus secured the Muslim votes, Rajiv thought, like a clever heir of a clever Dynasty, why not try and secure Hindu votes too. So allow opening of the lock of Ayodhya Temple/Masjid to have the conservative Hindus also on your side. Like Indians are still struggling with the consequences of his grandfather's acts on Kashmir, Tibet and India-China border-dispute; they—particularly, the minority Muslim community—are also suffering from the consequences of Rajiv Gandhi's disastrous acts on Shah Bano case and Ayodhya.

Wrote Ramchandra Guha in the *Hindustan Times* of 13 September 2008: "In April 1985, in awarding alimony to a divorced woman named Shah Bano, the Supreme Court called for honouring the constitutional commitment to a Uniform Civil Code. The Congress had a two-thirds majority in Parliament. However, instead of taking the Court's verdict forward, Rajiv Gandhi had a Bill passed overturning it. Less than a year later, the locks of the shrine in the Babri Masjid were opened. As the political analyst Neerja Chowdhury wrote at the time, 'Mr Rajiv Gandhi wants both to run with the hare and hunt with the hounds.' Chowdhury remarked that 'a policy of appeasement of both communities being pursued by the government for electoral gains is a vicious cycle which will become difficult to break'.... Rajiv Gandhi had 400 MPs, a Supreme Court verdict, and a liberal Muslim willing to bat for him (Arif Mohammed Khan). That he still flunked it may be attributed either to a lack of a sense of history or a lack of a robust commitment to liberal principles—or perhaps both."

MORE OF THE SAME WORN-OUT SOCIALISM

Finding that there is all round praise for the liberalisation heralded by Narasimha Rao, the Dynasty chamchas were quick to pass on the credit to Rajiv, claiming that the liberalisation actually commenced with Rajiv.

They conveniently forget—knowing no one would remember it—what Rajiv himself said on the subject. He stated at the Qinghua University, "The focus of our socialism is the uplift of the poor, succour to the weak, justice to the oppressed and balanced regional development. To attain these ends, we believe the State must control the commanding heights of the economy...."

In fact, the manifesto of the Congress under Rajiv promised another heavy dose of socialism as the 1991 elections approached. Despite this, people are mislead into believing that it was Rajiv who ushered in reforms.

The financial bankruptcy and the severe economic crisis that India faced in 1991 was thanks to gross economic mismanagement of the past decades ruled by Nehru, Indira and, of course, Rajiv Gandhi, who was at the helm during the immediate preceding years—foreign debt had doubled between 1985 and 1991.

IPKF

The naive Rajiv Gandhi and his advisers thought the Sri Lankan Tamil issue provided them an opportunity to show off their great prowess in International Affairs. You are a big guy, so you unilaterally decide with Sri Lanka what the solution of Tamil issue should be, without involving LTTE and Prabhakaran. And, later, you just call Pirbhakaran to Delhi and want him to sign on the dotted line, and expect he would do so!

Then, you dream you are a super power. And, to show to the world your responsibility as a super power, you send in your IPKF to Sri Lanka. What happens? LTTE becomes your sworn enemy. Your soldiers, who do not have full freedom to act, are killed by scores. Sri Lanka itself treats you as an alien, enemy force, which should be thrown out. So you make a mess of the whole Sri Lankan Tamil issue, and your soldiers come back bruised and despised, having failed in the thankless task.

MR. CLEAN

Media, ever ready to please those in power, dubbed Rajiv Gandhi Mr. Clean. He responded with Bofors. And it was not just Bofors. There were other financial scandals, including HDW. There are unconfirmed reports that Bofors was not necessarily the first such case, and that even as a pilot during the time of his mother, Rajiv Gandhi was perhaps associated with certain defence deals.

The extent to which the government and Rajiv, personally, went to mislead the public and scuttle the probe itself proved their involvement in some way or the other. What is interesting about the Bofors case is not its main focus—the bribe. By today's standards it was too less. What was indeed interesting, rather revealing, was the way, the machinations, and the extent to which the government under Rajiv, and even successive government, could go to save the possible culprits, mislead the public, and scuttle the probe they themselves instituted.

So what if we do something wrong, and are caught in the act—we know how to save ourselves and the other wrong-doers. That's our competence! So, don't mess with us and waste the country's time and money in probes and enquiries. What is notable about the Bofors probe is the sheer brazenness with which it was scuttled.

Sadly, we have no reliable institutional process—most of the institutions have been compromised or co-opted by the political class and babus—to prevent or catch wrong-doers. It is thanks to the foreign countries and their anti-bribery laws that many wrong-doings in India come to light, the latest being the Augusta-Westland Helicopter Bribery Scandal of 2013. The role of our "investigative" agencies, thanks to their political masters, has been not to investigate but to somehow suppress what is revealed abroad.

Sten Lindstrom, since retired, was the head of Swedish police, and had led the investigations into the Bofors deal in the late eighties and the nineties. He was a conscientious, honest cop, who did his best to bring the corrupt to justice. Chitra Subramaniam, now Chitra Subramaniam-Duella, was a journalist for *The Hindu* based in Geneva when the Bofors scandal broke. She did path-breaking investigative work on the Bofors deal. She shifted to *The Indian Express* when *The Hindu* reportedly discontinued her investigative reports on Bofors under political pressure. It is thanks to her that the government failed to suppress the scandal. Ottavio Quattrocchi, or Q, was an Italian businessman and reportedly a friend of the Gandhis. During Indira Gandhi and Rajiv Gandhi's time in the 1980s, Snamprogetti, an Italian company, won dozens of projects (around 60) from the Indian Government. That was thanks to Quattrocchi, who reportedly had free access to the PM's residence, could freely barge into the rooms of ministers and secretaries. Those in the government who dared to oppose him risked being humiliated or side-lined. Wrote Ashok Malik in *The Pioneer* of 28 April 2012, "Those who stood up to him [Quattrocchi]—opposing him on grounds of technology (Thal Vaishet project, 1980) or price (Hazira-Bijapur-Jagdishpur pipeline, 1985) were humiliated or side-lined. HBJ destroyed several careers. Mr Nawal Kishore Sharma lost his job as Petroleum Minister. Mr PK Kaul was sacked as Cabinet secretary. Mr GV Ramakrishna and Mr AS Gill, two outstanding Petroleum Secretaries, were thwarted from being considered for Cabinet Secretary-ship. In the case of Thal Vaishet, Mr KV Ramananthan, then Secretary for chemicals and fertilisers and frontrunner for the Cabinet Secretary's post, was shunted out to the Planning Commission."

Sten, in an interview to Chitra published on *The Hoot* on 24 April 2012 explaining why he turned a whistleblower, said: "I knew what I was doing when I leaked the documents to you. I could not count on my government or Bofors or the Government of India to get to the bottom of this....

"We were conducting several search and seize operations in the premises of Bofors and their executives.... In the pile were one set of documents to Swiss banks with instructions that the name of the recipient should be blocked out.... Bofors was unable to explain and then we found more and more documents leading to India....

"But he [Rajiv Gandhi] watched the massive cover-up in India and Sweden and did nothing. Many Indian institutions were tarred, innocent people were punished while the guilty got away. The evidence against Ottavio Quattrocchi was conclusive. Through a front company called A.E. Services, bribes paid by Bofors landed in Quattrocchi's account which he subsequently cleaned out because India said there was no evidence linking him to the Bofors deal. Nobody in Sweden or Switzerland was allowed to interrogate him....

"Ardbo was also concerned about the role of Arun Nehru who had told Bofors in 1985 that his name and Rajiv Gandhi's name should not appear anywhere. As the stories began to appear, Ardbo knew what I knew. He had written in his notes that the identity of N (Nehru) becoming public was a minor concern but at no cost could the identity of Q (Quattrocchi) be revealed because of his closeness to R (Rajiv Gandhi). He had also mentioned a meeting between an A.E. Services official and a Gandhi trustee lawyer in Geneva. This was a political payment. These payments are made when the deal has to be inked and all the numbers are on the table....

"During that trip to Sweden, the Indian investigators planted the Bachchan angle on DN (Swedish Newspaper *Dagens Nyheter*). The Bachchan's took them to court in the UK and won. DN had to apologise and they said the story had come from Indian investigators. I was disappointed with the role of many senior journalists and politicians during that period. They muddied the waters....

"After the LR [Letter-Rogatory] was lodged in Switzerland, I was waiting for the official track with India and Switzerland to begin. It never did. Whenever the public prosecutor Ekblom and I heard of any Indian visits to Stockholm, we would speak to the media expressing our desire to meet them. Can you imagine a situation where no one from India met the real investigators of the gun deal?"

The above clearly shows how the investigation was a hogwash.

Funnily, while the foreign governments—Swedish and the Swiss—were willing to cooperate and furnish documents that could help identify the guilty; our CBI was reluctant to acquire the documents and welcome the cooperation voluntarily offered by them! Such is the level of political control over CBI, and such is the pathetic state of our investigative machinery!!

Even though the Bofors scandal came to light in 1987, a case was registered only when VP Singh became the PM in 1989. His government lasted barely a year. Chandrashekhar government followed, with the backing of the Congress. Thanks to the same, the CBI lawyer started arguing in the court against the government's case itself!

In 1991, unknown persons—obviously those who must have received bribes—went to court in Geneva to ask the Swiss authorities not tell the Indian Government who the accounts belonged to! Then in 1992, India gave a note to the Swiss Foreign Minister saying the Bofors case was politically motivated, and requested the Swiss authorities not to cooperate with the Indian investigators and to ignore any requests made by other arms of the government. Guess, who gave the note? India's Foreign Minister in the Congress Government, Madhavsinh Solanki, when he met his Swiss counterpart at the WEF meeting.

Soon after Interpol advised India in July 1993 that Ottavio Quattrocchi was one of the persons appealing against the transfer of the Swiss bank documents, Quattrocchi flew out of India. A Congress politician reportedly helped him fly out.

India finally received documents from Switzerland in 1997 that established payment of kickback to Quattrocchi. Quattrocchi was then living in Malaysia. NDA Government tried his extradition, but failed—it lost in a lower court on a Friday, appealed to a higher court on the following Monday, but, over the weekend, Quattrocchi fled Malaysia.

To allow the case to die a natural death, UPA allowed two unfavourable court verdicts to go unchallenged. One was quashing of bribery charges in 2004. The second was quashing of charges against Hindujas in 2005 on the ground that papers presented to the court were authenticated photocopies, not originals. UPA allowed de-freezing of Quattrocchi's bank accounts in London in December 2005, and he was allowed to have his ill-gotten money. Argentina police detained Quattrocchi in 2007 on account of then still existing Interpol alert, but, as expected, UPA so handled the matter that Quattrocchi again got away.

Writes Seema Mustafa in her article, "Why there won't be any progress on Bofors", in DNA of 27 April 2012: "In 2004, when I asked Lindstrom to name some living persons who had full details of the Bofors kickbacks he responded without hesitation, 'Martin Ardbo, Ottavio Quattrocchi and Sonia Gandhi...' Ardbo has since died...."

If you look at it in perspective, you find that while in certain ways it was unique, in many ways the script was similar to many such things in the past, and also many since.

You can clearly see this manipulative tendency even in Nehru's handling of the Netaji Subhash Bose death mystery. Reading Anuj Dhar's *India's Biggest Cover-up*, you would be amazed by the road-blocks Nehru put in getting at the truth, the way he dragged his feet on setting up a Commission of Enquiry; and once it was setup, the way he manipulated it through the various agencies of the government to ensure it produced a report as the government wanted. One has to read that book to get an idea. Why manipulate a Commission you have agreed to setup?

The legacy has continued. Several enquiries into the *Anti-Sikh Attacks of 1984* were similarly aborted during Rajiv Gandhi's time. Check the latest: How the 2G PAC and JPC Reports were handled by the Congress.

Writes Kuldip Nayar in *Beyond the Lines*: "Rajiv Gandhi had bent all the rules to order Bofors' howitzers. Even the circumstantial evidence testified to his involvement. A close friend of his told me that Rajiv Gandhi had opened a new account abroad and had deposited the kickbacks there. This benefited his Italian in-laws, parents of Sonia Gandhi. Ottavio Quattrocchi, an Italian middleman in Delhi, close to Sonia Gandhi and Rajiv Gandhi, was responsible for the clandestine payment.

"Quattrocchi had once threatened to sue me for defamation because of what I had written about his 'nefarious activities' in my book *The Judgement* (1977). He escaped punishment for all he had done and was eventually allowed to leave India, the CBI ensuring that no harm came to an individual so close to the Dynasty. When I checked with some senior officers in the agency, their reply was that there were orders from above. H.R. Bharadwaj told me in Bangalore that he had 'put everything in order' before moving to Karnataka as governor. According to former CBI director Joginder Singh, Quattrocchi was aware in advance of every move the agency proposed to take against him. For example, he was shown all official papers before he appeared for extradition proceedings at a Malaysian court. I once asked Foreign Minister Madhavsinh Solanki in the Narasimha Rao government about the documents he had delivered to the Swedish government regarding the kickbacks. New Delhi was keen that the Swedish authorities remained silent. He did not comment on the documents but said that the Bofors gun deal was 'as messy as Narmada's non-use of water'."

~~~

Schweizer Illustrierte, a reputed Swiss magazine, carried an expose on the Swiss bank accounts of 14 politicians in its issue of 11 November 1991 that included USD 25.5 billion of Suharto of Indonesia, 22.5 billion of Haile Selassie of Ethiopia, 6 billion of Mobutu of Zaire, 5.7 billion of Shah Pehlvi of Iran, and so on. Shockingly, it also captioned under the photo of Rajiv Gandhi: '2.5 billion [Swiss] francs on the Indian secret accounts in Switzerland of Rajiv Gandhi, Indian.' Today that should amount to about USD 15 billion or ₹ 90,000 crores. Such a serious allegation against our ex-PM should not have gone unchallenged. Surprisingly, the Indian Government did not deem it fit either to file a defamation case against the magazine or to investigate the matter! When it was in power, BJP too did
~~~

nothing in the matter even though the report was brought to the notice of the NDA Government in 2002. Is the Indian public being fooled on the issue of illicit wealth parked abroad?

1984 BHOPAL GAS TRAGEDY

Bhopal Gas Tragedy was consequent to the leakage of poisonous gas from Union Carbide plant at Bhopal on 2 December 1984 causing over 10,000 deaths and about 500,000 injuries, making it the worst ever industrial accident in world history.

Warren Anderson, the CEO of Union Carbide, was arrested on charges of manslaughter. Strangely, he was allowed to post bail and escape to the US. All subsequent extradition efforts by India were unsuccessful. It has been reported that Arjun Singh, the then CM of MP facilitated Anderson's escape at the instance of Rajiv Gandhi.

EVALUATING RAJIV

A pilot yesterday, with no relevant experience, no proven competence, and scant knowledge never fitted the bill. Why step into something you cannot handle. Would Rajiv, as a pilot, have considered it reasonable if a novice with no skills in flying aircrafts was deputed to fly a Boeing from Delhi to Mumbai. Wouldn't he, as a responsible person, have objected to putting the life of passengers in peril, and of being callous with such a costly machine! Why then, as a responsible person, should he have taken the responsibility for India for which he was a misfit?

Positives? From political and leadership angle—hardly any. The major negatives are summarised below.

Economy. Rajiv Gandhi continued the dynasty's socialistic-babudom tradition. India remained poor, corrupt and backward.

Anti-Sikh Attacks: the worst carnage in post-independence India. Rajiv's government failed to stop the anti-Sikh attacks of 1984, post the assassination of Indira Gandhi. Complicity of the State, the Administration and the Police both in not stopping the attacks and in not booking the guilty was obvious. There was no subsequent action against the guilty. They were actually shielded. Even rewarded! Work of all Probes and Enquiry Commissions were scuttled. Brazenness in justifying the pogroms: "When a tree falls...."

Bhopal Gas Tragedy. Allowing Anderson to escape.

Sri Lankan Tamil Problem and IPKF. Unwise policy, poor execution and poor management.

Massive Fillip to Communalisation. Rajiv's myopic policies for political gains encouraged both the Muslim and the Hindu fundamentalists. The following two were his two major blunders. Bringing in a law to reverse Supreme Court's *Shah Bano verdict* was clearly a regressive decision that harmed the Muslim women at large. *Disturbing the status quo at Ayodhya*—that was yet another unwise decision.

Kashmir. The rise of the insurgency in Kashmir in the late eighties was partly stoked by the Rajiv Gandhi's government rigging of the 1987 elections in cahoots with the National Conference. Among those defeated, thanks to rigging, were some of the future leaders of the jihad.

Institutionalised corruption. Bofors and other cases.

Rajiv Gandhi's "achievements" notwithstanding, here is a sample from an intellectual and a thought-leader from the top ranks of the MSM (Main Stream Media): "...All this [about Rajiv Gandhi] is true enough, but I think it misses some of his deeper achievements. We forget, for instance, how bad things were when he took over.... Many people, predicted that the Indian experiment was at an end and that chaos was around the corner.... It was Rajiv Gandhi's five years in office—from the autumn of 1984 to the winter of 1989—that showed the world that India was here to stay. We had our problems. But our survival was not in doubt. Even if Rajiv had not done anything else, that single achievement alone is enough for an entire nation to owe him a debt of gratitude...."

What an audacious statement! So, 42 years after independence, ruled mostly by the Dynasty, and after 5 years of rule by Rajiv Gandhi, Indians must thank the Dynasty, because but for them India as a nation would not have survived! What a wise concoction and a clever counterfactual! With nothing worthwhile to show for their achievements, declare that India would have gone to pieces but for the dynasty.

What if a contrary counterfactual is posed: India would have been far more integrated and united and prosperous had the dynasty not weighted India down! Had Mahatma Gandhi not ushered in the dynasty by making Nehru the PM, and had the non-socialists like Sardar Patel or Rajaji taken over the reins and guided India along with competitive capitalism and free enterprise economy, India would have been a much more united, rich, prosperous, first-rate, first-world nation by 1980!

What is even more galling is the "vision" of such "eminent" intellectuals, and the liberties they take with the facts of history. While many countries who were behind or far behind India when India gained independence have already become prosperous and part of the first world, such "intellectuals" are relieved India has at least survived! Given such abysmally low expectations, any dumb of the dynasty would come out in flying colours.

6
They Also Ruled!

Non-dynasty persons such as Gulzarilal Nanda and Morarji Desai, apart from the trinity of gems—Lal Bahadur Shastri, Narasimha Rao and Atal Bihari Vajpayee—also served as India's prime ministers, though for relatively short durations. Non-entities (in the sense of those belonging to minor parties with but a few seats) too adorned the PM's chair thanks to the uncertain times in the Indian politics when no significant party could muster a majority. These included Charan Singh, V.P. Singh, Chandra Shekhar, Deve Gowda and I.K. Gujaral, some of whom are forgettables who wasted the precious time of the nation and its citizens—not that the Nehru-Gandhi Dynasty did any good.

Gulzarilal Nanda was a freedom fighter who twice became the PM for 13 days each, first after the death of Nehru in 1964, and later after the death of Lal Bahadur Shastri in 1966. He was a leader of the *Congress Forum for Socialist Action* which along with other such bodies and led by Nehru and Indira helped India run into the ground. Nanda left active politics in protest against the imposition of the Emergency by Indira Gandhi in 1975. Although he had been a central minister for a long time, he lead an austere, Gandhian life, and reportedly his bank balance never exceeded a few thousand rupees.

Like Gulzarilal Nanda, Morarji Desai too was a freedom fighter. His first attempt at the top post was after the demise of

Nehru. Fortunately for India, Shastri beat him to it. His next attempt was after Shastri's death, but ultimately Indira Gandhi triumphed. Jayaprakash Narayan (JP) finally handed him the crown following the victory of the Janata Party at the hustings after the Emergency in 1977. He remained the PM between March 1977 and July 1979. The defeat of Indira–Sanjay-Gandhi & Co, the perpetrators of the Emergency and destroyers of people's freedom, had fired people with bright hope of a new dawn. However, most of the Janata Party leaders were old wine in a new bottle, with little fresh, uplifting ideas. Morarji Desai was a self-righteous, obstinate, and hugely arrogant leader who was incapable of taking the party with him or give any new direction. He was long past the age of idealism. His son Kanti Desai gave him a bad name through his wheelings and dealings.

Along with Nehru and others, Desai entertained misplaced notions on the creation of additional states. They falsely regarded meeting the regional aspirations of people by creation of new states as being against the unity of India, and hence unpatriotic. As the Chief Minister of the then Bombay State (combined Maharashtra and Gujarat), Desai opposed bifurcation and even used force against the agitationists that ultimately led to his removal.

Desai had the distinction of being the only Indian to be conferred with Pakistan's highest civilian award, *Nishan-e-Pakistan*. Some connect this to the reported dismantling of India's RAW's assets in Pakistan during Morarji's time that severely affected India's intelligence operations.

Charan Singh, a farmer and a freedom fighter, served as the PM for about six months between July 1979 and January 1980. He thankfully opposed and succeeded in thwarting Nehru's Soviet-style socialistic/collectivist land-use policies in the fifties.

V.P. Singh was the PM for about a year between December 1989 and November 1990. To create his caste-support base and vote-bank, he implemented the *Mandal Commission Report* for reservation of jobs in the government/public sector for OBCs (Other Backward Classes), despite stiff opposition. When Arvind Kejriwal and AAP talk ad nauseam against corruption and for honest leadership, one is reminded of demagogues like V.P. Singh, who also rose on the bandwagon of honesty-corruption and took India to dogs.

He was followed by Chandra Shekhar as the PM for about 7 months from November 1990 to June 1991. Chandra Shekhar became the PM with the outside support of the Congress/Rajiv Gandhi and remained in that position till Rajiv withdrew support. However, that brief period of this once 'young turk' was among the most corrupt period. That's why one has to be vary of the current 'young turks'—a misnomer for the dynasts who have risen up the easy way thanks to their family. Chandra Shekhar, who had fought the Emergency and was jailed during that period, did not hesitate to appoint one of the monsters of the Emergency, V.C. Shukla, as his foreign minister!

Sleepy-head H.D. Deve Gowda adorned the PM's post for about 11 months between June 1996 and April 1997.

He was followed by I.K. Gujaral who was the PM for about 11 months between April 1997 and March 1998. Thanks to his faulty understanding, Gujaral scaled down RAW and did things that adversely affected its ability in vital intelligence operations. A controversial decision of his time was to transfer the CBI director Joginder Singh then investigating Lalu Prasad Yadav in the Fodder Scam case, reportedly in return for Lalu's support.

7

P.V. Narasimha Rao: Who Really Made a Difference

THE SECOND FREEDOM

P.V. Narasimha Rao (PVN) deserves credit for lifting India out of the economic quagmire it had sunk into and taking it on the path of relative prosperity. It was Rao who made a break from the populist and disastrous economic policies of the Nehru-Indira Dynasty prevalent till 1991 and ushered in economic liberalisation. Rao was the prime minister from 21 June 1991 to 16 May 1996.

Rao became the PM in the background of both India and the world in turmoil. In Eastern Europe, communism had collapsed. Berlin Wall had at last fallen and the East had reunited with the West Germany. The Soviet Union was nearing dissolution. The Iraq was under attack by the US over its invasion of Kuwait. In India, between November 1990 and March 1991, two governments had fallen. Rajiv Gandhi, the PM candidate then campaigning, was assassinated in May 1991. The Indian economy was on the cusp of disaster with the doubling of foreign debt between 1985 and 1991, spike in oil prices, and foreign currency reserves shrinking to less than two weeks of imports. The government had to pawn its gold abroad.

India was in such difficult economic situation that it had little option but to liberalise. But, had Nehru-Gandhi Dynasty been in power they would never have taken the bold steps that

Rao took. They would have somehow blundered along with their moth-eaten socialism, fooling people with their populism. Even earlier there had been difficult economic times, but did they open up the economy? No.

If thousands of freedom-fighters brought about India's political freedom; if the Nehru-Indira Dynasty plunged us into poverty, misery and economic disaster; then it was Narasimha Rao who ushered in economic freedom—the Second Freedom.

In a limited way, it was a good start. Atal Bihari Vajpayee's government gave it a further push. But, with the dynasty back in power since 2004, while there has been little progress in extending the reforms process, attempts have been made to partially reverse the past achievement—and that too with the Rao's ally, Manmohan Singh, as the prime minister. This itself shows that the reforms were actually thanks to Narasimha Rao—Manmohan Singh was only doing his bidding. With Sonia in power, it is gradually gravitating back to the bad old days of Nehru-Indira-Rajiv socialism and bureaucratism. The hard-earned surplus, thanks to liberalisation, is sought to be thrown around to garner votes—what with MNREGA, Food Security and such other schemes, which do little of any long-term good for the poor, and mostly helps fill pockets of the bloated bureaucracy and politicians. India is yet to overcome its leftism and socialism which did no good to anybody, except the dynasty.

The abstract terms like leftism, socialism, liberalisation do not convey the actual impact of such systems. It is necessary, therefore, to talk about these in concrete terms, as ground realities, and then appreciate the real difference; else it sounds like some abstract socialism vs. liberalisation debate. What were the state of affairs from the time of independence till 1991? Just picture them.

Famine conditions during several years in the fifties and the sixties. Thousands dying. Millions of men, women, boys, girls, children and infants going hungry for months on end.

Rampant unemployment. Bleak future for the majority of educated. Poor quality of jobs even for the well-educated.

Poor prospects for educated women. Most doing graduation and post-graduation merely to find a good marriage match, and not to pursue a career, the job prospects being very bleak. Country not getting the productivity benefit of the educated women, with most remaining just housewives, or remaining under-employed.

Highways like side roads: narrow and one lane. Pathetic city roads. Metros and cities inadequately inter-connected. Poor urban infrastructure. Rural infrastructure—a far cry. Rural people did not count.

Only two types of cars. Fiat and Ambassador. Relics of the time long ago. No changes or improvements through the decades. Only two types of scooters. If you want Bajaj, wait for a minimum of five years! No loans for cars or two-wheelers.

One airline. Only a few airports. Poor connections.

You want cooking gas. Apply. If you are lucky, you may get a cylinder after three-four years.

Refrigerator. Air-conditioners. They were all luxury—white goods. Subject to high taxes. Only the very rich and the corrupt could afford them. No loans for consumer goods.

You want a good TV or VCR or music system. Go abroad and get it, after paying heavy customs duty, or bribe the guy at the customs.

You want to have a house of your own? Wait till retirement. After retirement, take loan on your LIC policy, use your PF and acquire one. Till retirement, live in a rented accommodation, or a government-provided accommodation. Housing Loans for the general public from banks were unheard of.

Higher education and career. If you are good in studies, become a doctor or an engineer. If you are not so good, do arts, cram up, and try IAS. Alternately, become a teacher or a lawyer or something. The options ended. Contrast this with the wide variety of careers now.

Villages and villagers and agriculture. Who cared! Dynasty was elitist and city-centric. If nothing much was done for the cities, where did the villages come in? They were used to living on their fate for decades. So be it, post-independence too.

Tribals didn't count. Why has Naxalism and Maoism reared its ugly head in large swathes of tribal India? Thanks to sheer neglect and exploitation since the Nehru period.

Further, it was not just a case of economic deprivation. For many, it was the mental agony which was much worse.

Imagine being looked down upon or humiliated abroad, and even by foreigners who visited India. It was unfortunately like the current treatment of Biharis in Mumbai, or of East-UP persons as *Bhaiyaas* in Punjab! Now what fault is it of Biharis or the persons of East-UP? They both are among the most intelligent and capable people. Both East-UP and Bihar were the most prosperous and civilised areas in India. Where was Nalanda? Where was the capital of Chandragupta Maurya? Chanakya belonged to which area? Where was Sri Ram born? Where did Buddha achieve his enlightenment? Where did Mahavir propagate his religion? All these places are either in Bihar or in East-UP. But look what first the Congress, since independence, and then Lalu did to them in Bihar. And what did Nehru Dynasty, which belongs to East-UP and has been winning elections from there, did to it!

In Punjab and elsewhere people contemptuously call persons from East-UP as *Bhaiyyas*. Well then Sri Ram, and Laxman, and Sita were also *Bhaiyyas*! So is the Nehru Dynasty! The place of Sri Ram definitely deserves to be on the top. Who would do it? Certainly not the Dynasty. They have won so many elections from there, and also ruled it for a long time—but did nothing. The point is that the Dynasty's rule has made all Indians *Bhaiyyas* in the eyes of the world.

If you ask people who have survived those times, and ask them to compare it with the times now, they would certainly not say "Good old times!" for the times before 1991. They were like the dark ages. Practically three generations went to dogs!

Piloo Mody of Swatantra Party had addressed a revealing parliamentary question to Indira Gandhi: "Madam Prime Minister, can you tell this august House why Indians are successful everywhere in the world except under the rule of your government?" It took a Narasimha Rao to prove Piloo Mody wrong.

Consequent to Nehru-Indira-Rajiv socialistic claptrap, by 1991 India had become the world's greatest aid recipient—beggar #1. However, thanks to Narasimha Rao led economic reforms, India has since been aiding other countries, even if modestly. It has been remarked by many that Narasimha Rao was the best prime minister India has ever had. That way, the current generation is a lucky generation that grew up in the post-Nehru-Indira-Rajiv era. Many among the young already have a car and a flat of their own—something unimaginable in the Nehru-Indira-Rajiv era.

Come to think of it, could a Narayan Murthy—given his value-system—succeeded in pre-Rao times? Doubtful. Infosys did commence business in post-Indira and pre-Rao times, but it could flourish only thanks to Rao and his liberalisation.

Nehru grafted on the predominantly-feudal post-colonial India an intrusive socialist-bureaucratic state that strangulated innovation, stifled economic growth, vitiated value-systems and led to social stagnation. Indira Gandhi strengthened these structural weaknesses and prescribed "more of the same". Rajiv was no better.

COMPETENCE, FOR A CHANGE

Unlike the deficiently-educated Dynasty members, P.V. Narasimha Rao was an experienced, well-read, perspicacious polyglot and an exceptionally wise person. No wonder he managed to make a big difference for the country. In fact, if there is one person whom the current generation should thank for having good, well-paying jobs, if there is one person the Indians should thank for the nation having turned the corner and now over a trillion dollar economy, it is PVN.

But for his decisive break from the socialism of the Dynasty, this would not have been possible. It was not easy. The hangers-on of the Dynasty like Rajesh Pilot, Arjun Singh and many others opposed him tooth and nail. They and the Dynasty felt that without the leftist rhetoric and policies that allowed them to be seen as pro-poor, how would they get votes to continue in power? PVN had made a very perceptive remark: *Why rule for the sake of ruling if there is nothing specific to achieve.*

That is in sharp contrast to the Dynasty for whom vote and power come first, even if the national interest is hurt. Achievement and national good are secondary. The primary concern is the continuation of the Dynasty.

Yes, for any dynasty—Nehru-Gandhi or any other—remaining in power is the primary concern. Hence, they are risk averse. They do not want to disturb the apple cart. Start charities at government expense, allow wages for 100 days of unproductive labour, or do some such thing to get votes. Not something that can give 365 days of productive work!

It was ultimately PVN who managed to calm down Punjab, set on fire by the acts of the Dynasty. Had he more time, he would certainly have done something positive on the India-China front, on India-Pakistan relations, and on Kashmir, for he was indeed wise and clever.

BEING UNGRATEFUL

It was sad the way PVN was treated by the Congress Party upon his death—for all the good he did for the country. Although PVN had been both the AICC President and the PM, his body was not even kept inside the AICC office at New Delhi to allow people to pay homage. It was brought outside the gate of the AICC office at 24, Akbar Road and just kept there for 20 minutes! Was it 'to pay homage' to him, or to insult him?

His samadhi should have been on the banks of Yamuna in Delhi where there are samadhis of Mahatma Gandhi, Nehru, Indira Gandhi, Lal Bahadur Shastri, Charan Singh, Zail Singh, Rajiv Gandhi, Sanjay Gandhi, and so on. Narasimha Rao's family requested for a plot for his samadhi in Delhi on the banks of Yamuna, but the request was rejected. Instead, his body was flown to Hyderabad. So a person like Sanjay Gandhi who never held any official position could have his samadhi among the worthies, adjacent to Shantivan, but not Rao, who was perhaps the best PM of India. The way PVN was treated upon his death was, of course, shocking, but not surprising—it is the Dynasty tradition to ill-treat non-Dynasty leaders upon their death. For Jawaharlal Nehru's and Indira Gandhi's shockingly disgraceful behaviour in similar respect please see respectively *Foundations of Misery: Blunders of the Nehruvian Era* and the earlier chapter on Lal Bahadur Shastri in this book.

Incidentally, it was PVN who gave Manmohan Singh [MMS] a break into politics, made him Finance Minister, and supported him to the hilt, despite severe opposition to the policies from many in the Congress itself. And how did MMS, the gentleman, express his gratitude? MMS was to be the main speaker at the 91st birth anniversary event of PVN on 28 June 2012 organised at Andhra Bhavan in New Delhi by some Congress leaders from Andhra Pradesh, but MMS gave it a miss on the flimsy pretext of being busy, even though he was in the capital. Would the fellow do so if the event was of the Nehru-Gandhis?

Writes A Surya Prakash in an article "Manmohan joins league of the ungrateful" in *DNA* of 4 July 2012: "We are all aware of the churlishness of the Nehru-Gandhi family and its reluctance to acknowledge the contribution of political leaders who are not part of the family. This pettiness has been on display since the days of Jawaharlal Nehru when everything was done to run down the contribution of Subhash Chandra Bose, Sardar Patel and BR Ambedkar. Likewise, despite the spectacular turnaround of the nation's economy under Rao's stewardship, the Nehru-Gandhi family has never acknowledged his contribution. But it is sad to see Singh [MMS], who owes everything he has achieved over the last 21 years to Rao, lacking the courage to speak up for his mentor...."

8

NDA and Vajpayee

Atal Bihari Vajpayee, the leader of the Bharatiya Janata Party (BJP) and a parliamentarian since 1957, served as the Prime Minister of India in three non-consecutive terms: first for 13 days from 16 May 1996 to 1 June 1996, then for 13 months from 19 March 1998 to April 1999, and finally for five years from 13 October 1999 to 19 May 2004.

Vajpayee was a gifted speaker with unmatched oratorical and debating skills. He was also a poet.

It was under him that India went nuclear, when in May 1998 India conducted five underground nuclear tests in Pokhran desert in Rajasthan.

The crisis points during his tenure were the June-1999 Kargil War with Pakistan, which was ably handled by India; the December-1999 Indian Airlines flight IC 814 hijack that was incompetently handled; the December-2001 terrorist attack on the Indian Parliament that was adequately tackled; and the 2002 Post-Godhra Riots that could have been better handled.

Vajpayee tried his best to better relations with Pakistan, but couldn't make much headway, thanks to Pakistani politics. He tried to improve relations with China. During his time, India established strategic and military cooperation with Israel, including that for fighting terrorism. Bill Clinton visited India in 2000, becoming the first US president to visit India since Jimmy Carter.

Vajpayee ably carried forward the economic reforms started by Narasimha Rao. Disinvestment Ministry did notable work under Arun Shourie, supported by Vajpayee, undertaking privatisation of a part of the state sector, including the VSNL. Vajpayee government promoted special export processing zones, Information Technology Parks and Industrial Parks across the country to bolster industrial production and exports. Among the excellent initiatives of his term was the *National Highway Development Project* including the *Golden Quadrilateral* and the *Pradhan Mantri Gram Sadak Yojana*. During his tenure the infrastructure hugely improved, the economic growth picked up, and job and business opportunities multiplied. People in India and abroad began to see hope in India and felt India was well on its way to becoming a superpower, rivalling China's growth.

NDA managed to keep inflation under control—in sharp contrast to the run-away inflation and price-rise during the UPA rule of the last decade.

The NDA Government during its six years of rule was able to create about 60 million jobs compared to mere 15 million jobs created by the UPA in its first eight years till 2012 (for which the data is available).

It's a mystery why the National Democratic Alliance (NDA) under Vajpayee failed to get re-elected in 2004 despite its much superior performance than the Congress ever. The combination of the powerful vested interests around the dynasty and the Congress that includes the leftist/"secularist" intellectuals, and sections of the NGOs and the media perhaps proved lethal.

Vajpayee is surely among the three best prime ministers of India, the other two being Lal Bahadur Shastri and Narasimha Rao.

9

4G Part-B: Sonia Gandhi

Sonia Gandhi (SG), the Italian wife of late Rajiv Gandhi and the President of the Congress, has been the *de facto* head of the government, along with her son, Rahul Gandhi, since 2004. UPA-I (2004-09) and UPA-II (2009-14) would have hopefully performed better had Manmohan Singh (MMS), the *de jure* head of the government, been also the *de facto* head, and had asserted himself. But, alas, that is only a counterfactual. There had been high hopes from MMS—all belied. However, there were never any high hopes, or even low hopes, from either Sonia Gandhi or Rahul Gandhi.

MYSTERY? NOT REALLY

If one does not go into the reasons, it indeed appears mysterious that while political leaders in general keep communicating—effectively or otherwise—and very often over-communicate, even when you wish they took long pauses and did some real work on the ground, here is a political leader sitting right at the top and refusing to communicate. It is rare to hear Sonia Gandhi hold forth on any topic of importance. Has she ever tried to explain her viewpoints on TV, or through articles in print media? Has she allowed herself to be subjected to grilling interviews? No.

Why? It's not that she is busy devoting herself to any great national cause and does not find time to communicate. The plain reason—deductible and extrapolatable from whatever little sound bites leave her lips—appears to be that she just does not have the stuff. She lacks depth and understanding and is incapable of holding forth on any topic. So why make a spectacle of oneself in interviews and discussions. Restrict yourself to non-risky one-way inane communication.

The pathetic performance of UPA-I and UPA-II, preponderance of mega-scandals, financial hera-pheri of amounts unheard of before, no movement on economic liberalisation and financial reforms, paralysis in the government, throwing of money at populist schemes to garner votes, throw-back to the bad old days of socialism tell their own story—the massive cost to the nation of the gross incompetence of the current rulers from the dynasty.

But that should not come as a surprise. What can be expected from a person with no worthwhile credentials holding power merely on account of being a member of the dynasty. India is far too vast and complex a country to be managed by dynasty dumbs. One wonders what crimes have Indians done in their present and past lives to have to suffer at the hands of such leadership. The original culprit was perhaps Motilal Nehru who promoted Jawaharlal blindly, followed by Jawaharlal promoting Indira, followed by.... Well, it's sickeningly long and disappointing list.

Here is an extract from an article, "Rich MPs, Poor Voters" by Minhaz Merchant in *The Economic Times*, Mumbai of June 9, 2012: "...The Rae Bareli seat in Uttar Pradesh has been a Gandhi family bastion since 1967 when Indira Gandhi first stood for election from there. Sonia Gandhi adopted the constituency in 2004 and was re-elected with a huge majority in 2009. It should, therefore, be one of India's most developed districts. Right? Wrong. The Hunger and Malnutrition, or HUNGaMA, survey, released by the Prime Minister earlier this year, was carried out amongst children under the age of five in 112 rural districts across 3,360 villages in nine states. The results should shame politicians of every major party who represent the poor in these districts. Rae Bareli is a sprawling district spread over 4,608 sqkm with a population of 34.04 lakh. How does it fare? Poorly—even by the abysmal standards of the other 111 districts surveyed.

According to the report, coordinated by the Naandi Foundation and reviewed, among others, by economists Dr Abhijeet Banerjee and Dr Isher Judge Ahluwalia, 'Rae Bareli with 70.40%, Koraput in Orissa with 68.86% and Dumka in Jharkhand with 63.65% have the highest number of stunted children.'"

The dynasty and the Congress who in their overlong rule of over five decades did nothing effective on the ground—like massive educational and social campaigns, good governance, firm implementation of the "rule of law"—to root out communalism and casteism forever and consign it to history, and instead leveraged the two curses for votes, are currently back at their dirty old game of polarising voters on communal lines to stay in the game in the parliamentary election, even though the parties they accuse of being communal have shunned campaign on communal lines and have stuck to developmental agenda and welfare for all communities, irrespective of religion. Shows the hypocrisy of the dynasty, the Congress and all similar parties loudly professing secularism, but keeping the communal campaign in the forefront (as they have no worthwhile achievements to seek votes on). Also, exposes the hypocrisy of their intellectual supporters and the media.

10
5G : Rahul Gandhi

DEFICIENT EDUCATION : A DYNASTIC TRAIT

Deficient education is a dynasty attribute, despite all the money, and all the facilities at their disposal.

Nehru's academic achievements were rather modest. He was a graduate and had passed the bar exams. Writes M.J. Akbar in *Nehru: The Making of India*: "Eventually when he [Jawaharlal] passed in the second half of the second class, Motilal was relieved enough to celebrate lavishly.... Motilal was acutely terrified that his son might fail, so even such moderate results were cause for celebrations.... Motilal had set his heart on sending his son to the Indian Civil Service.... He called the ICS the 'greatest of services in the world'.... But the weak Second [class of Jawaharlal Nehru] at the end of Cambridge persuaded Motilal that his son was unlikely to get through the tough ICS examinations.... His [Jawaharlal's] expenditure in 1911 was £800, enough to pay for three years of an ordinary student's existence...."

Contrast this with Ambedkar who often skipped meals or ate frugally to save money when he was studying in London. In *Dr Ambedkar: Life and Mission*, Dhananjay Keer mentions that Ambedkar subsisted in London on mere £8 a month! That amounts to £96 a year. Compare this with £800 a year of Nehru, which excluded expenses for several other requirements that were separately arranged by Nehru's father.

Indira Gandhi failed to complete her graduation despite spending considerable time and money in prestigious institutions in India, Europe and Britain.

Sanjay Gandhi never attended college!

Rajiv Gandhi did not do his graduation despite all the expenses at London. He was at Cambridge till 1965, but left it without a degree, because he did not appear for the examinations. He joined Imperial College, London in 1966, but again left it after a year, without a degree.

Sonia Gandhi? A graduate? Not clear. Most probably not.

Rahul Gandhi. Educational details are not available with due clarity, although he is reported to be a graduate. Like his father he had the habit of joining a college or a course, and leaving it mid-way, perhaps finding the load too much to tackle.

All the members of the dynasty, despite all the money, support and facilities, have been gross under-achievers academically. Yet, they are qualified enough to rule India! And naming educational institutes after their name is justified!

It can of course be argued that academics is not all. It is not necessary to be highly qualified to be a good leader. That's fine. If a certain leader was unable to go in for higher studies on account of paucity of money, or because of some special circumstances, one can understand. But, when you do take admission in a college, and have all the monetary support, and all the facilities, and yet you either fail to finish your education or do poorly, it does reflect on you as a person. Perhaps, you have no self-discipline, or you lack commitment, or you possess no determination, or you are too casual and irresponsible and while away time, or you have low IQ. You need not be a topper, but blessed with all facilities, you do need to do reasonably well.

Another queer thing about the Nehru-Gandhi Dynasty has been pursuing studies and courses abroad at considerable expense when those courses of similar or better standards were available in India. Indira tried to engage in elementary studies abroad, Rajiv tried to do engineering in London. Why? Didn't the family, which flaunted its patriotism, find good schools and colleges in India! One could understand if they were academically brilliant and went abroad to do some specialised courses not available in India, or went to prestigious colleges abroad for their better teaching. But, no. They went for ordinary courses; and mostly, they whiled away their time there.

STUFF?

Like his mother, Rahul Gandhi has never held forth on any topic of importance, nor has he participated in any TV debates. He has never tried to explain and defend his viewpoints either in speeches or on TV or through articles in print media. How then to know if he has any stuff? Actually, the very fact that he avoids all these is because he is afraid he would stand exposed. He has also not allowed himself to be subjected to grilling interviews. *Times Now* interview was an exception, and he got badly mauled in it. It's doubtful if he would again take the risk. Why expose oneself?

TV debates and questioning, like they happen among US presidential and other contestants, must be made mandatory. Let us at least know our leaders. He just makes a statement, and runs away.

One of Rahul's campaign complaint against the opposition across the states is: "We at the Centre send money for the schemes for the poor to the State, and the State does not pass it on to the poor or swallows it or gives it to the rich!" Is he a king at the Centre? Is it his money that he dispenses? Are states beggars getting his doles? Do the Congress-ruled states utilise the money properly? No answers to these vital questions. Does he think Indian voters are fools? Why does he indulge in such silly comments? Did he not have anything substantial to say?

In Gujarat, much before the last state elections, hinting at Modi, he said something to the effect that evil man like Mao Zedong also did development. This remark educated us on several things about Rahul. *One*, he has no historical knowledge. Mao's period was an economic disaster for China, like Rahul's father's, his grandmother's and his great-grandfather's was for India. *Two*, he has no idea about world leaders. Mao was certainly not an evil person. Yes, many of his ideas, which he genuinely believed in, thinking they would benefit China, proved disastrous. But then, many of the things Nehru and Indira Gandhi and Rajiv Gandhi did also proved disastrous. Were they evil? *Three*, the person having ambition to be the PM of India seems to have no idea on diplomacy, and how to refer to leaders of other countries. China still reveres Mao. *Four*, Rahul does not know how to articulate what he wants to say. *Five*, anything impromptu, and Rahul is likely to blunder.

Campaigning in Kerala in 2011 assembly elections, he commented on the advanced age of Achuthanandan to gain some political mileage, when Karunanidhi was in the same age bracket, and DMK was an ally of the Congress in Tamil Nadu, going to polls simultaneously with Kerala. Where was the application of mind? What does it tell about Rahul?

During the Mayawati period in UP, Rahul Gandhi said in a certain context: "I feel ashamed to call myself an Indian after seeing what has happened here in UP." Sure, there is much to feel ashamed about, not only in UP, but elsewhere too. Six PMs of India have been from UP—three from his own dynasty. Congress ruled it since the pre-independence period, after the elections in the thirties. Post-independence, Congress-ruled UP for the first 40 years, barring some periods in-between. All through, since the late 1930s, the dynasty members have been getting elected from UP, without a break. It is because Rahul's dynasty did little for UP that the other parties displaced Congress. So, if Rahul feels ashamed, it is a genuine sentiment. He ought to feel ashamed of how his dynasty has shamed all Indians—in UP and elsewhere in India! He, his dynasty and the Congress have plenty of reasons to feel ashamed: India's pathetic poverty, crores in hunger, millions of children victim of malnutrition, widespread illiteracy, poor infrastructure, wretched living conditions, yet crores being looted through mega-scams—CWG, 2G, Coalgate,...it's a long list.

In 2012, in the UP elections, Rahul led a negative campaign against all—BSP, SP and BJP—totalling ignoring the pathetic record of the UPA-II at the Centre, and that of the Congress when it was in power in UP, and of his own dynasty which has been getting elected from east UP for decades with nothing positive to show for it achievements. Good, people gave Congress a sound thrashing and showed the brother-sister pair their place!

As per the WikiLeaks, Rahul had told the US Ambassador to India in all seriousness that the Hindu terror was a greater challenge than the Islamic terror! What does it tell about his understanding of this serious issue of terror?

He is unable to even speak cogently on any issue. And when things get politically controversial, he just disappears from the scene—unable to face repercussions.

Look at his so-called "mass" contacts. All these publicised contacts happen only in the opposition-ruled states, not in the Congress-ruled ones, where the situation may be much worse.

His visit to Dalit homes; suddenly showing up at a tribal village in Orissa as their champion in Delhi; not doing or saying anything on Team Anna's agitation since April 2011 or on Lokpal, and then suddenly, after many months of deafening public silence, pouring forth inanities in Parliament, inter-mixed with Lokpal-like-Election-Commissioner comment lapped up by chamchas and media as "game-changer"; suddenly noticing the weaver's conditions before elections—all demonstrate a transparent lack of any genuine concern, concern only with votes, and raise more questions than they answer. It is in crises that weaknesses are thrown up in sharp relief; and the Brand Rahul stood totally exposed in the Anna crisis, showing up all its inadequacies.

Rahul's attempts to project himself as the messiah of the *other* India, to cultivate the rural Bharat, and show off himself as the protector of those who seemingly lost out on the reforms cannot fool anyone. It is the same old wine in the same old bottle—the hackneyed socialist rhetoric of his grandmother, now imitated by his mother. A genuine leader cannot speak down at the people. He has to engage with them. He has to participate in debates. He has to address difficult issues. And he has to get his hands dirty and stick it out. He cannot suddenly emerge, say or do something, and then disappear. His is a cosy, cocooned political style.

Lately, he has been vociferous about "Empowerment" of general public, of common man. Isn't it ironic that the dynasty that has unfairly concentrated most powers within it talks of empowering others! He also talks of empowerment in terms of laws: RTI, RTE, and so on (most of which the Congress was forced to pass, not that the Congress took the initiative). What matters is delivery on the ground. What's the worth of laws that you can't or don't implement. First implement (what the Congress has miserably failed to implement in over five decades of its rule) the most basic of all sets of laws—that of "law and order"—that would ensure the most basic of rights to citizens—that of security and safety—then ventilate on grand schemes.

He is also seen lecturing small and big groups, including FICCI. If you hear him you feel baffled at his banalities, meanderings and generalities and lack of understanding, analysis and specifics, and wonder if he is so dumb as to be unconscious that others bear him out and don't walk out only out of courtesy.

If Rahul Gandhi is indeed honest and sincere, he must ask himself the following questions, and also share the answers with the general public. Does he realise that the Congress Party—the shape that it is in: full of chamchas; corrupt netas; ambitious, incompetent, arrogant ex-bureaucrats; self-seeking lawyers—is incapable of delivering goods for the country? What has he done for all these years—when he is not in the government, and has only been doing party work—to stem the rot? Is the Congress significantly better, and significantly less corrupt, as a body compared to what it was when he got involved with the Congress? In short, what has been his concrete contribution in terms of practical results on the ground? If he has utterly failed in this task, what hope is there that he would do better when in the government?

What is his track record? Has he headed a panchayat or a municipal corporation and achieved significant results? Has he worked as a junior or a senior minister in any state and done some work? Has he worked as a junior or a senior minister at the Centre and achieved results? Has he made a single speech that has impressed people? Has he given a single interview that has shown him to be sharp and intelligent? If he has done none of these, why should any reasonable person believe he can do anything worthwhile as the PM?

Is he aware how complex India is, how difficult are its problems, and how difficult is the job of a PM? What makes him feel he is experienced and qualified for the job? As a patriot, does he not think it would be disastrous for India to be managed by people not competent for the job? Would he ask an unskilled and inexperienced driver to drive him? All those who are promoting him to be the future PM must re-examine their act and re-evaluate it to make sure it is not inappropriate, irresponsible and unpatriotic.

Wrote M.J. Akbar in his column "Out of Turn" in *The Times of India*, Mumbai of 6 October 2013: "...This paradox will be lost on those Congresspersons who have become so subservient to dynasty that nothing matters other than ritual hallelujahs before a prince who has aged, or at least middle-aged, without having matured politically. Rahul Gandhi's interventions are a step-up from the extra-Constitutional authority formula. His preferred style is beyond anything known in democracy: press conference dictatorship. A privileged individual is more important in the current dispensation than the complex edifice of constitutional government in which any decision has to be nudged and nurtured carefully through numerous checks and balances.... For three years at least this UPA government has been imploding. It is now exploding, and its fragments are scattered across the news. Each Cabinet meeting ends with the grinding sound of Congress crumbling just a little more...."

Comments Sanjay Baru in an article titled "Inheritor as insurgent: Why Rahul Gandhi's outburst against the government strains credibility" in *The Financial Express* of 30 September 2013 in the context of Rahul Gandhi having torn his own government's ordinance: "It would have been one thing if Rahul had in fact publicly upbraided someone known to be sleazy or corrupt and ejected him from a position of power. That would turn him into a hero. Instead, he chose to embarrass his own party spokesperson, who was first defending a decision of the party's own government and was then forced to criticise it, and worse, he embarrassed the entire government by describing a decision of the Union cabinet as 'nonsense'.... Even if it was the case that wisdom suddenly dawned on a newly enlightened party vice-president, was the method adopted to seek change of policy and the language used appropriate?... Then followed the Pavlovian response of sycophantic junior ministers, supplicants in the Delhi durbar, jumping up to praise their leader's criticism of their own government. None considered it necessary to quit as minister, give up the Lutyens bungalow, white Ambassador with red light, and all the perks of office before belittling one's own government. Will such self-serving radicalism be rewarded with votes?... This is not the first time that members of the Sonia Gandhi Congress and ministers in the Manmohan Singh Government have happily hunted with the hounds and run with the hares.... Rahul has for long toyed with the option of either succeeding Manmohan Singh or dethroning him. Part of the problem with the second Manmohan Singh Government has been this confusion. Should the Rahul loyalists praise the government and inherit their success or criticise the government and grab the reins?... *Can an inheritor of power also be the rebel, the radical, the outsider*?"

When sycophants shout about his fitness to be the next prime minister, the Indian public has a right to know the basis of such claims. His views and comments have always been very simplistic, and show neither intellectual spark, nor wide reading, nor the ability to think deeply and analyse, nor experience, nor wisdom; and his leadership has not been proved in practice. So far, his track record has been less than mediocre. Congress would be doing a tremendous disservice to India by imposing him on the nation.

If you look at the sequence from the beginning to hopefully the end—Nehru, Indira, Rajiv, Sonia and Rahul—you find a steep deterioration. Nehru himself did not measure up to what our first PM should have been—if you go by the facts, the concrete results of his reign, his many blunders whose consequences we are still suffering, and not the fiction trotted out by the fawners. However, his successors have been progressively worse. The general trend in most families, which are well-to-do and can afford education, is that each generation is better than the previous. Nehru Dynasty is an exception. Each generation is worse than the previous.

It is important to realise that managing a country as large and as complex as India requires deep knowledge of India's different regions and people, its politics, its administration, its economy, its culture, its history, its strengths, its weaknesses and its international relations; intelligence to absorb them, experience to manage, competence to deal with complexities, and wisdom to take right decisions. Do Rahul-Sonia, and in due course, perhaps Priyanka, measure up? Certainly not.

In the interest of the nation, an iron law should be laid down: First prove your leadership competence in a public or private or political organisation or an NGO; then as a minister in a state or at the Centre or as a chief minister of a state for at least five years; and then only a candidate should be allowed to put himself or herself up as a prime minister.

Of course, the Nehru Dynasty would never like to follow such a rule. They know they would badly flunk in the first two stages, depriving them a chance at the top slot. They want to fail only at the top-slot!

We study, analyse and implement risk-mitigation in all walks of life: finance, banking, management, software, health, transport, security and so on. Practically, no segment is left untouched by it. However, when it comes to the biggest risk of all—that of the position of the prime minister—we seem to be casual, rather criminally callous.

"NAMUNAS" (SAMPLES)

Here are some samples ("namunas") of Rahul Gandhi's wisdom. They speak for themselves. Only short comments, where warranted, are therefore included.

Rahul at the AICC session in Jaipur on 21 January 2013: "...Last night each one of you congratulated me. My mother came to my room and she sat with me and she cried...because she understands that power so many people seek is actually a poison...."

~~~

As per reports in the media, the Election Commission on Friday, 9 May 2014, issued a show cause notice to the Congress
~~~

vice-president Rahul Gandhi for his alleged remarks at an election rally in Solan, Himachal Pradesh on May 1: "People from Japan ask me.... They say we are scared over one issue. We will help you, we will prepare roads. But we are scared whether there will be peace.... They say whether people of India will fight with each other or not?... This fear is there in our lives as well. If there is BJP, there will be violence. If there is BJP, 22,000 people will die, because they spread anger.... This question was never raised before...."

~~~

Given below are extracts from Rahul Gandhi's interview to Arnab Goswami of *Times Now* on 27 January 2014.

Rahul: "...but what one has to do and this is central to what I keep saying is that democracy is about respect of processes. Democracy is about non-arbitrary decisions. Democracy is about spreading decisions; it is not about destroying processes. There is a process in the constitution and that process says, and it is clearly written in the constitution, and it says members of parliament are to be elected by the population and members of parliament are to elect the Prime Minister. All I am doing is respecting that process."

Comments: Where was the democratic process when, rather than reversing the cabinet decision on the "ordinance on convicted lawmakers" internally through discussions, Rahul chose to crudely stomp into meet-the-press programme of his party's general secretary Ajay Maken at the Press Club at New Delhi on 27 September 2013, and declared the ordinance as "complete nonsense" deserving to be "torn up and thrown away". Prime Minister's former-advisor Sanjaya Baru has said, inter alia: "This type of blame on the government for a decision which was obviously taken in consultation with the party amounts to insubordination.... You can't pretend to be a great hero at the cost of dignity of your Prime Minister.... The principle of this government is that all credits will go to the party leadership and all blame for anything will go to the Prime Minister that has been the principle on which this government has been run for more than nine years...." So much for the "democratic" spirit!
~~~

And, how does his own position in the party thanks to his being a dynasty scion and his projection as a prime minister candidate match with the democratic spirit?

~~~

Rahul: "What Rahul Gandhi wants to do, is Rahul Gandhi and millions of youngsters in this country want to change the way the system in this country works. What Rahul Gandhi wants to do is empower the women in this country, wants to unleash the power of these women, I mean we talk about being a superpower...."

Comments: Who prevented him from doing so during the decade of UPA-I and UPA-II? Did he achieve anything?

~~~

Rahul: "The BJP has prime ministerial candidate, the BJP believes in concentration of power in the hands of one person, I fundamentally disagree with that, I believe in democracy, I believe in opening up the system. I believe in the RTI, I believe in giving power to our people. We have fundamentally different philosophies...."

Comments: Let Rahul first relinquish power derived thanks to being a dynasty scion.

~~~

Rahul: "The Congress Party and the BJP have two completely different philosophies, our attack on the BJP is based on the idea that this country needs to move forward democratically, it needs push democracy deeper into the country, it needs to push democracy into the villagers, it needs to give women democratic powers, it needs to give youngsters democratic powers. It is about opening the doors of the congress party, about empowering the youth..."

Comments: For a dynast to talk of democracy—what could be more hypocritical!

~~~

Rahul: "Our political party is fighting an ideological battle against the BJP and let me draw out the two pillars—our party believes that women should be empowered, democracy should go to every house, that RTI, and the MNREGA paradigm should be further expanded. The BJP believes power should be extremely concentrated in this country, few people should run this country and the large mass of this country should have no voice...."

Comments: Just throw random lies!

~~~

Rahul: "...The Gujarat riots took place frankly because of the way our system is structured, because of the fact that people do not have a voice in the system. And what I want to do. And I have said it and I will say it again. What I want to do is question the fundamentals over here. What I want to do is ask a couple of questions. I want to ask why candidates that are chosen in every single party are chosen by a tiny number of people. I want to ask why women have to be scared to go out on the street. I want to ask these questions. These are fundamental questions...."

Comments: His party has been in power, and the mother-son duo have been running the government for a decade. What have they done? They must answer this question, rather than asking it!

~~~

Rahul: "I don't actually keep invoking my family name, I have mentioned my family name once or twice and then people report that. The real issue is that I didn't choose to be born in this family, I didn't sign up and say that I like to be born in this family it happened, so the choice in front of me is pretty simple I can either turn around and say okay I will just walk away from this thing and leave it alone or I can say I can try and improve something. Pretty much every single thing I have done in my political career has been to bring in youngsters, has been to open up, has been to democratise. I am absolutely against the concept of dynasty, anybody who knows me knows that and understands that. But you are not going to wish away dynasty in a closed system, you have to open the system. Dynasty or children of politicians becoming powerful happens in the BJP, it happens in the DMK, it happens in the SP, it happens in the Congress party, it happens everywhere."

Arnab: "Then how are you different?"

Rahul: "You have to go into why it is happening."

Arnab: "It is happening because dynasties are allowed to proliferate, it is because a Scindia's son is a minister, a Deora's son is a minister, a Pilot's son is a minister. A PM's son is the Congress VP that is dynasty. Change is not happening at the top, you want change at the bottom. There are people out there who are saying that we want change at the top."

Rahul: "The reason children of politicians keep getting repositioned is because the system is closed. You are not going to change that without opening the system, you are not going to open the system without having processes, the system is not going to open by waving a wand and saying Abracadabra let us open the system. It is going to take time, it is going to take effort and it is going to take structure. That is the work that I do. That is the work I spent a whole bunch of my time doing that is the revolutionary work I have done in the IYC and the NSUI that is the work we are doing when we talk of an open manifesto. That is the work we are doing when we talk of 15 parliamentary seats being chosen."

Comments: What to comment? Can't blame Modi when he says Rahul is a *namuna* (a sample)!

~~~

Here are extracts from Rahul Gandhi's Speech (drivel!) at CII on 4 April, 2014:

"There is a tendency to look at India as a country. In our everyday life we see India as a national structure. But if you go back slightly more than that, go back a hundred, two hundred years, you would find that India is energy, it is a force. If you go back a thousand years, two thousand years, you would find that force came from our rivers, Ganga, Yamuna, Saraswati. We worshiped these rivers and the reason we worshiped these rivers was because that is where our energy came from, and everything we had was built on these rivers. Now we have gone way beyond that. We have built structures that are allowing this energy to rise, to explode...."

"...Democracy and technology have triggered a non-reversible chain reaction in India. This reaction is unstoppable. Nobody can
~~~

stop it. We have to channel this reaction. We need to nurture it. We need to make it harmonious. We need to make this happen smoothly. We need to use the energy generated by this movement of people and ideas, the force this movement is generating, and we need to use it to empower everybody. Not one person, not almost everybody, but everybody..."

Comments: Speechless! Rather "*comments-less*"!!

~~~

A few more gems from Rahul Gandhi:

"Yahan Hindustan mein hamara jaat ka concept hai. Is mein bhi escape velocity hoti hai. Dalit community ko is dharti pe Jupiter ki escape velocity chahiye. (In India we have caste. Dalits need ***Jupiter's escape velocity*** on Earth)."

"Isiliye agar aap history ko dekhe, jo dalit log hai, hum sab hai, Ambedkarji ko bahut garv se dekhte hai. Wo pehle aadmi hain jo escape velocity kar ke US chale gaye (Ambedkar was the first to achieve *escape velocity* and go to the US)."

"Jo leadership hai wo Mayawati ji ne capture kar liya hai aur doosre logon ko ubharne nahin deti. (Mayawati has captured the leadership and she does not allow others to emerge)."

Comments: What about Rahul and his dynasty who never allow capable Congress leaders to emerge, lest they threaten their position! Rahul seems to be so dumb the irony of what he says doesn't hit him.
~~~

11
Sonia-Rahul-MMS-UPA

The Sonia-Rahul Gandhi-Manmohan Singh government or simply the MMS government is surely the most corrupt and inept government in the history of independent India. It would win hands-down in incompetence with any other democratic government in the world.

The golden prospects that India looked forward to in 2004 thanks first to Narasimha Rao and then to the Vajpayee government have all but evaporated thanks to lack of vision of the dynasty-driven Congress and their stale, uninspiring policies, utter lack of governance, appalling administrative deterioration and gross corruption.

MANMOHAN SINGH (MMS)

Manmohan Singh (MMS) has frittered away all the approbation he had received as the Finance Minister under Narasimha Rao. He presents a pathetic picture of an incompetent and ineffective prime minister (PM) passing his time. He has been an obsequious babu ever-grateful to the dynasty for having him elevated to the position of the PM. Many now view him as an underachieving and overrated prime minister.

Vinod Jose in his article "Falling Man" in *The Caravan* magazine of 1 October 2011 quotes Sanjaya Baru, a business journalist who served as Singh's media advisor from 2004 to

2008: "In politics, it's alright to be loved or hated, but you should never be ridiculed. And his [MMS] problem today is that he has become an object of ridicule."

The article further says: "The prominent historian Ramachandra Guha, who has described the current administration as 'inept and incompetent beyond words', told me that he now regards Singh 'increasingly as a tragic figure'. 'He's intelligent, upright, and possesses all these vast experience of working in the government for over four decades,' Guha said. 'But the timidity, complacency and intellectual dishonesty will make him a tragic figure in our history.'"

The article also includes a comment by a former senior secretary: "Manmohan Singh is an honest man in a pecuniary sense, but not in the high political-moral sense, as someone who wants to correct wrongs in governance by taking on dishonest people or practices."

Wrote Simon Denyer in the article titled "India's 'silent' prime minister becomes a tragic figure" in *The Washington Post* of 5 September 2012: "...But the image of the scrupulously honorable, humble and intellectual technocrat has slowly given way to a completely different one: a dithering, ineffectual bureaucrat presiding over a deeply corrupt government.... As India's economy has slowed and as its reputation for rampant corruption has reasserted itself, the idea that the country was on an inexorable road to becoming a global power has increasingly come into question.... The irony is that Singh's greatest selling points—his incorruptibility and economic experience—are the mirror image of his government's greatest failings.... Under Singh, economic reforms have stalled, growth has slowed sharply and the rupee has collapsed. But just as damaging to his reputation is the accusation that he looked the other way and remained silent as his cabinet colleagues filled their own pockets...."

These extracts are from the blog dated 13 September 2013 titled 'The "Man" who betrayed himself' by Sanjeev Ahluwalia, IAS (retired): "We assume that knowledge, learning and professionalism is what makes the difference between an 'extractive' policracy and a 'developmental' one.... In 2004, when Dr Manmohan Singh...became PM, there was relief that.... India would again be led by an 'intellectual' far above the hurly burly of election politics, with no personal stake and no motive, except to 'wipe the tears from the eyes of the poorest Indian' (the Mahatma).... Like the collapse of the mountains above Kedarnath, the lofty edifice built up by reputation and public expectations cracked and collapsed under the weight of timidity, poor political instincts but most importantly self-betrayal. Dr Singh betrayed himself time and again as he turned a Nelson's eye to massive corruption, allowed decision making to be subverted by unconscionably partisan politics and sloth. He defined the integrity of the highest executive position in India as a narrowly construed 'personal' integrity and in doing so reverted to his essentially 'babu' roots of keeping 'his desk clean'. Even this is questioned in the 2G scam and Coalgate, though most would put down the seeming links to him, to a secretariat, outside of his control. He betrayed his profession, since economics played, at best a marginal role, in the working of his cabinet. He betrayed his earlier characterization of himself as a Sher (Singh) and appeared to meekly toe the backward looking, ineffective and contradictory party line. In acting thus, he debased the high office he holds...."

MEGA SCAMS AND GROSS FAILURES

Although the well-publicised Nirbhaya case of 2013 is sufficient to illustrate the sad state of security for women in India and the depth to which India has fallen under the watch of the Nehru-Gandhi dynasty, here is another shocking case from yet another Congress-ruled state described in an article "The Death of Kali" by Samar Harlankar in *Hindustan Times* of 19 July 2012: "As India fulminates after a 16-year-old student was slapped, dragged, groped and stripped on a Guwahati street last week, it is clear this abomination is not about one woman against a mob of opportunistic, brutal men. This is a story of a dangerous decline in Indians and India itself, of not just failing morality but disintegrating public governance when it comes to women...Second, the governance failures. The first calls to a local police station go unanswered, and the station house officer is suspended for dereliction of duty but only after national attention. The search for suspects does not get underway after the broadcast of the assault. It starts nearly two days later, after the video goes viral and posters of the assailants appear in Guwahati. Only after the video hits national television do the police chief and a deputy make public statements, deeply insensitive ones (chief—the police are not an ATM machine dispensing instant service; deputy—a stray incident hyped by the national media). The government reacts to the outrage with strange, tired logic, ordering a 10 pm shutdown for Guwahati's 127 bars, never mind that the assault occurred just after 9 pm. To calm the victim, the National Commission of Women (NCW) sends a representative, who promptly reveals the girl's name. The chief minister does the same, even emailing photos of his meeting with the girl to the media. Later, the NCW chief cautions women to be 'careful' of how they dress because 'such incidents are a result of blindly aping the West', and the CM now sees the assault as 'a conspiracy' against his government...."

One spectacular achievement that the Sonia-Rahul-MMS government can be credited with is massively upping the scale of scams and corruption. Not the insignificant loose-change of a few lacs and crores. Even a 100-crore is viewed with contempt. Unless it is hundreds or thousands of crores, it is not in keeping with the high watermarks set by UPA-I and II. Covering details of mega scams like Adarsh, CWG, 2G, Coalgate, AgustaWestland and NavyGate and others would require a separate exclusive book. However, the extent and the spread, the amounts involved and the brazenness of the scams illustrate the depths to which the government, the politicians and the Babudom has fallen under the Sonia-Rahul-MMS dispension.

Taking briefly just the Coalgate for illustration, the 2012-report of the Comptroller and Auditor General of India (CAG) terms the government's allotment policy of allocation of coal blocks as arbitrary and non-transparent causing undue gains amounting to an estimated ₹ 1.86 lakh crore (₹ 1860 billion = USD 31 billion @1USD = ₹ 60) to private parties. Naresh Gujaral, in his article "Denationalise Coal, Now" in *The Indian Express* of 1 Sept. 2013, regards this figure as an underestimate, and pegs the figure at 5.1 lakh core (USD 85 billion). When the draft-report was leaked, while the coal minister pooh-poohed the losses as 'notional and imaginary', the honest PM MMS dismissed the honest findings as 'uninformed allegations'.

Writes Naresh Gujaral in the aforementioned article, "This scenario is reminiscent of the one that arose in a disintegrating Soviet Union, when oligarchs, in connivance with state officials, captured the state's mineral resources. Here in India, paan masala wallahs, TV manufacturers and newspaper owners have jumped into the fray—people who have no other known expertise except their ability to manage the powers that be. It is no surprise that names of MPs and ministers are also surfacing in this context."

Rather than responding to the serious accusations, coming clean on the scam and commencing necessary legal action, the PM's arrogant care two hoots retort was to unabashedly recite an Urdu couplet on the virtues of silence! Cabinet ministers' credibility-straining zero loss arguments, brazen lies and the PM reciting a poem!! Was it a government or a joke?

Here are extracts from a report from another Congress-NCP run state, Maharashtra, by Hemali Chhapia in *The Times of India*, Mumbai of 8 June 2012: "Even as large parts of Maharashtra reel under drought, dams initiated as long ago as 45 years are still works-in-progress. Construction deadlines have been postponed endlessly and costs have been inflated, sometimes leading to a project itself getting drowned. The Warna irrigation project, approved 45 years ago in January 1967, remains incomplete due to land acquisition troubles and insufficient funds. Its cost has risen 6,704% from ₹ 31.6 crore to ₹ 2,150 crore. The Chaskamam project, initiated 38 years ago, has had a 6,708% cost escalation, from ₹ 10.7 crore to ₹ 728.5 crore. Other projects—like the Kadavi, Chikotra, Patgaon and Kumbi—were initiated 32 to 35 years ago. Some of the talukas that would have benefited from the oldest projects are Shirala, Walwa, Palus, Miraj, Shahuwadi, Panhala, Hatkanangale, Shirol, Khed, Shirur, Shahuwadi, Panhala and Bhudargad. Consultant to the World Bank Prakash Sanglikar said that had the dams been built, the state would have stored enough water during the past five monsoons and not faced the droughtlike situation.

Many feel there is a chronic weaselling that doesn't allow one to unravel the mystery behind the delays...."

CONGRESS/UPA'S NON-PERFORMANCE

Here is a representative example to illustrate UPA's gross under-performance. The Central Government advised the Supreme Court in an affidavit in July 2013 that the length of the national highways in 1980 was 29,000 km, which expanded to 77,000 km in 2012—an increase of 48,000 km in 32 years. Of this 48000 km, 24000 km (50%) were added during the 9th five-year plan of 1997-2002, when the NDA was in power—highest during any plan period since independence; and 16000 km during the 10-year UPA rule since 2004. That is, the UPA constructed only one-third that of the NDA in as much time. Rather than increasing the pace further, the laggards UPA slumped to one-third.

Wrote N. Madhavan, K.R. Balasubramanyam and Anilesh Mahajan in an article "Paucity Amidst Plenty: Why a country flush with natural resources finds itself grappling with their shortage" in the *Business Today* of 22 December 2013: "Billionaire Lakshmi Niwas Mittal has the uncanny ability to work successfully with governments of all kinds across the globe. That, and his unbridled ambition, have enabled him to set up or acquire steel factories in 20 countries. But the man who created the world's largest steel empire from scratch tasted the bitter fruit of failure when he decided to invest in his country of birth—India. In a bid to capitalise on India's huge iron ore deposits and rising steel consumption, Mittal in 2005 announced plans to set up a steel project in Jharkhand that year and in Orissa the next. Later, he proposed another mill in Karnataka. The total intended investment was $30 billion. In July this year, Arcelor Mittal, Mittal's company, scrapped its $12 billion mill in Orissa after having failed to acquire land and iron ore mines for seven years. Its other projects have not yet been called off, but are also facing delays. Mittal's decision came just a day after South Korean steelmaker Posco, the world's fifth-largest, abandoned a $5.3 billion project in Karnataka for similar reasons. The two developments highlight how the Indian mining environment is scaring investors away. So, what is going wrong?..."

The callousness with which the Congress has been determinedly putting India's prospects at risk is highly disconcerting. The UPA has been busy throttling the dynamism of the economy, and has already put India's growth story at risk. The government has become a dismal farce, and is only busy running the country into the ground.

The Congress talks of 'inclusive growth', but does not understand either the desirability or the demands of inclusive governance and federalism. Besides, how does 'inclusive' growth fit-in with UPA's mega scams that are cumulatively far larger than UPA's designed-for-votes-and-corruption dole-outs like MNREGA and FSB? This UPA-sympathetic Nobel-laureate economists and leftist intellectuals must explain.

Even after 66 years of independence and the bitter results of its disastrous policies, the Congress and the Dynasty have been moronic enough not to have understood what causes poverty and what leads to its removal and prosperity, and foolishly pursue Nehru-Indira socialistic claptrap and fritter away precious money in dole-outs, only 20 per cent of which reaches the intended beneficiaries—thinking that's the way to garner votes.

Small-mindedness is the hallmark of the Dynasty and the Congress. They are medieval and feudal in their workings. Most of the Congress leaders, young and old, are but courtiers and hangers on, adept at palace intrigue, and aware that loyalty matters more than good work and competence. The political strategy of the government, the Congress and the Dynasty is the brutal strategy of using the state machinery to fix all critics, rather than try and learn from them. The vital democratic institutions are unravelling, and the Congress, led by the Dynasty, is presiding over this appalling administrative deterioration. From an apex, decisive political office, the PMO has been reduced to a bureaucratic post office. There is a general rot.

Wrote Pratap Bhanu Mehta in an article titled "Phantom democracy" in *The Indian Express* of 9 May 2013: "...But the fact that the government did not even feel it proper to keep up appearances is a mark of how narcissistic and hubris-driven it had become. The responsibility for a culture of corruption, evasion, lying and sheer contempt for institutions lies directly at the door of Sonia Gandhi and Manmohan Singh. Their air of injured innocence has become nauseating...."

12

Doomed by Dynacracy (Feudal Dynastic Democracy)

India is a country whose culture and thinking has been so vitiated by the dynasts and their hangers-on and direct and indirect beneficiaries that even the indefensible—dynastic democracy—is defended by an exotic class of politicians, academics, media-persons and "intellectuals". It is therefore necessary to take up certain relevant questions about dynacracy upfront.

WHY IS DYNACRACY UNFAIR AND AGAINST THE SPIRIT OF THE CONSTITUTION?

Dynacracy-tolerant or Dynacracy-"neutral" "intellectuals" often question: Are the dynasts trying to get in undemocratically? No. Then, what is the problem? If one fights an election, gets elected, and becomes a political leader, what illegality or wrong is committed—everything is democratic and above board.

Although obviously absurd, one is not surprised to hear such pleas. What is happening dynasty-wise, be it Nehru-Gandhi or DMK or Lalu or any of the scores of other dynasties, is so obviously wrong that it should neither attract any defence, nor any arguments to demolish that defence. However, the original Dynasty has been able to do such publicity over the decades through the compliant MSM, intellectuals and netas that the reverse has happened: questioning the dynastic succession has become questionable!

A prominent argument advanced goes like this. Dhirubhai Ambani's sons are also businessmen. That is, businessmen's wards generally become businessmen. Progeny of artists—singers, musicians, writers, and others—also become artists. Sons or daughters of Bollywood actors also become actors. Doctor's wards also become doctors. Farmer's son is often a farmer. Dynasty is everywhere. So why pick on only political dynasties? This superficial argument can fool only the gullible. Progeny of doctors, artists, actors, businessmen becoming also doctors, artists, actors, businessmen affect them only, not others. However, progeny of a neta/politician becoming a neta affects people at large. It is the requirement of a democracy to be representative and hence non-dynastic. Business houses or art houses or professional establishments are not required to be representative.

In politics too, you once had hereditary rajas and maharajas and kings and queens. But the days of those retrograde systems are gone—now replaced by a democratic system. In a way, therefore, hereditary or dynastic succession is unconstitutional. Then, why bring it in from the backdoor. It is against the spirit of the Constitution. Dynastic succession is feudal, inappropriate, unjust, and harmful for the nation, whether it happens in the communist North Korea or the Islamic Saudi Arabia or in the democratic or dynacratic India.

To the pro-dynasty "Don't they fight elections and win" argument, the question is: How do they win? A far more competent competitor would not even get the party-ticket. But for the dynasty scion, it is for the asking. They get on a platter the constituency nursed for years by their parents. And they have money to splurge to get elected. After getting elected, a high position within the party-organisation or the government is assured to them—something denied to the many much more competent but less-connected contenders. The whole thing is unjust, unfair and undemocratic.

Don't those who defend dynasties on the specious plea that "after all they get elected" realise that it is thanks to their running, or rather, running down the country for decades that

India could do no better than rank among the poorest and the most corrupt countries in the world and remains in "dark" ages, with millions of malnourished children, unjust criminal-justice system loaded against the poor and the powerless; continuing reprehensible caste, class and religious distinctions and social evils; and vicious, indifferent and incompetent Babudom.

CAN'T A DYNAST ENTER POLITICS?

The sophists question: "Are you saying that children of a politician should be denied a political career? Would that be democratic?"

It is not that the progeny or relatives of a politician should be denied a political career. Only thing is that they should not be allowed to derive an unfair advantage. That is possible when things are enforced to be genuinely democratic, nepotism is rooted-out, and talent and ability take the front-seat. Is there any inner-party democracy in the political parties?

What if the person from the so-called dynasty also has merit? Well, does he or she have more merit compared to the many with merit? If yes, fine. But, let there be a fair comparison, competition and debates.

WHY DYNACRACY IS DISASTROUS?

The principal hazards of dynasty politics are as under:

1. It discounts merit and prevents competent from rising.
2. It thwarts internal democracy in political parties.
3. Dynastic politics, nepotism, institutionalised corruption and non-accountability go together.
4. Dynastic politics is always at the expense of the nation.
5. It is the biggest menace. It's the foundation of India's misery.

DISCOUNTS MERIT; PREVENTS COMPETENT FROM RISING

Dynasty chamchas and politicians and pro-dynasty self-serving section of the media and "intellectuals", even after you exhaust all their pro-dynasty arguments, don't give up: "What's so bad about dynacracy, except perhaps it is apparently a bit unfair? But, look at the positive side. Politics is a difficult art, and it takes a long time to learn the ropes. Thanks to political dynasties, you get ready-made politicians!"

The above argument is totally bogus. Dynacracy is bad not just because we resent some having unfair advantage, it is bad because it results in mediocrity, and it discounts merit. The quality of leadership emerging out of a dynastic process can never be really good. For proof, check for yourself the unutterable underachievements of the underwhelming leadership of the dynasts, at the state or at the Centre, and how it has become worse and worse down the generations.

Real political leaders come from real political movements, while dynasts—the pretenders—come up from the cosy and secure family environments, without having to struggle or prove themselves, and are sustained by entitlements.

The results are there for anyone to see. None of the young dynasts that we see is a real reformist or revolutionary, ready to sacrifice to better India. Like their fawning parents, who came up ingratiating themselves with those who mattered, these young, covetous self-seekers are amazingly enlightened on the benefits of being a toady and do not miss out any opportunity to show their servility by trooping behind yet another scion in an obsequious manner.

Dynastic democracy is the main stumbling block in the creation and emergence of capable, young leadership.

THWARTS INTERNAL DEMOCRACY IN POLITICAL PARTIES

How can a country have a healthy democracy where the participant political parties fail to practice it internally. Internal democracy could mean emergence of non-dynasty leaders and curtailment of unfair privileges to the scions. Hence, dynasties ensure the parties founded by them or inherited by them do not engage in the luxury of internal democracy. In the US, the UK and other mature democracies, leaders of parties are elected after a tough inner-party contest. In India, leaders do not get elected, they get anointed.

Congress, DMK, NCP, SAD, RJD, SP, SS, and the like are all family firms. It is ironic that those participating in the democratic electoral process are themselves responsible for throttling democracy in their own party.

DYNASTIC POLITICS, CORRUPTION, NON-ACCOUNTABILITY GO TOGETHER

The hazards of our hereditary democracy stare us in our face: the spoilt, incompetent, unemployable scions of political leaders are thrust into public life because they know that politics is about power and making money—much faster than what the Ambanis or Birlas or Tatas are capable of.

Dynastic politics is not about alternative visions of India and contest of ideas; it is about winning power and controlling patronage, which in turn generates money to fuel electoral politics and perpetuating the family hold. Dynasts are there to protect the family inheritance and to further expand it.

Dynasties control party finance. In the US, politicians raise finance independently and openly. Not so in India. If that were so, individual politicians could challenge the party leadership. Election funds and campaign contributions are collected centrally by the dynasties secretly in black, and they remain undisclosed. Central leadership of the parties, that is, dynasties, allocate funds for election campaigns, and thereby control those elected. Black money and corruption is therefore part and parcel of the dynastic politics—that's what fuels the election campaigns.

Nepotism, corruption, dilution of accountability, and other negatives are the components of a complicit environment promoted by dynacracy to survive and continue.

Writes Vasundhara Sirnate in an article "Disassembling dynasty" in *The Indian Express* of 8 June 2012: "As long as politicians raise their own campaign finances illegally, their best insurance against disclosure is to keep the money in the family. If all politicians in India raised funds independently and openly (as they do in the United States) individual politicians could challenge the party leadership. In India this independence is discouraged and substantial campaign contributions are undisclosed or "black" and collected centrally. This centralisation of finances is essential to avoid detection... In India, and elsewhere, if a political party does not have a cadre-based organisation, is not rooted in an independent civil society association and has centralised financing of elections, it is much more likely to be dynastic."

DYNASTIC POLITICS AT THE EXPENSE OF THE NATION

Remain Secretive, Hide Misdeeds

Yet another negative is that dynasties have a vested interest in continuance at the expense of the nation. They also cover up all the wrong doings of the dynasty. Family-centric parties are bound to put their self-interest above public and national interest.

Nehru never appointed a deputy prime minister (after Patel) or a senior minister who would take his place in his absence (when abroad or unwell or on holiday), which was desirable from all angles. It was his national responsibility to build up a capable successor. But he didn't do it. Why? Because, while he could not have anointed Indira Gandhi in that position knowing the just and severe criticism it would attract, he didn't wish anyone else to get precedence, while building up meanwhile Indira's stature gradually.

So many countries have a law to release records after a certain period. This helps researchers delve into them, analyse reasons, and publish details. It serves a very useful national purpose. You can know what you did right, and what you did wrong—so that you do not repeat the same mistakes. But, in India, even where the law permits, the documents are not disclosed for one reason or the other. Mostly, because it would expose the incompetence of the government of the day. And so long as the same Dynasty has control, generation after generation, they would keep doing blunders, and ensure nothing comes out. Successive Nehru-Gandhi dynasts have ensured that any document or record that could embarrass the dynasty, even if it benefits the nation, is forever kept top-secret, like the Henderson-Brooks-Bhagat Report on the India-China War 1962, Netaji Subhash papers, Shimla Agreement with Pakistan, and so on. Similarly, any finding or revelation in India or abroad, if it could be embarrassing to the dynasty, is immediately suppressed or ignored, like the Mitrokhin Archives.

DYNACRACY: THE BIGGEST MENACE

The biggest menace threatening India is not poverty or backwardness or corruption or lack of governance or socialism-babudom, but feudal dynastic-democracy, because that is at the root of the former deficiencies.

There is no doubt India has great potential, talent and favourable demographics, but those by themselves can't trump bad governance and crumbling institutions, when politics has degenerated into family enterprises designed to plunder the country.

Thanks to the dynasty, India is now led by Congress leadership that is centralized and opaque. You have a mother-son pair whose thinking and opinion on various issues or their vision people have no idea about. A secret? Democracy propelled by *secret* ideas! A loyalty-based, and not merit-based, select servile and sycophantic group takes all key decisions.

At the foundation of India's misery and poverty is the feudal dynastic-democracy. Dynasty is necessarily vote-focussed and not nation-focussed, because its priority is to somehow continue in power. Hence, the logic of the myopic policies for vote-gain through dole-outs and sops to the poor, rather than engaging and delivering on a medium to long term economic vision that would eliminate the need for dole-outs and sops.

If India is poor, wretched and backward, it is thanks to dynacracy. If the states like UP are going to dogs, it is again thanks to Mulayam-Dynasty.

Rahul Gandhi goes around distributing unsought free gyan on his mission of "empowerment"! If he wants to walk his talk, he must first free himself from his own inherited "empowerment" and let the non-dynasty capables emerge in his party and take over reins of both the party and the government in the times to come.

Dynastic politics is an anachronism, and Indian democracy can become a mature, genuine and prosperous democracy only by discarding it. Privileges and entitlements have no place in modern democracy.

THE SPREADING TENTACLES OF DYNACRACY

The dynastic politics that Nehru started and thus sanctified has now vitiated and poisoned our whole democratic system. When people talk of Nehru as a great democrat, one can't help but laugh. How can a person who laid the foundation of the dynastic-rule in democratic India be ever called a democrat? Democracy grafted on a nation with a strong feudal mindset is likely to degenerate into dynacracy, unless the leaders who matter consciously devote themselves to ensuring it does not happen, both by setting an example themselves (like Sardar Patel and Gandhi) and by putting in place appropriate systems. Rather than doing that, Nehru sanctified dynacracy through his actions, and Indira Gandhi unabashedly promoted it. Following in their footsteps, now most leaders promote their own dynasty in politics. It has now become all pervasive and has vitiated and poisoned our whole democratic system.

Now, it's not just Nehru's heirs—we now have heirs in nearly every state. Abdullah and Sons and Mufti and Daughter in J&K; Mulayam Singh Yadav, Son and Family in UP; Badal and Sons in Punjab; Chautala and Sons, Hooda and Sons in Haryana; Lalu-Rabri and Sons in Bihar; Sharad Pawar and Daughter and Nephew, Thackery and Sons and Nephew in Maharashtra; YSR's family in Andhra; Karunanidhi and Sons in Tamil Nadu; and, of course, spouses and sons and daughters and relatives of many other politicians. Many legislative and parliamentary constituencies are now private estates. Ours is now a feudal democracy. Most political parties from Kashmir to Kanyakumari are private jagirs. Election tickets are distributed mostly on feudal grounds. Talk of reservation of seats for women—reserved seats are likely to go wives, sisters, sisters-in-law, aunts and mothers of politicians, as the situation in the municipal elections in Mumbai shows.

As per a study detailed in Patrick French's book, *India: A Portrait*, about 28.6% of the MPs in the Indian parliament are HMPs—Hereditary MPs. Even more revealing are the figures that while over two-thirds of the 66 MPs aged 40 years or less are HMPs, all the MPs below 30 are HMPs!

Going by this trend, we would soon be back to where we were in the 'good' old pre-independence period: ruled by hereditary rajas and maharajas and princes.

YOUNG "TURKS"

The funny thing is that the younger political leaders from the dynasties, who have got the position for free, thanks to the power-structure built by their parents, are being called by the media the *young turks*! How can successors in a dynastic-line be ever *young turks*! They may be young, but certainly not *turks*. The nomenclature "*Young Turks*" or "*Jön Türkler*" in Turkish came to signify young reformists and revolutionaries—not the dynasts and the status-quoist lording over their parental turf that the current Indian crop is. In any case, how can HMPs—Hereditary MPs—be young turks?

Many of the MLAs, MPs and party-controllers are scions who are no leaders at all. None of them is fired with any reformist zeal or ready to sacrifice anything to better India—they are there to protect the family inheritance and to further expand it. Just look at the young politicians who are sons and daughters of the seniors. They are following the footsteps of their parents. And, like their parents who came up ingratiating themselves with the party boss, you have these young—not turks, as the media mistakenly labels them—enlightened self-seekers, amazing enlightened on which side the bread is buttered. Like their fawning, servile elders, they too have learnt the benefits of being a toady and behaving in an obsequious manner. They are ever-ready to troop behind yet another scion.

Thanks to the way India has been ruled and governed, we are not only a country of impoverished villages, we are also a country of stinking slums, ugly and haphazard "development" and execrable overcrowded urban spaces. Most of the Indian towns and cities are dirty, foul smelling and hideous. They look like a defacement of what once might have been unspoilt greenery. They are a blot on the landscape. Cities in the West and in the South-East Asia get better, cleaner, smarter and spiffier year after year, while ours get worse, more congested, more difficult to live in and more squalid. Our municipal system and civic leadership in towns and cities is an embarrassment. Why don't our *young "turks"* try and do something about them and demonstrate what they are capable of, before hankering after ministerial positions and the positions of a CM or PM.

These so-called young "turks" are only biologically younger to their parents; their thinking, or lack of thinking, is at the same level as their parents—maybe, even worse. They are simply incompetent, not young, for that gives a different flavour. What did the young "turk" Sanjay Gandhi do? He was far worse that his mother—he not only engaged in unscrupulous wheeling and dealing, he didn't flinch in trying to deprive the Indian people of their hard-won freedom, and even wanted the Emergency to continue! What did the young "turk" Rajiv Gandhi do? His tenure was heralded by butchering of the Sikhs; and his Bofors and other doings and undoings we have already discussed. What is the brand new young "turk" Akhilesh Yadav as the Chief Minister of the largest state of India up to? In less than two years of his rule there have been over a hundred minor and major communal incidents, and the law and order situation in UP is pathetic.

The Nirbhaya example glares you in the face. When young and old, men and women, boys and girls, and overwhelmingly the youth, were peacefully out in the streets and at India Gate and Jantar Mantar expressing their shock at the brutal Nirbhaya gangrape and were demanding security for half the population of Delhi and India, where were these incompetent dynacrats, whom media calls young "turks", hiding. These "representatives" of the people are so afraid of the ones they claim to represent that they just barricaded themselves in the safety of Lutyens Delhi, and only communicated with them, and that too only when forced, like haughty maharajas from the SPG-security of their cosy, colonial homes. All these incompetent dynacrats, the young "turks", have been staying in Delhi for long. Do they not know the terrible security environment in Delhi, and of the violence against women in general all over India. What have they done about it? They have proved themselves in nothing even at the village or town or city level. They have tried to improve nothing. All they seek are seats in the parliament, thanks to the ground work done by their parents—cosy and secure environment of Lutyens Delhi, and ministerial berths, if possible.

Many media anchors wondered why the youth "icons" didn't communicate with the youth at Jantar Mantar or at India Gate—"golden opportunity missed!" they lamented. One can't sometimes help feeling these over-wise anchors are but simpletons. It is they who have labelled these incompetent dynacrats as young "turks" or youth "icons" and have raised expectations from them—when they are actually worse than even their parents! For example, recall what the son (another young turk?) of the President commented—"dented and painted". They just can't measure up to an assertive, self-respecting, enlightened and fiercely aspirational India.

THE NONSENSE CALLED "CHARISMA"

Rather than strengthening the party by making it democratic, hereditary politicians start talking in terms of the *charisma* of the family! They also engage pliant section of the media and "intellectuals" to promote this nonsense. It helps eliminate all others. Who was it who said, "*Let the others have the charisma, I've got the class.*"

But, what is this childish '*charisma*' business? Are we saying that Mahatma Gandhi or Lal Bahadur Shastri or Sardar Patel or Narsimha Rao did not fit the bill, as they lacked good looks, or the so-called 'charisma'. Any sensible person would admit that people become 'charismatic' through their deeds, and not cheaply through their appearance.

Building a person cheaply as 'charismatic' is very easy, if you have the money and the clout. Keep projecting a person positively through TV, radio, newspapers and magazines. It is a Goebbelsian technique. In due course, the person would start seeming 'charismatic'! And the dynasties with money and power get the publicity very cheaply. There are so many in the media ready to oblige in return for favours.

DYNASTIC RIGHT TO BE PM

Those defending the dynasty often question: If Rahul fights an election, gets elected, and if members of his party choose to make him the PM, and he becomes the PM, what illegality or wrong is committed—everything is democratic and above board.

Let us logically analyse. The argument is if the party chooses to make Rahul PM, what is wrong? The question is: does the party have a choice? Has the party evolved a rational criteria for choosing a PM? Are several persons allowed to put themselves up for the post? Is one person out of them democratically chosen? No. The party itself has been hijacked. There is only one candidate, and he is from the dynasty. Only the form is maintained, the spirit of democracy has long since been strangulated. It is political *dadagiri*. Whoever has usurped the party calls the shots. Where does the democracy come in?

The sophists argue: "Even in US you have political dynasties. What about Kennedys and Bush Senior and Bush Junior?" Bush Senior did not own the Republican Party like the Nehru-Gandhis own the Congress, or Mulayam owns the Samajwadi Party, or Karunanidhi owns the DMK. George Bush Junior did not follow the Senior Bush soon after he demitted office. The Senior Bush was President between 1989 and 1993, while the Junior Bush was President between 2001 and 2009. Junior Bush did not become President out of nowhere; he was previously Governor of Texas. He was a graduate from Yale University and from Harvard Business School.

You just can't have a person becoming a senior office-bearer of a party or a minister or a CM or a PM out of nowhere. You have intelligence test, comprehension test, skill test, practical test, personality test even for entry-level job positions, and you need decades of all-round experience for a professional to become a CEO or an IAS to become Cabinet Secretary, but it is all right for a novice to man a senior post in the party or become a minister or a CM or even take up the highest post of the PM!

People talk of 21st century as the *Indian Century*! With the dynasty dumbs lined up to take over, India has a long, long way to go. And we dare to compare ourselves with China. China is way, way ahead, and it would remain so. Their leaders are far too competent. Most of them are engineers or scientists or professionals, who have risen the hard way—not like dynasty dumbs. China is not under the curse of dynacracy.

13
BJP and NaMo

BJP'S OLD, STAID CENTRAL-LEADERSHIP

The AAP has been claiming right since its inception that there is little essential difference between the Congress and the BJP, that both have similar policies on many issues and both are corrupt to the core. The BJP alleges that AAP is the B team of the Congress. Looking to its culture of freebies, its socialistic bent and its pronouncements on various issues, it seems 'AAP = Congress LESS Corruption'. Of course, one is likely to become corrupt only after being in power for some time. Hence, one would have to wait for at least a year to arrive at a definitive conclusion in this regard.

But, if the above is indeed so, it is really sad for the country. All we have after over six decades of democracy are the Congress and its mirror images! Regional parties—SP, RJD, NCP, DMK and so on—with barely an exception are no different. They are all thoroughly corrupt and incompetent and resemble the Congress.

The BJP, under the old-Advani-Sushma-Driven-Central-leadership, has been trying to match the Congress not only in having similar economic and political policies and tolerance for corruption, but also in petty-mindedness, cornering of privileges, crass display of egos, and lack of intellectual honesty. It has also been displaying utter bankruptcy of imagination and a singular lack of will to do anything worthwhile for the nation.

Here are the extracts from Arun Shourie's comments in his talks of 3 December 2010 with rediff.com's Sheela Bhatt titled 'BJP and Congress are One Party': "This [Radia tapes] shows the extent of corporate penetration into government, into the media and into details of policy making.... These tapes have shown that everybody is now linked to everybody else. ...now the Opposition is no different from the ruling party, whichever is the ruling party. The influence of those puppeteers [corporate interests] behind the scene works on both sides. As a result, no issue is pursued to conclusion.... Is the 2G issue a new one? No. It is two years old. I know how I have taken documents to editors, to senior people in government. How can it be that only one reporter in one newspaper *The Pioneer* was following it? He was not withholding information, but not one newspaper or television channel touched it.... I don't see the difference between the two. I feel they (the BJP and the Congress) are one party. They are jointly ruling. It is a dinner party.... See, issues are not taken up in New Delhi by anybody. The political parties and corporates have complete liaison with the media."

You don't find the BJP-Old-Guard having any substantial conflict or differing views with the Congress on the economic front. When the Congress came to power in 2004, they gave a new spin to economic growth and reforms, that had been shaping fine under Atal Bihari Vajpayee, ably assisted by his Disinvestment Minister, Arun Shourie. Growth, thanks to Nehru-Indira brand of vote-catching and the poverty-perpetuating socialism of Sonia-NAC, was adjectivised with "inclusive" to become "Inclusive Growth", and reforms were "humanised" to "reforms with a human face". The BJP-Old-Guard, happy in their cosy Lutyens Delhi, went along. They even went along with the regressive measures (including the Vodafone case) of Pranab Mukherjee when he was the UPA Finance Minister. In fact, the BJP-Old-Guard had hardly any issues with the UPA's back-to-socialism economic policies. Pranab Mukherjee, who as Finance Minister wrecked the Indian economy, was a favourite of Advani and Sushma Swaraj. Strangely, if the BJP-Old-Guard had any issues, it was with some good reformist measures of the Congress like FDI in Multi-brand Retail!

The BJP's defeat in 2004 general election should have lead to a rethink in its political ideas and formulation of a new strategy. But, nothing of the sort happened. It grew even more stale in the opposition. Rather than being a positive, constructive opposition, it became a disruptive obstructionist. Their senior parliamentarians seemed happy scoring brownie points like children in school debates. No one knew where they really stood on various important issues. Even on Team-Anna Agitation and Jan Lokpal Bill, BJP's role was dubious, and as bad, if not worse than the Congress.

Till Narendra Modi (NaMo) came onto the scene, BJP's central leadership led by Advani, who thought he had a natural claim to prime ministership, and the BJP's Delhi elites had put their faith in a number of organisations to bring them into power at the Centre in 2014. Foremost among them was the Congress, in which they had an abiding faith and trust. Even though they kept neutralising through their own unwise acts the advantages they gained from time to time through the scams and the blunders of the Congress, still, they had been depending upon Congress to further solidify its credentials as a natural party of bad governance and to continue with its scams till the elections in 2014, hogging global headlines on mega corruptions and gross mismanagement.

Among the other organisations the BJP had depended upon was TA—Team Anna. As all agitations are necessarily anti-those-in-power, BJP's logic had been that the benefit would automatically accrue to them. But, BJP is not a foolish, passive party. In fact, they thought they were very clever. They outwardly supported TA-demands, and then proceeded to tactfully abort it lest their political turf was affected. They just paid lip service to the independence of the investigation agency, and forcefully made sure the dreaded Lokpal did not morph into Lokayukt for the states, for they rule several states. All the while they kept up the appearance of being pro-TA. Ride two horses. Get the pro-TA votes in the next elections, and yet make sure the irritating provisions of the proposed Lokpal Bill are set aside. Now, did they think TA-members and the public in general were so gullible? Had they been honest and genuine they would have easily got willing support from a large section of people who backed TA. But, what did they ultimately get? Severance of support from an influential section. Such were their clever tactics.

One wonders why, despite being the main opposition party, their central leadership did not build any worthwhile movement against corruption and black-money and host of such issues. They only talked about it, but failed to launch an effective movement. Why didn't they also build some positive movements for economic reforms and liberalisation, and for police reforms, judicial reforms, administrative reforms, social reforms, urban and rural planning and cleanliness, and so on. Why did their central leaders just talk sitting in Delhi, doing nothing worthwhile. How could they just depend upon the ill-performance of the Congress and the movements against the government by other organisations to deliver them votes?

In many states, the BJP does not have any presence. Rather than trying to expand their presence, they had managed to shrink it, particularly in Karnataka, the only south Indian state they managed to have presence in. Rather than progressing, Karnataka under the BJP tried to imitate UP.

The BJP, under the old-Guard, has done little to expand its influence in the states it had little presence. The South, but for Karnataka, remains out-of-bound. In UP, the state which sends maximum MPs to the Parliament, it has been reduced to a fringe player. It has little influence in Assam and the Northeast.

The BJP's old-Guard had no fresh economic or political ideas. Rather than expressing their considered opinion on various matters, they would always claim it was the duty of the ruling party to first put forth their policy. The BJP's policy was the policy of avoidance, of maintaining calculated ambiguity. And, when the ruling party did formulate its policy, the BJP would find some way to criticise it. Do nothing constructive or original. Just criticise sitting in the cosy comfort of Lutyen's Delhi—any activity or mobilisation or groundwork being a far cry.

The BJP's old-Central-leadership, rather than being an asset and serving to integrate the state-units together and providing added-value, has been more of a liability, playing factional wars and setting one state-unit against the other or setting one state-faction against the other. It is the state-units which help the leaders in the old-Central-leadership win parliamentary elections, rather than the leaders in the old-Central-leadership helping state-units and state-leaders win state-elections, for they hardly command any popular support. Their political activism is confined to only being obstructionist in parliament. They lead no movements. They gather popular support for no causes. They don't do anything worthwhile even for their own parliamentary constituencies. They hardly visit them.

Rather than opposing and abusing each other, there are scores of positive campaigns or mini-revolutions political parties can lead that are not directed against another political party or establishment, and help change the face of India. It would also give them visibility and votes in the elections. For example, "Clean India, Garbage-Free India!", "Potable Water to All!", "Pollution-Free Rivers", "Safety for Women!", "Casteism-Free India!", "Communalism-Free India! Safety for All!", "Educational Reforms!", "Police Reforms! Better Facilities to Constabulary!", "Complete Overhaul of IAS-IFS-IPS-IRS and Bureaucracy!", and so on. But, has a single political party done so? Particularly the BJP which keeps slamming the UPA day-in and day-out. Has the BJP-Old-Guard engaged in any such positive campaign? Can political parties not rise above engaging only in Ram Janmabhoomi or Reservation or one-day Anti-Price-Rise campaigns?

NAMO

Is There an Alternative?

It's not a question of NaMo—Narendra Modi. The question is: Can this nation afford more of the same—the same Congress government and the same Dynasty?

The DDC—Dynasty-driven Congress—has ensured India remains forever a third-rate third-world country. Yet they keep scheming to somehow continue to rule. Why rule when you can't deliver? Or, is it that one must keep ruling for the sake of self and one's own dynasty and keep having a nice time in Lutyen's Delhi at the expense of the whole nation.

India started out as a poor, underdeveloped, developing nation in 1947. Unfortunately, condemned as it was to the mercy of the DDC, it has continued to remain so. There was a hope in-between during the non-dynasty period when Narasimha Rao and then Vajpayee were in power, but with the Dynasty back in the saddle during the last decade, it has been a downhill ride. Thanks to the efforts of Narasimha Rao and Vajpayee, we progressed to be an emerging nation and were on our way to becoming an emerging superpower, but thanks to the brakes applied by the Dynasty during the last decade, we are now not an emerging but a submerging nation!

India simply cannot afford Third-Front comprising SP, BSP, JDU, DMK, AIDMK, TMC and assorted parties? SP is yet another dynastic party. They would turn out to be far worse than the Congress.

It is not as if there is something indisputably good about BJP, but compared to others, one does hope they would do better for the sake of the country, and would measure up to their promises. Particularly, with Modi at the helm.

WHY NAMO?

Modi does hold out hope given his excellent track record in Gujarat. One has to admire Modi for the development work he has done in Gujarat. As the facts show, he has done far, far more than any chief minister of any state since independence.

He has also been quite innovative. Besides his high competence in good governance, he is a man with the right ideas and an impressive vision, and a drive and passion to realise them. His talks and speeches enthuse the public and give them hope in an otherwise hopeless environment. Among the current leaders none measures up to him or comes even close.

He is also an honest leader. Modi is one leader against whom there are no charges of corruption.

Stating that "Modi is *decisive*, not *divisive*", commented Arun Shourie in a lighter vein, "Manmohan Singh is the main election agent of Narendra Modi today, *kyuki jab ye koi kaam hi nahi karte hai to log kehte hai ki yar Modi ko lao, Modi ko lao* (because when he—Manmohan Singh—doesn't do any work at all, people say "bring Modi, bring Modi")."

What India needs is a person capable of ensuring good governance, and Modi is such a leader. In case he doesn't measure up he can always be unseated—after all we are in a parliamentary democracy. But, he sure deserves a shot at the top spot, we need to give him that chance.

Of course, it is nobody's case that one Modi can solve India's problems. The states are governed by chief ministers where a prime minister can't do much beyond a point. And, even at the Centre you would need a large competent cohesive team to bring about results. But then it is a good leader's primary job to build such a team and deliver results. Just because the job is tough and a single person by himself or herself can't achieve all, one can't advance a plea that a competent leader is immaterial, and therefore anyone would do—even a dynasty dumb!

India now desperately needs a leader at the top like Modi if India has to rise above its debilitating poverty and deprivation to which it has been condemned since independence thanks to the poverty-perpetuating and misery-multiplying policies, misrule and misgovernance by the DDC [Dynasty-driven Congress]. There is no alternative. You can't afford to have more of the same. Frankly, one dreads that fate. One dreads India being again condemned to be ruled by yet another dynasty scion. One doesn't know what God has against India that He has been showing no mercy to its citizens since Independence (but for short intervals when Narasimha Rao and Vajpayee were at the helm). High time God took pity on us.

"Abki baar Modi sarkar!" is a slogan most would love to see transform into a ground reality.

NAMO'S WCS—"WISE" CRITICS

There are many WCs—the "wise" critics—against Modi. It is a varied combination of politicians, NGOs, economists, editors, media-persons, essayists and other groups and intellectuals, and lately, sanctimonious, holier-than-thou slam-all-abuse-all lying-is-my-birth-right party, AAP.

If anyone talks of Modi's development, they would say it is not inclusive. But, they are careful to make only a concocted generalisation and a sweeping statement. They won't ever come to specifics and facts and list each item or aspect of Gujarat development and then state whether or not it is inclusive, and if not inclusive, why so? One has to know if 24-hour electricity supply to all urban and rural homes is inclusive or not. Whether drinking water supply to all is inclusive or not? Whether good roads help only the rich? Whether the higher employment on account of increased industrialisation can be considered inclusive or not? Whether annual agricultural growth of over 10% helps or does not help the farmers and the agricultural labourers, and is effectively inclusive?

Ignoring the facts about Gujarat on the ground, and aware that the ruling dispension at the Centre and in many states is incapable of ever achieving those heights, the Dynasty and their supporters, and even the Delhi-deserters AAP, have decided to either deny the facts themselves, or twist them or be selective about them. Or, bring out only the negatives or the deficiencies. While many vital things have been set right, not everything is hunky-dory in Gujarat. Modi himself does not claim that. What more can be done in a decade. He has done enough, but there are still many things remaining to be done. *What is worth acknowledging is that if Modi has not yet done "x" things in Gujarat, most states haven't yet done "2x to 20x or more "; if he has achieved "y", others have achieved only "y/2 to y/20 or less".*

And who is AAP to point a finger, who have no practical achievements on the ground to their credit, and who just ran away from governing Delhi. Similarly, have the Congress and the other parties like the SP achieved anything worthwhile to find fault with Modi and Gujarat. "I do nothing or my score-card is negative, but ignoring all your achievements, I would dig out or concoct some shortcomings and would condemn you!"

Even the MSM—Main Stream Media—won't do the hard work of going around Gujarat and reporting the facts. Sitting in Mumbai or New Delhi in their air-conditioned offices they would just call a few jokers from the Congress and the NGOs and intellectuals from the anti-Modi brigade, and a person from BJP, to pretend it's a balanced discussion group, and keep highlighting the negatives on Modi and Gujarat. One is reminded of the book *Mother India* by Katherine Mayo that contained all kinds of negatives on India, and which was termed by Mahatma Gandhi as a drain or gutter inspector's report. That's what most of the media and other critics do for Modi and Gujarat. Dig up and report only on the negatives or concoct negatives, ignoring the many, many positives.

The book, *Gujarat: Governance for Growth and Development* by the reputed economist Bibek Debroy of the Centre for Policy Research, Delhi, is worth reading if one wishes to know the facts about Gujarat. One also needs to read "Modinama" by Madhu Kishwar available at manushi.in.

As it is, most of our netas, whether chief ministers or prime minister or ministers at the state or the central level or MLAs or MPs or those who are powers behind the throne, don't deliver, and most are corrupt and unfit and incompetent for the job. In such a pathetic and miserable setting, you have one person who has delivered—yet you choose to pan him! If this is not intellectual bankruptcy and dishonesty, what is! It is indeed a misfortune for India that most of its so-called intellectuals lack guts and prefer always to be on the right side of those in power.

DTD: DIRTY TRICKS DEPARTMENT

It is strange this persistent negative propaganda against Modi? The viciousness and persistence of the DTD, Dirty Tricks Department, of the Congress and their ability to rope in intellectuals, babus, policewallas, ex-judges, NGOs, media-persons and others in their designs and disinformation campaigns is astounding.

Don't do anything worthwhile to get votes and get elected. Throw sops treating Indians as beggars to get votes—and ensure they remain beggars for ever to give you votes—and demolish or bring round the opposition not through good work but by entangling them in legal cases or unleashing CBI, IT and Enforcement agencies on them. Also, get the media, babus and policewallas on your side either through sops or through intimidation or both. DDC is totally unprincipled and unscrupulous, its revered Guru and inspiration being late Indira Gandhi who, to preserve her power, had even gone to the extent of imposing Emergency.

A canard has been spread by the DDC [Dynasty-Driven Congress] that while Gujarat's development is not inclusive; Modi is divisive, communal and dictatorial, hence unfit to govern the country. Their Goebbelsian technique of repeating these canards incessantly through their spokespersons, pet MSM [Main Stream Media] and intellectuals, and lately through always-game-for-being-abusive AAP, has been so effective that many who don't have the time or the inclination to do some R&D on the web and check the facts tend to believe the same. The fact is that those adjectives fit the DDC like a T. It is thanks to the non-inclusive growth over the last 66 years post Independence mostly ruled by the DDC that poverty in India is so high. It is the non-development and deprivation thanks to them that has been giving rise to divisive tendencies in India, with too many deprived chasing too few resources. There have been many more communal riots under the DDC than under anyone else. The backwardness and poverty among Muslims is thanks to the policies of the DDC. As for democratic or dictatorial methods, no one can ever accuse the DDC of ever being democratic. The DDC is a Dynasty-driven dictatorial party that has never had any qualms on using unfair methods to demolish all opposition.

The DDC looks upon Modi as the only person who is capable of unseating them. Hence, they have all guns blazing against him—through their own brigade, and through their bought-over Media, NGOs and others. They are afraid that if Modi comes to power he may do a Gujarat on India for development and may ensure communal harmony in India like that in Gujarat for the last 12 years. If that happens what would happen to their (Congress/SP/RJD/JDU/...) communal vote-banks?

The Dynasty can't countenance others. They think they have an inalienable right to misgovern India; and they feel they are not finished with India yet—there is still a great scope to take it further to dogs.

GUJARAT MODEL VS. THE DYNASTY MODEL

Surfing the news channels for the 9 pm inanities today (25 April 2014), one chanced upon the headline "Gujarat Model: Solution or Curse?" on *Headlines Today* with Karan Thapar as the anchor. It tended to legitimise the relevance of the nonsense on the GMD (Gujarat Model of Development) spouted by the Dynasty-trio.

One is amazed at such discussions. Why haven't Karan Thapar and other media people themselves taken an intensive tour of Gujarat, studied all the relevant aspects, and reported to us the ground-level facts first-hand? That's their duty as media-persons. Especially, when it is such an important issue. Why must the TV audience depend on the "views" of the participants in the discussions whose only agenda is to contradict one another? Or, is the purpose to simply muddy the water and create grave doubts on the GMD—not to really enlighten the audience?

The Dynasty-trio; the spokespersons of the DDC (Dynasty-Driven Congress); the sanctimonious, holier-than-thou, slam-all-abuse-all, lying-is-my-birth-right Delhi-deserters AAP; the sundries like the SP, RJD, JDU fearful of wipe-out; and, of course, the LIDS (Leftist Intellectual Deformists ventilating their Socialistic/Nehruvian, Staid, Stale, Self-Serving, 'Secular' claptrap) infesting the academe, NGOs, media had been busy slamming the *Gujarat Model* to somehow shore up the chances of the Congress.

They were adopting Goebbelsian techniques of the Hitler era: keep repeating the lies, and it seem like "truth", or at least some of it would stick, especially because most voters don't have the time to know and examine all the facts.

Proof of pudding being in the eating, to cut the crap, rather than talking of the models in general that lead you nowhere, let's examine the net results of the two models: the Dynasty Model, and the Gujarat Model.

First, let's look at the model being panned, the Gujarat Model.

THE GUJARAT MODEL

Out of the many, many positive end-results of the Gujarat Model, highlighted here are a few for the sake of illustration:

Twenty-four hour electricity for all rural and urban households, thanks to sweeping power sector reforms post-2001. When Modi took over in 2001, Gujarat's power sector was in the ICU; but thanks to the turn-around under Modi, Gujarat's electricity companies are in profit (in 2000-01, Gujarat Electricity Board had made a loss of ₹ 2246 crores), even as the cumulative losses of DICOMs (electricity distribution companies) in India are over rupees 2 lakh crores! In 2010, the Jyotigram Yojana of Gujarat bagged the Innovation for India Award of the Marico Innovation Foundation.

Innovative practices in solar electricity generation, including canal top and roof top solar panel projects. Gujarat Solar Park, Charanka, is the single largest such installation in Asia.

Gujarat's Tidal Based Power Projects at Gulf of Kachchh near Mandvi and at Gulf of Khambhat near Hajira with a 200 MW to 300 MW capacity are coming up.

Gujarat's power utility companies and its officials have bagged three awards at the 7th Enertia Award 2013 for sustainable energy and power. Gujarat has won award for being India's top investment and infrastructure excellent state for energy and power. It is for the sixth consecutive time since the introduction of this category in 2008 that the state has won award in this category.

Piped drinking water-supply; drinking-water to all.

Good roads—even to villages. A 2009 letter from the World Bank stated that "the Governance frame work and institutional arrangement in the Gujarat Road Sector were found exemplary". Another report in August 2010, 'Good Governance in Highway Sector: Learning from Gujarat', said, "The exemplary reforms in Gujarat's roads sector should be replicated by other states." A *Times of India* report of 10 October 2010 stated: "In its latest report, the Independent Evaluation Group (IEG) of the World Bank has said that Gujarat state highways' International

Roughness Index (IRI)—the commonly used method worldwide for evaluating quality of road—is better than the internationally desirable level.

Increasing industrialisation, leading to job-creation. Manufacturing growth accelerated under Modi, compared to pre-Modi period.

Services sector growth also accelerated under Modi, compared to pre-Modi period. It climbed to 10.7%.

Over 5 lakh water-management structures. Increase in groundwater level—compared to depletion elsewhere.

Over 10% agricultural growth has been a boon to farmers and agricultural labourers. This massive, inclusive growth has benefitted lakhs of poor.

Compared to the other states, the tribals have fared much better in Gujarat: against an all-India decline of 22 ppt (percentage point) in poverty among the ST since 1999-2000, the decline in Gujarat has been 29 ppt.

In the Modi period, wages of the "rich" (non-disadvantaged) group increased at an annual rate of 2.2 ppa (per cent per annum) compared to a higher 3.5 ppa rate for the poor, as per Surjit S. Bhalla's article "Gujarat's Inclusive Growth" in *The Indian Express* of 12 April 2014.

Gujarat has been having the lowest unemployment rate in the country.

Grand Sabarmati Riverfront. KPMG has included the Project in the list of '100 Most Innovative Projects' towards urban regeneration that make cities liveable as well as sustainable.

BRTS: Bus Rapid Transport System. The Ahmedabad's BRTS was chosen as a part of UN's Lighthouse Project.

Writes Surjit S. Bhalla in his article "Lessons from the Gujarat Model" in *The Indian Express* of 26 October 2013: "The latest 2011-12 NSSO data radically changes the conclusions and interpretation of the nature of Inclusive Growth in Gujarat. The sharpest decline in poverty between 2009-10 and 2011-12 is observed for Muslims, the very community against which a Gujarati-Modi bias is assumed and presumed. The poverty ratio for Muslims, which had not shown much change between 1999-2000 and 2009-10, now collapses to only a 11.4 per cent level from the high 37.6 per cent level observed just two years earlier. At this level, the Muslim poverty rate is marginally below the 12.4 per cent poverty rate of the non-disadvantaged group consisting of OBCs and upper-caste Hindus.... For Gujarat, the non-disadvantaged have a poverty decline of 15 percentage points (ppt) between 1999-2000 and 2011-12. For SC/STs, the poverty decline is 28 ppt for the same period. So the excess poverty decline for SC/STs is 13 ppt, and this is the third-largest excess decline in the country for SC/STs. In the case of Muslims, Gujarat was the second best performing state.... Election 2014 should be about development, and about the aspirations and improvement in the lives of the bottom 40 per cent of the population.... If one looks jointly at poverty reduction and poverty levels, the preliminary conclusion has to be that the "Gujarat Model" of development seems to have performed much better than most models on offer."

Communal peace for over a decade. Compare this with hundreds of riots in UP ruled by the "pro-minorities" SP during the last two years; and many riots in Rajasthan and Assam ruled by the "secular" Congress.

Awards Unlimited: Gujarat government under Modi has won many awards from the government and non-government organisations—too many to be enumerated here. Those who pan the Gujarat Model must explain why has Gujarat then won so many Indian and international awards. As per *The Times of India* report of 6 February 2013: "The Gujarat government seems to be on a roll these days. Following the urban development ministry asking other states to follow Gujarat models for urban infrastructure projects, the BJP-ruled state has now bagged four of the 16 national awards for e-governance initiatives. No other state got more than two. One of the awards for Gujarat was for its Online Voting System (OVS), implemented successfully in the state local body polls, showing others how such a system can be useful in getting people to vote in the internet age." Gujarat's Kaushalya Vardhan Kendra, the flagship scheme of the Directorate of Employment and Training to enhance skill development among the people won the Prime Minister's Award for Excellence in Public Administration for the year 2011-12. Gujarat Tourism has bagged three National Tourism Awards for best tourism film, innovative use of information and technology and one of the best States for comprehensive development of tourism in the country. Gujarat received Krishi Commendation Award for excellent food grain production.

Overall: Gujarat Model has proved to be a very successful model for massive inclusive growth.

Rider: True, not everything is hunky-dory in Gujarat. Modi himself does not claim that. What more can be done in a decade. Modi has done enough, but there are still many more things to be done.

Comparison with Other States: What is worth acknowledging is that if Modi has not yet done "x" things in Gujarat, most states haven't yet done "2x to 20x or more"; if he has achieved "y", others have achieved only "y/2 to y/20 or less".

Now, let's look at the Dynasty model.

RAHUL'S AMETHI MODEL OF DEVELOPMENT

Amethi was represented by Sanjay Gandhi since 1980, by Rajiv Gandhi between 1981 and 1991, by Satish Sharma (family friend of the Gandhis) between 1991 and 1998, by Sonia Gandhi between 1999 and 2004, and by Rahul Gandhi since 2004. That is, it is with the Gandhis for over last thirty years.

And, what is its current status?

Road conditions are pathetic. Union minister for road transport and highways Oscar Fernandes of the Congress himself admitted the fact.

The electricity supply is totally erratic making the lives of the residents miserable, especially in the terribly hot summer months. Many residents complain they are not even able to charge their mobile, what to speak of watching TV. There are villages who have lived without electricity for long. Only about 20 per cent of the families have electricity.

Most of the schools don't have drinking water facilities and toilets. Forty-four per cent of the schools have no toilets for girls.

As per the Naandi Foundation report, 70 per cent of its kids below five are stunted.

There is no organised way of supplying domestic gas cylinders. Rowdies rule the roost. Considering that this is within the purview of the Union government being run by Sonia-Rahul by proxy, how come Rahul could not even manage this. It's a case of gross indifference. Same is the case with the PDS.

There is rampant unemployment and under-employment. Per capita income of Amethi is sliding instead of soaring under Rahul—it is one-third the national average!

Can a family which can't take care of even one constituency that has been with it for over three decades take care of the nation?

THE DYNASTY MODEL OF DEVELOPMENT

Even though *The Economist* wrote some nonsense recently in the context of the Indian elections, here is what it had to say in its issue of 29 June 2013: "As a conundrum it could hardly be bigger. Six decades of laudably fair elections, a free press, rule of law and much else should have delivered rulers who are responsive to the ruled. India's development record, however, is worse than poor. It is host to some of the world's worst failures in health and education. If democracy works there, why are so many Indian lives still so wretched? Social indicators leave that in no doubt. A massive blackout last summer caught global attention, yet 400 m Indians had (and still have) no electricity. Sanitation and public hygiene are awful, especially in the north: half of all Indians still defecate in the open, resulting in many deaths from diarrhoea and encephalitis.... Twice as many Indian children (43%) as African ones go hungry. Many adults, especially women, are also undernourished.... Compared even with its poorer neighbours, Bangladesh and Nepal, India's social record is unusually grim.... State-provided education, too, is in a shocking state. One survey of state schools in seven big northern states found no teaching activity in half of them. But sacking a teacher in India is hard. Teachers are well paid and many new schools have been built. Yet quality of instruction, the authors say, remains generally 'horrifying'. Even the poor prefer private tuition; at least the teachers show up...."

That about sums up the net results of the Dynasty Model which has reigned supreme in India for over five decades.

Of course, the DEDs (the unabashed Defenders and apologists of the Establishment and the Dynasty) would point to various items of progress and development. Some progress would anyway be made with the passage of time. The point is whether the progress was as much as it could or should have been. For example, say five IITs were opened in the first 17 years after independence. Could or should they have been 50? Were only 5 out of the possible 50 opened? That has to be evaluated. We have to compare ourselves with nations who were about as good or as bad as us, or were worse off than us, around the time India got independence—like China, Japan, South Korea, Taiwan, Singapore (formed later), and so on—but are now far ahead of India. How is it that all of them have long since been part of the first-world, while we plod along as a third-rate, third-world country? Could we not have been part of the first-world by say 1980 itself or earlier (with poverty a distant memory), had proper policies been followed?

When you look at their (countries listed above) airports, their roads, their metros, their city-buses, their well laid-out cities, their infrastructure, their cleanliness, their everything, you wonder why you have remained a country of crumbling roads, overcrowded locals, overhanging scary ugly mess of mesh of electrical, TV and internet cables blotting the skyline and brutally assaulting even the "chalta hai" sense of terribly intolerable tolerance of the "have given up" generations; a country of absent pavements or encroached pavements or pavements that stink from the use they are not meant for, and where mercifully for the walkers this is not so, they are but patches of broken down pavers, punctuated by uncovered, or partially covered, or precariously or deceptively covered manholes, awaiting their catch; a nation of stinking slums and impoverished villages, open drains and sewers, rotting garbage, squalor and stink all around, children and men defecating by the roadside—all testimony to criminal absence of the very basics of being civilised.

And all this unmitigated misery despite the overwhelming advantage of India as a nation with first-rate people, plentiful natural resources, relatively better position in all fields—infrastructure, trained manpower, bureaucracy, army—at the time of independence compared to all other nations who have since overtaken us, grand civilisational heritage, rich culture and languages, and unmatched ethical and spiritual traditions.

Why did we fail to leverage such rich assets of a gifted country?

That's because India has been at the mercy of the Dynasty Model for over five decades. Let's examine the net results of the various sub-models of the Dynasty Model for various segments. One finds that the Dynasty-driven Nehruvian-socialistic-populist-babudom-dominated dynacratic India rarely disappoints in scoring the top grade—when it comes to the negatives.

Net Results of the Dynasty Model of "Inclusive" Development

We have the largest number of poor—a third of the world's poor! As per the World Bank's estimate for 2011, while 69 per cent Indians live on less than US$2 per day, 33 per cent fall below the international poverty line of US$1.25 per day.

In terms of GDP per capita, India stands at 129 among 183 countries as per IMF tabulation for 2011. Per capita income in India is little more than half that of Sri Lanka, about a sixth that of Malaysia, and a third that of Jamaica.

Says Darryl D'Monte in an article, Living off the Land, that appeared in the *Hindustan Times* of 7 August 2012: "In 2010, Oxford University and the UN Development Programme brought out a *Multidimensional Poverty Index* or MPI which replaced the Human Poverty Index. The researchers analysed data from 104 countries with a combined population of 5.2 billion, constituting 78 per cent of the world's total. It found that about 1.7 billion people in these countries live in multidimensional poverty. If income alone is taken into account, at less than $1.25 a day, a standard measure throughout the world, this amounts to 1.3 billion. The startling fact that emerges from this analysis, which made headlines throughout the world, is that using the MPI, just eight Indian states have more poor people than the 26 poorest African countries combined. These sub-Saharan countries—like Ethiopia—are considered the worst-off in the world, with pictures of starving children there becoming symptomatic of a deep malaise."

Murshidabad used to be one of the richest areas in India in the pre-British times. While the British, the foreigners, did wreck Murshidabad and Bengal, have the Indians, the natives, done any better since independence. Whether it was the Congress or the CPM—these socialists of different hues—they both further took it to dogs. The 12 August 2013 issue of the *India Today* magazine has a special report titled "A day in the life of India's poorest", with a sub-title, "In Murshidabad, India's poorest district, survival is a daily burden and hope is a luxury afforded only by faith".

Things are so pathetic even after over six decades of independence, ruled predominantly by the Nehru Dynasty, that while the politicians and babus and businessmen have stashed away millions in black money here and abroad, handouts of mere 100 days of subsistence wages per poor rural household—not even per person—under the MNREGA, or meagre cash transfers in lieu of subsidies in kind are considered "game changers", something that can fetch votes for the descendents of the Nehru-Gandhi clan! Such is the level of destitution, thanks to their gross misgovernance and policies that are effectively anti-poor! Forget about providing steady monthly income, even if measly, and a stable employment even after more than 60 years of independence, we can't even provide 100 days of manual work per needy rural adult!

Net Results of the Dynasty Model to Tackle Hunger and Malnutrition

The Hunger and Malnutrition (HUNGaMA) report by the Naandi Foundation points out that 42 per cent of under-five Indian children are severely or moderately underweight and that 59 per cent of them suffer from moderate to severe stunting.

The Global Hunger Index (GHI) computed each year by the International Food Policy Research Institute (IFPRI) is designed to comprehensively measure and track hunger globally and by country and region. If you look at the GHI global colour map displayed at the IFPRI website, you find only India and certain countries in Africa are painted dark yellow indicating the status as "alarming"! India ranks 15th among 57 nations ranked (those who have eliminated hunger—and there are many—are not included in the list), rank 1 being the worst-case. That is, out of 57 nations still afflicted, 14 are worse than India and 42 are better off than India. Even countries like Sudan, Pakistan, Cambodia, North Korea, Zimbabwe, Uganda, Nigeria are much better than India!

Net Results of the Dynasty Model of Economic Development

The Legatum Prosperity Index ranks countries based on a mix of parameters that include economy, entrepreneurship and opportunity, governance, education, health, safety and security, personal freedom, and social capital. For 2012, India ranks 101 among 142 countries. Countries like Algeria, Bosnia, Armenia, Albania, Ghana, Lebanon, Sri Lanka were ahead of India!

Net Results of the Dynasty Model of Promoting Business

The latest "Doing Business" Report of the World Bank for June 2013 ranks 189 countries on various ease of doing business parameters, rank 1 being for the country with the most conducive environment for business. The report is available at *www.doingbusiness.org*. As per the report, the overall ranking of India is 134. Singapore is at number 1, USA at 4, and even countries like Azerbaijan are ahead of India at 70, Mongolia at 76, Sri Lanka at 85, Vietnam at 99, and Pakistan at 110! The report also gives 10 sub-rankings like for ease of "starting a business", "enforcing contracts", "dealing with construction permits", etc. India ranks shockingly low at 179 (11th from the bottom) on "ease of starting a business", 182 (8th from the bottom) on "ease of dealing with construction permits" and 186 (4th from the bottom) on "ease of enforcing contracts". Why so? Pathetic, incompetent political management, governance and babudom, and all-pervading corruption.

Net Results of the Dynasty Model of Economic Growth Rate

While the developing countries of SE-Asia, which had been far behind India in 1947, raced ahead at over 9% growth and became highly prosperous, with infrastructure rivalling Western countries, India plodded along at just 3%, and became a basket-case, begging aid and food from all.

Post Narasimha Rao and Vajpayee, with the dynasty back in the saddle in UPA-I and II, the growth rate and the economy again took a beating.

Net Results of the Dynasty Model for Curbing Corruption

Transparency International, TI, ranks countries annually on the Corruption Perceptions Index, CPI, on a scale from 100 for very clean to 0 for highly corrupt. In 2012, India ranked 94 among 176 countries, with a CPI score of 36. Denmark, Finland and New Zealand tied for the first place of the least corrupt with a score of 90. Sweden, Singapore and Switzerland were ranked 4th, 5th and 6th with scores of 88, 87 and 86 respectively. Countries like Zambia, Jamaica, Sri Lanka and Rwanda were ahead of us, being less corrupt.

Maplecroft (maplecroft.com), a Global Risk Analytics company, also evaluates risks associated with doing business in a country on account of the prevalent levels of corruption there—encapsulated in Corruption Risk Index (CRI). It categorises countries as Low-Risk, Medium-Risk, High-Risk and Extreme-Risk based on levels of corruption. *India* is consistently categorised under *Extreme-Risk*. As per the latest index, India ranks as 69th worst (rank 1 being for most-corrupt) among 197 nations. That is, 128 countries are better off (less corrupt) than India, and 68 worse off. India is in the 'august' company of Congo, Somalia, Sudan, Zimbabwe, North Korea and the like, 'proudly' sharing its Extreme-Risk categorisation with them.

Maplecroft highlights the consequences of corruption for the concerned countries: detrimental effect on the economic performance and political environment; public disillusionment with government corruption; rising levels of societal unrest, and so on. The World Economic Forum estimates that corruption adds up to 10% to the total cost of doing business globally and up to 25% to the cost of procurement contracts in developing countries. Corruption also raises the cost of capital by worsening a country's risk rating. That is, corruption is criminal not merely because it makes the dishonest rich and facilitates dishonest win elections or get unfairly ahead in business; but because it adversely affects economy, and therefore, its people in general.

Increasingly, it is making foreign companies vary of investing in and doing business in a country like India, for it exposes them to high risk of complicity when conducting business with government officials and local partners, potentially resulting in reputational damage and legal repercussions under extraterritorial anti-corruption legislation, such as the UK Bribery Act and the US Foreign Corrupt Practices Act (FCPA).

Thanks to our corrupt and shameless babudom and politicians, we have now reached a stage that the little check (vis-à-vis at least foreign companies and investments from the UK and the US) that would be on our corruption would be thanks to foreign laws and their strict implementation by foreign countries. Insofar as we are concerned, we would not only not do anything effective against corruption, we would continue to throttle messengers.

Net Results of the Dynasty Model of External Security and Foreign Policy

Thanks to Nehru and his dynasty's policies, we have no friends in the neighbourhood and have unsettled borders with the two major neighbours, forcing us to spend disproportionately massive amounts on defence and security. The problems are mostly self-created, rather, dynasty-created. Kashmir, and hence Pakistan-problem, is thanks to Nehru. China problem is also thanks to Nehru's Tibet policy and to his ill-informed border policy. Sri Lankan problem too is thanks to Nehru having ignored the Tamil question, and not having attempted a solution in the fifties.

Net Results of the Dynasty Model of Internal Security

The internal security situation is alarming. You are unable to tackle the unrest and the insurgency in the northeast and in Kashmir. On top of it, the red corridor now straddles nine states—106 of the total of about 600 districts, that is, about 18%, are worst-affected! Why? Because the tribal districts were neglected and left to fend for themselves since independence. Nobody bothered about them. They were ungoverned. If an interest was shown about them, that was only from the mining angle. When now questioned, it is claimed that one is unable to develop them on account of the Maoists. Well, were Maoists calling the shots there right since independence? Further, are other tribal areas that are free from Maoists witnessing progress and development?

Further, it is not just tribal areas that are neglected and ungoverned. There are vast swathes of countryside and small towns in UP, Bihar and many other states that are hopeless, depressing, lawless, dangerous *Omkaralands*.

Net Results of the Dynasty Model to Deal with Terror Attacks

There have been a large number of terror attacks, but you neither had the preventive mechanisms in place, nor the measures to deal with the attacks or its aftermath: 26/11 totally exposed your gross incompetence. You just don't care if people die. Yes, there would be commotion for a few days. Then, it would be life as usual. There was an *IBN Live* report titled 'Five years after 26/11 attacks, coastal security remains vulnerable'.

Net Results of the Dynasty Model of Tourism

India earns merely USD 8 billion in tourism compared to USD 54 billion by France and USD 49 billion by China! It affects employment too, for tourism is a labour intensive industry. According to the World Economic Forum, tourism accounts for nine per cent of global gross domestic product and is projected to represent one in every 10 jobs by 2022.

States Tavleen Singh in an article, "Two Ideas of India", in the *Indian Express*, Mumbai of 10 February 2013: "Some of our poorest states are poor only because they have not understood how to use pristine beaches, high mountains and magnificent temples as their unique selling point. The real advantage of using tourism as a tool for economic growth is that the infrastructure tourism needs benefits local people even more. Roads, modern telecommunications and high standards of civic infrastructure are not things that benefit only tourists. But, since tourists do not come to places that do not have them, state governments investing in tourism build them with speed."

The "Incredible India!" tourism campaign by the Government of India seems to be a sarcasm on itself: incredibly awful security environment for tourists; incredibly ill-behaved auto and taxi wallas out to fleece their clients, with no control by the concerned government agencies; incredibly ill-maintained government-owned resorts, hotels and tourist places; incredibly filthy surroundings; and incredibly pathetic infrastructure.

Net Results of the Dynasty Model of Upkeep of Urban/ Rural Spaces

Most of the Indian towns, cities and metros are dirty, foul smelling and hideous. They look like a defacement of spaces and a blot on the landscape. Cities in the West, SE-Asia, China and elsewhere get better, cleaner, smarter and spiffier year after year, while ours get worse, more congested, more difficult to live in and more squalid.

When you have visitors from abroad, you try to avoid taking them around—you feel so embarrassed. With what face to take them around on pot-holed roads through traffic-jams to witness dirt and filth all around? Living in Indian cities is an ordeal, and not a pleasure.

Worldwide rankings for 2012 by the Mercer Quality of Living Survey lists 49 cities. No Indian city makes the grade. Mercer City Infrastructure Ranking, 2012 lists 50 cities. No Indian city appears in the list.

As per the Cities of Opportunity 2012 report of Pricewaterhouse Coopers, Mumbai is considered to be the worst city to live in. The report ranked 27 cities across the world based on variables such as cultural vibrancy, quality of living, working age population and traffic congestion.

Net Results of the Dynasty Model for Housing and Slums

Government's recent housing survey reveals that 53% of Indian homes are without toilets, 68% are without access to clean tap water, 39% do not have indoor kitchens, and 70% make do with one or two room homes. Figures don't reveal the real horror. Of course, all—men, women and children—suffer; but the main sufferers are women: having to defecate in the open in the absence of toilets, having to fetch water in the absence of tap-water at home, having to cook without a kitchen!

There are nearly 97 million urban poor living in 50,000 slums in India, 24% of which are located along nallahs and drains and 12% along railway lines. And, thanks to our lack of planning and neglect, the number of slums and the slum population is on the rise. The worst affected are the children—our future—in these slums.

Net Results of the Dynasty Model of Pollution Control

Two cities in India, Sukinda and Vapi, rank third and fourth in the world as the most polluted cities!

Even our water bodies and rivers, including the most sacred ones, get dirtier by the year. The sacred rivers have been reduced to sewers. The waters of the Ganga are pure and sparkling when it starts from Gangotri, with a BOD, that is, Biochemical Oxygen Demand, of zero, and a DO, Dissolved Oxygen, of over 10. Water with BOD level of less than 2 mg per litre can be consumed without treatment; that with BOD level between 2 and 3 mg per litre can be consumed, but only after treatment; and that with BOD level above 3 mg per litre is unfit even for bathing. Ganga-Yamuna water at Sangam in Allahabad has a BOD level of 7.3 mg per litre! It is totally unfit even for bathing!! Such is the state of affairs even after spending more than rupees 8,000 crores over the years on various schemes to clean the Ganga-Yamuna waters. Where does all the money go?

Reportedly, over 10 million took a dip in the Sangam this Kumbh—in waters far, far more polluted than the level that make it unfit even for bathing!

To summarise a ToI report, "A pitcherful of poison: India's water woes set to get worse", India ranks third-lowest, a lowly 120, in a list of 122 countries rated on quality of potable water. By 2020, India is likely to become a water-stressed nation. Nearly 50% of Indian villages still do not have any source of protected drinking water. Of the 1.42 million villages in India, 1.95 lacs are affected by chemical contamination of water. 37.7 million are afflicted by waterborne diseases every year. Nearly 66 million people in 20 Indian states are at risk because of excessive fluoride in their water. Nearly six million children below 14 suffer from dental, skeletal and non-skeletal fluorosis. In Jhabua district, bone deformities are common among children. Arsenic is the other big killer lurking in ground water, putting at risk nearly 10 million people. The problem is acute in several districts of West Bengal. The deeper aquifers in the entire Gangetic plains contain arsenic. In UP's Ballia district, the problem is so acute that almost every family has been affected—most people are suffering from skin rashes, some have lost their limbs; many are dying a slow death due to arsenic-induced cancer. Bacteriological contamination, which leads to diarrhoea, cholera and hepatitis, is most widespread in India.

Net Results of the Dynasty Model for Human Development

The HDI, *Human Development Index*, is a composite statistic of life expectancy, education, and income indices and was published by the UNDP, United Nations Development Programme. In 2011, India ranked 134 on HDI among 187 countries, below even Iraq and Egypt!

Net Results of the Dynasty Model on Education

Singapore and Finland recruit teachers in schools from among the brightest 10% of graduates and offer them salaries on par with engineers. And, in India?

Quality of graduates from engineering and management colleges is so poor many remain unemployable. Our education system—it is a mess.

In literacy, India is 183 among 214 countries—below many African countries.

Reports *The Economic Times* of 18 January 2013: "The Annual Status of Education Report (ASER 2012) by NGO Pratham shows that the number of Class V students who could not read a Class II level text or solve a simple arithmetic problem has increased. In 2010, 46.3% of kids in this category failed to make the cut and this shot up to 51.8% in 2011 and 53.2% in 2012.... In 2010, 29.1% children in Class V could not solve a two-digit subtraction problem without seeking help. This proportion increased to 39% in 2011 and 46.5% in 2012."

Not a single Indian university or institute of higher learning, including the premier IITs, figure in the top 200 universities of the world, listed by the QS World Rankings 2012! The only ones close to the best are IIT-Delhi at 212, IIT-Mumbai at 227 and IIT-Kanpur at 278. India remains the only BRICS nation without a university in the top 200.

Net Results of the Dynasty Model of Health Care

As per another study released on *Mother's Day*, India ranks 76th among 80 "less developed countries" in the world on Mother-care Index, that is fifth worst. Health-care system—we beat even the poorest countries in Africa in infant mortality rates! The rate is a measure of number of deaths of infants under one year old in a given year per 1,000 live births. Among 221 countries, India ranks 50—rank 1 being the worst—with an infant mortality rate of 46. That is, among 221 countries, 171 countries are better off than India. China's infant mortality rate is 15.62, Singapore's 2.65, while India's is 46.07. Over 400,000 newborns die within the first 24 hours of their birth every year in India, the highest anywhere in the world, a study by an international non-government organisation, "Save the Children", has declared.

Take MMR, the Maternal Mortality Rate, which is the annual number of female deaths per 100,000 live births from any cause related to or aggravated by pregnancy or its management. The MMR includes deaths during pregnancy, childbirth, or within 42 days of termination of pregnancy. India ranks 52—rank 1 being the worst—among 183 countries, with an MMR of 200 deaths per 100,000 live births. MMR is 37 for China and just 3 for Singapore.

Net Results of the Dynasty Model for Youth

By 2020 the average age of the Indian population would be 29, in comparison to 37, 45 and 48 for China, Western Europe and USA respectively. We would be the youngest nation! There have been talks of India reaping the demographic dividend to become rich and powerful. But, would merely being young yield the dividends? Given the way we are "caring for", "cultivating", "educating" and "training" the young, rather than converting this demographic dividend into social and economic dividend, we would most likely have a huge demographic liability upon us, as the current dismal statistics show. As per *Tehelka* issue of 20 April 2013, 20% of children have low birth weight; over 40% are underweight and stunted; 70% of children below five are anaemic; only 43% of children below two receive all their immunisation—compared to 90% in Bangladesh. Of the 27 million children who enrol annually in primary schools only 5.4 million, that is, only 20%, make it to class XII.

Net Results of the Dynasty Model for Quality of Life for Women

India is at the bottom or near the bottom of the heap. India ranked 134 out of 187 countries in terms of women's well-being as per a UN index of 2011—below even Saudi Arabia and Iraq!

The *Global Gender Gap Index* depicts the disparity between male and female population of a country on a scale of 0 to 1—0 for total inequality to 1 for total equality.

The index is worked out on four broad criteria of national gender gaps on (1) Economic participation and opportunity, (2) Educational attainment, (3) Political empowerment—representation in decision-making, and (4) Health and survival/life expectancy. Fourteen variables are used to create the index, 13 of which are from publicly available 'hard data' indicators.

The index was introduced by the *World Economic Forum* (*WEF*) in 2006. Its 2013 report is available at www.weforum.org/reports/global-gender-gap-report-2013.

The 2013-report covers 136 countries. India ranks a lowly 101. That is, 100 countries are better off than India, that even include Mauritius at rank 98, Bhutan at 93, Kenya at 78, Bangladesh at 75, Sri Lanka at 55 and Uganda at 46! Compared to the three highest indexes of 0.8731, 0.8421, 0.8417 for Iceland, Finland and Norway respectively, India's score is just 0.6551. However, even this low rank is inflated on account of the relatively higher political empowerment score, which is misleading—having had a female president and some ladies in high political positions does not really amount to women's political empowerment. India ranks (1) 124 on Economic Participation & Opportunity, (2) 120 on Educational Attainment, (3) 135 on Health & Survival, and (4) a high 9 on Political Empowerment. That is, if Political Empowerment component is excluded, India ranks near the bottom on all the other parameters—a shocking 16th-worst on Educational Attainment, 13th-worst on Economic Participation & Opportunity and 2nd-worst in the world on Health & Survival!!

Then there are those aspects that don't make headlines or that are not indexed or ranked or widely taken cognizance of—early marriage and motherhood that kills aspirations, forces young girls to play the onerous roles of wife and mother, making hell of their young lives and condemning them to life-long drudgery. As per 17 April 2013 report of *The Times of India*, Mumbai, India has the largest number of child brides in the world: 47% of girls are married off below the legal age of 18—that's almost half! *The Indian Express*, Mumbai of 18 July 2013 reports that in eight states of India over half the women are married as children. The shocking figures are 64% for Bihar, 60% for Jharkhand, 58% for Rajasthan, 56% for Andhra Pradesh, and so on.

As per *The Times of India*, Mumbai of 14 October 2013: "*India, the world's child marriage capital*, has once again failed its underage brides. The country has refused to sign the first-ever UN-led global resolution on early and forced marriage of children." One hundred and seven countries have supported the resolution, including even countries like Ethiopia, South Sudan, Sierra Leone, Chad, Guatemala, Honduras and Yemen—but not India! Continues *ToI*: "India has the record of having the highest absolute number of child brides: about 24 million. This represents 40% of the world's 60 million child marriages. The percentage of women between the ages of 20 and 24, who were married before 18 years of age, has decreased from 54% in 1992-93 to 43% in 2007-08, thus showing a reduction of 11% in 15 years. The improvement though is far too little, experts say." Says *The Centre for Reproductive Rights* as quoted in *ToI*: "Child marriage does not constitute a single rights violation—rather, every instance of child marriage triggers a continuum of violations that continues throughout a girl's life. Further, women and girls married as children are often denied educational opportunities, are isolated from society and face a lifetime of economic dependence."

The insecurity faced by half the population of India given our pathetic record of violence against women is alarming! This insecurity does not just affect women in India, it severely affects inflow of international tourists and hence the economy.

Talking of security of women and tourists, well, security has been usurped by the VIPs and VVIPs! As per a newspaper report, 61% of the Mumbai's 46,000-strong police force has been assigned the job of protecting VIPs and VVIPs, a whopping 1,184 per cent jump in deployment since 2007! As per another newspaper report, in Delhi, out of a sanctioned force of 83,000, only 30% is deployed for general public!! What does this show? Utter selfishness of the politicians and their total apathy and contempt for the public.

Net Results of the Dynasty Model for the Aged

The fate of the aged is no better. India happens to be among the worst countries to grow old in. Global AgeWatch Index 2013 (www.helpage.org/global-agewatch) ranks India at 73 out of 91 countries it studied. India has the dubious distinction of being far below Brazil at rank 31, China at 35, Sri Lanka at 36, Philippines at 44, and Vietnam at 53. India's overall score is 35 compared to the massive score of 89.9 of Sweden at rank 1. Almost 90% of the Indian elderly of about 100 million have to continue to work to survive.

Net Results of the Dynasty Model to Tackle "Modern Slavery"

The *Global Slavery Index 2013* report (available on the web) published by the Australia-based rights organisation *Walk Free Foundation* ('Walk Free'), committed to ending all forms of modern slavery by mobilising global activist movements, generating highest quality research, enlisting businesses, raising funds and driving changes, includes slavery and slavery-like practices—debt bondage, forced marriage, sale or exploitation of children, human trafficking and forced labour, and other practices described in key international treaties, voluntarily ratified by nearly every country in the world—under *Modern Slavery*.

As per the report, which surveyed 162 nations, of the 30 million across the world living in conditions of modern-day slavery, nearly half (14 million) are in India!

Following far behind India at 14 million are China at 2.9, Pakistan at 2.1, Nigeria at 0.7, Ethiopia at 0.65, Russia at 0.51, Thailand at 0.47 million, and so on.

Net Results of the Dynasty Model for Shelter Homes

The status of the shelter homes for women and children, and hostels for Dalits and Adivasis is pathetic. So many horrid reports appear on TV and in the newspapers from time to time. There is nothing that our babus cannot mismanage. There was a *Times of India* of 4 February 2013 titled, "Drugs, sex abuse of kids rampant at juvenile homes".

As per a report titled "Haryana cops raped us: Children's home inmates" of 6 June 2012 in *The Indian Express*: "Inmates of the Apna Ghar shelter in Rohtak told a four-member committee that visited them today that they were gangraped by Haryana Police officials, who made them dance naked and forcibly took them out of the home."

If you go through the reports on the juvenile homes, shelters for women and children, and hostels for Dalits and Adivasis, you feel that if there were to be an Indian Charles Dickens or Charlotte Brontë, they could write real-life stories that would make David Copperfield, Oliver Twist or Jane Eyre appear like fairy tales in comparison. India of the 21st century is competing with England of the 19th century!

MODI'S BJP OUGHT TO BE A 21ST CENTURY PARTY

If Modi's BJP has to be a much better national alternative, it has to rise much above and far beyond the current Left, Centre, Right, the Far Right, and the populist sops and doles and nonsense. It has to be a modern, non-dogmatic, daring, pragmatic, problem-solving, forward-looking innovative force with fresh ideas. It must steer India onwards on competitive capitalism and free enterprise economy.

Going forward, the BJP would have to curb an influential section of their conservative, narrow-minded ideologues, with their inward looking, jingoistic cultural, religious and economic nonsense. Also, the jokers from the fringe groups, owing allegiance to them and deriving clout through that association, who rampage as moral police telling women what to wear and what not to do. If Modi wants support from young women, he must promise he would firmly deal with such obnoxious characters. Of course, Modi appears to have already done so in Gujarat.

Says Shekhar Gupta in his article 'National Interest: Left, Right or Standstill' of 18 January 2014 in *The Indian Express*: "...Narendra Modi can look at this as a challenge or an opportunity. Challenge, because his own party, in its utter bankruptcy of imagination, has also chosen socialism as its economic philosophy. Years ago, confused and short of ideas, and inspired by the Neanderthals of Nagpur, it proposed the concept of Gandhian Socialism (1980),... Socialism is the most persistent virus in Indian politics and the party has never even tried to get rid of it. Atal Bihari Vajpayee's reforms, particularly disinvestment, were blocked more by his own party's pinkos than the Congress's or the Left's... The fuel growth needs, is entrepreneurship. Which, in turn, needs lesser, cleaner government, fair and clear regulation and a market-friendly environment. The Congress, and now the AAP, have fully vacated this space for him. He doesn't have to make the BJP the new Swatantra Party. But he can certainly benefit from moulding his party's economics more to the ideas of Vajpayee..."

14
Media and Intellectuals

POOR TV COVERAGE AND QUALITY

Looking to the miserable state of India, one would have expected a powerful medium like television, with its vast reach, to highlight problems and issues. But no. The Indian TV channels are happy broadcasting inanities.

News for Indian news channels is only some odd things happening at New Delhi or Mumbai. It is as if India of the other metros, over thousand cities and towns and over six hundred thousand villages does not exist. News is mostly what some political bloke said or what BCCI or IPL did. In June 2013, all the news channels remained focussed 24x7 for one whole week on only N. Srinivasan of BCCI—rest of India ceased to exist! And, what sort of discussions they have? Gossips based on guesses. News at 9 pm and discussions on most news channels seems like post-dinner prattle and time-pass.

The anchors on TV, even when they take up an issue, generate lots of heat, but no light. You schedule half-an-hour. Some eight minutes go in the ads. That leaves 22 minutes. Over one-third time is hogged by the moderator, who should actually take no more than 10 per cent of the time. That leaves only 14 minutes for the actual debate participants. If there are four participants, that works out to just over three minutes per person. What kind of worthwhile debate is possible in that much time. But the idea is not to throw light on anything. The whole drama is just to generate as much heat and acrimony as possible by engaging in unsubstantiated, controversial statements.

Those good at one-liners leave triumphant. Those who have something worthwhile to say find their time is over just when they are about to begin on a critical aspect. "We have completely run out of time," the moderator would shout, and then take another few minutes putting words in somebody's mouth or giving the matter a controversial spin. The moderator does not like to be a moderator. He or she is the wisest know-all around, hogging maximum time: wasting time on giving unnecessary background, interfering when others are talking, commenting after each has his or her say, and blabbering his/her own meagre knowledge.

Most TV debates are a waste of time. They are, in fact, as pointless and predictable as the Saas-Bahu serials, especially after the preponderance of lawyers as spokesmen from all parties. It is rare to watch a debate on TV on any Indian channel after listening to which one could say with satisfaction: it was worth it, it enlightened me.

Though, one does find several debates on BBC TV to be good. First, unlike the moderators on Indian channels, those moderators only moderate, taking as little time for themselves as possible, and giving maximum time to the participants and the audience. Second, the debate participants show respect to one another. They listen to others in silence allowing them to complete. They do not cross-talk. They do not try to hog the time for themselves, or accuse others.

Even Lok Sabha and Rajya Sabha TVs have a number of well-conducted debates. These Sarkari channels beat the commercial ones hands-down when it comes to quality of discussions. They also have a better variety of topics. Part of the reason is that for many of their discussions, Lok Sabha and Rajya Sabha TVs call experts in the field, who really enlighten you, and not politicians. Commercial channels deliberately call politicians from the opposition and the ruling groups so as to generate as much heat as possible—that being their only motive! That's why you see the pathetic spectacle of each participant trying to be one up, interrupting others, and saying his or her own thing, without listening to the others.

You even have people like that fellow who was given no quarters by the wise Narsimha Rao, but who has now warmed his way back through *chamchagiri*: writing appropriate book and articles and becoming self-appointed defender and propagator of the Nehru-Gandhis, and their defunct socialism and disastrous foreign policies. The obnoxious fellow considers himself very wise and knowledgeable and even witty—and says so himself, with no one willing to put in a good word for him. This babu turned politician is so crude and arrogant that he freely insults other participants on TV. One wonder why moderators do not shut him up or throw him out or ban him from appearance on TV. He even came on one BBC debate, and true to his crudeness told a participant, "you are completely wrong!" One can understand somebody saying, "I beg to differ." But to dismiss another guy like he did—it was shocking. And, it was not as if he himself had anything worthwhile to say. The creep flaunts his having been a babu! As if that is an achievement! It exposes the bankruptcy of that character. He is just a lapdog of the dynasty. However, it is a revelation to find that dogs can be arrogant too!

You have one-hour debates on some Indian channels where you collect a crowd and then let a score or more say a few sentences, and before anybody is wiser, an hour is over, and the moderator declares: "We are completely out of time." The participants in the debate and the TV audience waste an hour, and the moderator ends it in a grand manner as if some complex issues have been resolved, or some new light has been thrown on the topic under wasteful discussion.

Then there are some TV personalities who intimidate the person they are interviewing, behave in an aggressive and grossly ill-mannered fashion, and think they are great TV journalists—a particularly irritating journo among this tribe puts on a scowl, grits his teeth and growls menacingly to intimidate his guests. As if by behaving police-like they would ferret out information from the interviewee that the interviewee would not reveal if the interview was conducted in a cultured manner. Further, they do this in a selective manner. If this tribe perceives that the interviewee has the power that could bring harm to him or her or to the channel, the interview method changes, and takes a very pleasing, cultured form. However, if this tribe perceives the interviewee to be otherwise, and judges that by embarrassing or insulting him those in power would feel happy, the tribe sticks to its crude techniques.

PAID NEWS

Based on the report of the Press Council of India and other sources, it can be said that in recent years, corruption in the Indian media has gone way beyond the corruption of individual journalists and specific media organizations—from "planting" information and views in lieu of favours received in cash or kind, to more institutionalized and organized forms of corruption wherein newspapers and television channels receive funds for publishing or broadcasting information in favour of particular individuals, corporate entities, representatives of political parties and candidates contesting elections, that is sought to be disguised as "news".

Writes Kuldip Nayar in *Beyond The Lines*: "...Corruption is not confined to politicians, public servants, or the corporate world. The media too has blackened its face. Not only have reporters or correspondents changed their copy or withheld information for a consideration, but they are also involved in scams, vis-a-vis the appellate income tax tribunal... I do believe there should be greater transparency in relation to editors. My suggestion to the Editor's Guild of India was that editors should annually file with the Press Council of India a list of their assets and that of their spouse... Like Caesar's wife, editors should not only be honest but seen to be so. My suggestion was not to the liking of many editors... Whether journalists believe in anything at all is difficult to say but my general impression is they are primarily interested in themselves. They may speak about values, and they ceaselessly speak about principles but it is material rewards that they hanker after..."

INTELLECTUALS

There are thousands of topics in India waiting to be studied, researched and written about, but you don't find many analytical or interesting articles or books being written. A typical intellectual is a staid, leftist, "secular" intellectual who does not have anything much different to say from the hundreds others like him. It's like the RSS-types or the communists: all speak the same stale language. A typical Indian intellectual is a conformist who has learnt what types of opinions to vent and what sort of stand to take to be accepted as an "intellectual". He is not a rebel, he knows which side the bread is buttered, and is careful not to annoy the establishment.

In India, you just have to get familiar with the "leftist, anti-American, pro-Arab, anti-Israel, 'secularist', Hindu-baiting, Muslim-apologist, Nehruvian, JNU-type" refrain and jargon to qualify as an intellectual. It's that easy. No serious knowledge or expertise or research work or analytical ability or originality or depth or integrity is required. Besides, it is safe. Others won't heckle you. Because, these typical Indian leftists have an invisible, informal brotherhood. They support, defend and promote one another, ensure their predominance in the academe and government bodies, and stoutly defend their turf. They are also "eminent" invitees on TV and public functions, seriously ventilating their hackneyed, stale ideas. These windbags have not come up with a single original idea in the last 66 years.

These hypocrite "anti-Americans" are otherwise very keen to get to the US, get some position or assignment there, or send their children there. Their rabidly anti-American Guru, Nehru, also desperately sought help of the US during the 1962 India-China War by writing top-secret letters to the US President (still kept secret by the Indian government, but declassified in the US), when his favourite, the communist USSR, sided with China. Anti-Israel Nehru even took help from Israel then, and Israel readily provided it.

For ease of repeated reference, let's label this leftist cabal LIDS: Leftist Intellectual Deformists with Socialistic/Nehruvian, Staid, Stale, Self-Serving, 'Secular' claptrap. This parasitic cabal has its origin in the Nehruvian era with its debilitating socialism and deformed world-view. It still thrives on that discredited ideology, and has spawned the academe and sarkari establishments. It has infested the opinion-making arms including the media. It has become a major stumbling block in progress, for it has managed to pervert sensible discourse.

It is amazing that despite such rich history, diverse religions, such turbulent pre-independent and post-independent politics, scores of agitations, several wars, such diverse geography and people, some massive achievements and many gross underachievements, some successes and many failures, you have an insignificant number of genuine academic works and research or worth-reading non-fiction or movies from India since independence. It is pathetic. It is also thanks to the dominance of LIDS in the academe and other establishments. This small-minded cabal manages to prevent genuine ones from coming in or getting funded. LIDS also comprise the Indian History Mafia.

Leave apart the past, there is no honesty or depth even in recording the contemporary history. Reporting and writing has largely become biased and propagandist, and what suits the Establishment. A large motivated lobby keeps ranting against Narendra Modi. Fine, you criticise. That is also a legitimate aspect. But, have individuals or groups tried to fan across Gujarat to study first-hand the real or claimed developments on the ground in various cities, towns and villages, and write about them? Hardly. There is no serious journalistic or academic or research approach. A rare book is "Gujarat" by Bibek Debroy. Similarly, are there serious studies and reports and books on Tripura and its austere CM? No. You hardly have interesting and authentic books on various states and regions detailing the contemporary status and history.

Writes Kuldip Nayar in *Beyond The Lines*: "Intellectuals are no better. Conformism has become the badge of their community. They rationalize every occurrence in their lives. Independent thinking is only a facade behind which they live in security and prosperity. The rule, 'I sing the song of him whose bread I eat', sums up their philosophy. They would do anything to retain what they have. It is not that they do not appreciate the value of sacrifice or the suffering of others, but it is a precept they want others to follow but not themselves."

It would be grossly unfair not to credit the LIDS along with the dynasty for taking India to dogs, and for still persisting and resisting attempts to pull India out of the black hole they have jointly thrown India into. They can't imagine being dislodged from their cozy positions and are one with the dynasty in concocting rationale for their joint continuance.

In their book *Why Nations Fail: The Origins of Power, Prosperity and Poverty*, Daron Acemoglu and James Robinson define two types of institutions: *Extractive* and *Inclusive* (details in the last chapter). *Extractive* ones lead to misery and *Inclusive* ones lead to prosperity. The DDC (Dynasty-Driven Congress) and their support-structures like the LIDS represent the *Extractive* institutions.

Then there is another class of "intellectuals"—the RSS types. They have their own mythology. Despite diverse geographic regions and dozens of languages in India, you have to credit them for managing to speak in one language. These gentlemen (do they allow ladies?), whether from Assam or from Gujarat, whether from Himachal Pradesh or from Kerala, speak an identical language and expound a fixed mythology. They have their pet reasoning and their pet solutions, that do not vary from person to person, or from region to region. That's why their 5-to-15 minutes *Bauddhiki* (intellectual discourse/discussions) suffices. What is there to think or discuss or argue anew or different? Just repeat portions from the past or the contemporary mythology. Yes, they have a mythology for the past which goes back thousands of years. And, they have a contemporary mythology that Nagpur spins, and all thankfully and appreciatively accept. No questions asked. What happened to India with a golden past? Why is Kaliyug India weak, poor and wretched? Character! Lack of character! We need to first build character. Our mission: character-building across India. The pronounced diagnosis and the remedy are the last words—to echo across all *shakhas*, and be part of the *Bauddhikis*! Such a brilliant non-mind-straining diagnosis-remedy pair—uncomplicated, straight-forward and simple, and easy to absorb and repeat and spread! Blasphemy, if someone were to counter-question: "Why Australia of the characterless convicts progressed to be a first-rate, first-world country?"

You also have stiff-upper-lip, moralistic Gandhiites who think all woes are thanks to India having strayed from the Gandhian path. Simplicity and austerity is a personal choice. Those who are non-simple and non-austere may be as good or even better than the simple and the austere, as long as they live within legitimate means and are not ostentatious. However, the problem arises when simplicity-cum-austerity is elevated to a level where whatever the concerned austere person says is accepted as gospel truth and the path advocated by him as a path worth following. Dr. B.R. Ambedkar, who generally wore suit, tie and hat, talked and wrote far more sensible things than Gandhi did. Sardar Patel, who was as simple as Gandhi, talked far more sense and achieved much more than the dapper-dressed or simple-dressed (as it suited) Nehru. So how you live, simple or otherwise, does not have a bearing on the quality of your thinking or ideas. Before people advocate Gandhiism, they must read Mahatma Gandhi's "Hind Swaraj" and other similar writings. That would cure them of Gandhiism.

There are also fundamentalists of various hues for whom the emancipation of the nation starts and ends with women—what they should wear and what they should or should not do!

Unfortunately, there is no widely-accepted and publicised evaluation criteria and objective test on the anvil of which intellectual ideas could be accepted or rejected. One wishes there was one. Had it been so, LIDS would have been history long back. Also, the other two.

Strangely, the LIDS (the leftist intellectuals), the Gandhians and the RSS-types you thought were poles apart, share some common and critical ideas. They are all in favour of "swadeshi" and opposed to "videshi", foreign multi-nationals and foreign investments. Exposes their non-intellectual roots and closed minds. They keep their eyes and mind closed. They don't observe and study what is happening the world over. Which countries are doing what? Who are succeeding and who are failing and why? They don't want to look at facts and statistics. They don't take the trouble to analyse. They are not patriotic in the real sense. They care more in protecting their indefensible turf than taking the nation forward. They are comfortable being frogs-in-the-well. Either the nation should progress as per their pet theories or not at all. Scientific outlook, and scientific analysis and thinking are not part of their DNA. They are impervious to facts, neither are they swayed by reason. They can't ever be accused of analytical thinking.

Critical traits of an intellectual is to remain a keen observer, a person who does not ignore past, current and emerging facts, an empiricist, and a bit of a skepticist, not accepting anything as a final or gospel truth. Also, look globally. Study what the various countries did in the past, what they are currently doing and succeeding or failing, and what they plan doing. Most of what you are facing in your country, all or some of the others too must have faced. What did they do, and what were the results? While accepting a principle, a theory, an approach on the basis of current state of knowledge, the intellectuals know that things evolve and they therefore remain open to modifying their understanding and views. Capitalism itself has been an evolving system for over two centuries and it would further evolve and change.

PRIYANKA, MEDIA AND THE "INTELLECTUALS"

There are good reasons to believe in the existence of a camouflaged parasitic class that derives its power and pelf thanks to its direct or indirect association and defence of the Nehru-Gandhi dynasty. This class cuts across political and sarkari establishments, academe, research organisations, NGOs and media. Let's call them ***PDPC***: Pro-dynasty Parasitic Class. This PDPC needs the dynasty as much as the dynasty needs them. It's a mutual benefit society. They can't get or retain their positions and/or derive pelf without the dynasty in power, and the dynasty needs them to perpetuate its stranglehold. Both speak in the name of the poor, the minority and the marginalised to justify their relevance, yet thanks to them the facts on the ground are never-ending poverty and misery, continued insecurity of the minority, and further marginalisation of the marginalised. Is it that the continuance of this PDPC and the dynasty is actually dependent upon poverty and continued insecurity of the minority?

PDPC first projected 2014 elections as Modi vs. Rahul, as if the two were comparable, totally ignoring that an inexperienced, incompetent, moronic, unintelligent Rahul, with no track-record, was no match for the proven, brilliant, visionary Modi. They did their utmost to denigrate and defame Modi, labelling him as unsuited to the high-office of prime minister. However, they never bothered to establish why Rahul was fit for that high position.

To their dismay, the PDPC found that Rahul is unable to deliver, putting their position in jeopardy. As expected, in their self-interest, they began to promote Priyanka Gandhi Vadra as someone who could do what Rahul had failed to do. So, start focussing on her saries, dress-sense and style. Start highlighting her inane speeches, and ill-mannered and intemperate sound bytes as "befitting replies" and "grand hit-backs". Priyanka Gandhi Vadra spoke nothing of substance befitting any attention, yet the PDPC was all agog. She talked things like: "The more they attack my family, the stronger we would emerge... Amethi has witnessed tremendous development under Rahul Gandhi as its MP..." What development? The status of Amethi on all vital parameters is pathetic, despite its two-time MP Rahul and one-time MP Sonia Gandhi.

Actually, there is nothing new in what the PDPC, particularly a section of the media, is engaged in. They had engaged in similar antics when Rahul had failed in the state elections some years back.

Here is an extract from a very old article, but it is a good enough illustration of the ways of the PDPC—an article titled 'A political season of pappis, jhappis and thappads' by Shobhaa De in *The Times of India* of 3 May 2009:

"Oh me, oh my... Phase 3 of the Great Indian Circus is over, and there are so many people one feels like giving jhappis, pappis and thappads to. Let's start with a pappi. Mine is reserved for the Princess of India, Priyanka Gandhi (forget all the Vadra-Shadra business—Gandhi she was, and Gandhi she remains). Clearly, the Congress backed the wrong Gandhi."

"Rahul baba, the Dimpled Darling is sweet and likeable (gelato or jalebi? You decide). But Rahul baba is not a patch on Princess Priyanka when it comes to people skills... Which raises the million-dollar question—why did Sonia push Rahul the reluctant debutant into the fray, when Priyanka ought to have been the obvious choice? Maa ki mamtaa? A mother's blind spot for the beta? It may remain one of those annoying mysteries. Can, Rahul, the nominated heir to the Gandhi gaddi ever deliver? How long is the seat going to be kept hot for the political greenhorn?"

"Meanwhile, let us throw in an extra pyaar ki jhappi for the charming sis who campaigned convincingly, sincerely and tirelessly for the son who may or may not rise. Priyanka's theme song should be, 'Pari Hoon Mein...'..."

How amusing? Beautiful people deserve to be PMs. The only catch is, if it is the looks that matter, why not Priyanka Chopra, why Priyanka Vadra? She beats that Vadra-Shadra hands down. Besides, Chopra is a self-made person. She is beautiful, smart and intelligent. It is not a cake walk to win a world beauty contest, and it takes guts and stuff to survive the Bollywood. And hard work and talent to reach the top. What has the other Priyanka proved herself in?

Here are extracts from another gem of an article—again a very old one—from a senior journalist: Karan Thapar in the *Hindustan Times* of 9 May 2009:

"...Priyanka Gandhi will be Prime Minister of India one day. ...My hunch is we are going to see a messy outcome of the present elections...And the pain of endurance will determine the outcome of the next election. That could be as early as 2011... the process that brings Modi to power will fracture or shatter the NDA. ...And I'd say his government will probably serve its full term...So it's seven years down the road that Priyanka Gandhi will step on to the political stage. It will be the shock of the Modi victory...that will overcome both her philosophical distaste for politics as well as her emotional reluctance to replace her brother...Convincing Priyanka won't be easy and it won't happen quickly. In fact, she'll have to convince herself...by accepting, but perhaps never admitting, that Rahul, the brother she adores, cannot restore the Congress fortunes or India's self-image and self-respect. She'll have to convince herself that her party and her country need her. And now, why do I believe if Priyanka steps into politics she could end up as PM? Because she has a magical spark that makes her compelling. It's a combination of charm, charisma, presence, appearance and intelligence. You see it on TV, you sense it in her interviews and, if my colleagues are correct, it captivates the audiences she speaks to. She has one further quality which is particularly rare. She understands herself and is comfortable with who she is. It's a sort of Buddhist self-awareness and it's reassuring to encounter. It makes you want to believe in her. Yet this is why she will struggle and agonise over becoming a politician but, when she does, this is also why she will rise to the top..."

Do you notice what the senior journalist thought were her credentials to become PM: '*charm, charisma, presence, appearance, intelligence... Buddhist self-awareness*.' The first four '*charm, charisma, presence, appearance*' are all related to looks; '*intelligence*' ...this he senses; and finally, having run out of any further attributes, you have the mystical '*Buddhist self-awareness*'. The critical and the most vital attributes for becoming a PM do not seem to figure at all: experience, proven achievements, competence for the job, track record, thought process, views on matters of national importance, ability to deal with complexities,... Only trivialities seem to matter!

PRIYANKA, DYNASTY AND "NEECH" POLITICS

During the campaign for Elections-2014, days after Priyanka Vadra accused Narendra Modi of resorting to "neech rajniti (politics)", Congress president Sonia Gandhi levelled a similar charge.

While the examples of the dynasty's hubris-driven mean and "neech" politics since the time of Indira Gandhi have already been covered in the foregoing chapters (Shastri's death and Narsimha Rao's death), here are examples from the time of Nehru.

When Sardar died in Mumbai, Nehru, who himself attended the funeral, advised the then President, Rajendra Prasad, to not attend the funeral—the reason given by him was that as per the protocol, President need not attend funerals of ministers!

So he treated Sardar Patel as a mere minister—what arrogance! A disgraceful attitude, particularly when Sardar Patel had so selflessly supported him in the interest of the nation, even though Nehru had usurped the PM's post from him most undemocratically. Writes Stanley Wolpert in his book, *Nehru*, "Gandhi's death reunited Nehru and Patel. Their reconciliation not only saved Congress and India's central government from collapse, but it kept Nehru in power. Without the Sardar's strength and support Nehru might have broken down or been forced out of high office. Vallabhbhai ran India's administration for the next two years [before his death] while Nehru indulged mostly in foreign affairs and high Himalayan adventures."

That is what Sardar got for all he did for Nehru. But, of course, Rajendra Prasad went. Sardar was not just the Deputy PM, but was Rajendra Prasad's colleague of many, many years in the Independence Struggle. This incident is mentioned in *India from Curzon to Nehru & After* by Durga Das.

~~~

An article in *The Pioneer* of 30 October 2012, "Revealed: Nehru wanted to scuttle Sardar's Hyderabad plan" by Kumar Chellappani, based on "With No Ill Feeling to Anybody", the memoirs of an IAS officer MKK Nair, who was close to both Sardar Patel and VP Menon, states that while Sardar was for army action to liberate Hyderabad, Nehru desired the UN route, and had bitterly opposed Sardar. MKK Nair also states in his book: "Immediately after he got the news about Sardar Patel's death, Nehru sent two notes to the Ministry of States [which was headed by Sardar Patel]. The notes reached VP Menon, the then Secretary to the Ministry. In one of the notes, Nehru had asked Menon to send the official Cadillac car used by Sardar Patel to the former's office. The second note was shocking. Nehru wanted government secretaries desirous of attending Sardar Patel's last rites to do so at their own personal expenses." It is hard to believe the supposedly cultured person Nehru could be so ungracious and could go to such lengths upon death of a colleague and a great national leader and freedom fighter!

~~~

Rajendra Prasad was the person about whom Gandhi had himself said that his contribution to freedom struggle was second to none. As per *India from Curzon to Nehru & After* by Durga Das, when Rajendra Prasad was ill and it was suspected that he might not survive, Nehru was reported to have deputed Lal Bahadur Shastri, his trusted lieutenant, to search a place of funeral as far away as possible from that of Gandhi! However, Rajendra Prasad survived. When he died, and his funeral was held in Patna, Nehru did not attend, saying that he was busy with election campaign fund collection in Gujarat! That time Nehru had advised Dr. Radhakrishnan, then President, "I do not see any reason for you to go." Dr. Radhakrishnan had replied: "No, I think I must go and attend the funeral. That respect is due to him and must be paid. I think you should give up your tour and come with me." But, Nehru stuck to his programme.

~~~

This is from the foreword of S. Nijalingappa to the book, *Inside Story of Sardar Patel—The Diary of Maniben Patel: 1936-50*: "Strangely, however, while the collected works of many other leaders [notably, Nehru and Gandhi] have been published by the government since Independence, *the collected or selected works of two foremost leaders, namely Sardar Patel and Netaji Subhash Chandra Bose, were never taken up by any official agency*. It is for this reason that we constituted the *Sardar Patel Society*, had it registered, collected funds and published the *Collected works of Sardar Patel* in fifteen volumes..."

~~~

In the capital, in the prime area, you have Rajghat for Gandhiji, Shanti Van for Nehru, Shakti Sthal for Indira Gandhi, Veer Bhumi for Rajiv Gandhi, Vijay Ghat for Shastri, Kishan Ghat for Charan Singh, besides many museums or memorials for the Nehru-Gandhis, but no memorial to either Subhash Bose or to Sardar Patel in the capital, when next to Gandhiji the latter two deserve the highest respect! Dr. Ambedkar's memorial in Delhi and in Nagpur, and the Tilak Janmasthan Memorial at Ratnagiri are also in a state of neglect! Contrast them with Nehru-Gandhi memorials!

There is no samadhi of Sardar Patel in Delhi, or elsewhere in India, although people like Sanjay Gandhi have their samadhi at a prime location in Delhi! The residence in Delhi where Sardar lived when he was the Deputy Prime Minister of the country has been razed and there is no sign that he had ever lived there. Nehru's house, on the other hand, has been turned into a museum.

Writes Neha Bhatt in an article, "A Fall Into Sear And Yellow Leaf", in the *Outlook* magazine of 20 August 2012: "The untended grounds of 26, Alipur Road, in New Delhi's upscale Civil Lines neighbourhood, give a telling foretaste of the overall neglect of the building. It's hard to believe that this is the Dr. Ambedkar National Memorial, where the man spent his twilight years and breathed his last. The visitor's book here reveals more than the walls themselves—scribbled in by the few visitors it receives, some all the way from Maharashtra, Haryana, Gujarat, are urgent requests, not only for a 'better' memorial, but for basic amenities like fans, lights and some ventilation."

There is no memorial to Subhash Bose in the capital! And, what to speak of memorials or samadhis, Nehru-Gandhis refused to even put Netaji Bose's portrait in the Central House of the Parliament, that had portraits of other leaders. Only in 1978, when the first non-Congress Government came to the Centre that Netaji's portrait was put up!

~~~

In an article, "A Case For Bhim Rajya", in the *Outlook* issue of 20 August 2012 (a special issue on B.R. Ambedkar), the author S. Anand describes a shocking incident. It reads:

"Let us begin at the end, with one of the worst humiliations in Ambedkar's life, less than three months before his death. On September 14, 1956, exactly a month before he embraced Buddhism with half-a-million followers in Nagpur, he wrote a heart-breaking letter to prime minister Nehru from his 26, Alipore Road residence in Delhi. Enclosing two copies of the comprehensive Table of Contents of his mnemonic opus, *The Buddha and His Dhamma*, Ambedkar suppressed pride and sought Nehru's help in the publication of a book he had worked on for five years: 'The cost of printing is very heavy and will
~~~

come to about ₹ 20,000. This is beyond my capacity, and I am, therefore, canvassing help from all quarters. I wonder if the Government of India could purchase 500 copies for distribution among the various libraries and among the many scholars whom it is inviting during the course of this year for the celebration of Buddha's 2,500 years' anniversary. Ambedkar had perhaps gotten used to exclusion by then. The greatest exponent of Buddhism after Asoka had ruthlessly been kept out of this Buddha Jayanti committee presided over by S. Radhakrishnan, then vice president...Worse, when Nehru replied to Ambedkar the next day, he said that the sum set aside for publications related to Buddha Jayanti had been exhausted, and that he should approach Radhakrishnan, chairman of the commemorative committee. Nehru also offered some business advice, gratuitously: 'I might suggest that your books might be on sale in Delhi and elsewhere at the time of Buddha Jayanti celebrations when many people may come from abroad. It might find a good sale then.' Radhakrishnan is said to have informed Ambedkar on phone about his inability to help him.

"This is the vinaya that the prime minister and vice-president of the day extended to the former law minister and chairperson of the drafting committee of the Constitution. It was suggested with impertinence that Ambedkar could set up a stall, hawk copies and recover costs..."

It is a shocking lack of grace and courtesy. Couldn't they have spared a few thousand for Ambedkar's great works—when the Government could spend lacs on all kind of sundry and selected and collected works of Nehru and Gandhi. The Government had also refused to publish the collected or selected works of two other great leaders: Sardar Patel and Subhash Bose.

~~~

It has been alleged that the Indian government and its political leadership were aware that it was likely that Netaji was alive and in captivity in USSR, but chose to ignore the information, and perhaps even actively collaborated to suppress the information after independence.
~~~

It is believed by many that Netaji breathed his last in Soviet custody years after the alleged crash in Taiwan. There is also a startling report—unconfirmed—that India's the then ambassador to Russia, Dr. S. Radhakrishnan, was permitted to see Netaji from a distance in an undisclosed location in the Soviet Union. The details are not known.

In his book, *Back from Dead*, Anuj Dhar mentions that reportedly "the Ambassador was then taken to one of the labour camps in Siberia and he saw Bose from a distance of 10 metres. On his return, the Ambassador filed a report to the Prime Minister." As per the book, many witnesses before Khosla Commission charged that Radhakrishnan and his predecessor Vijaylakshmi Pandit knew something about Bose's presence in the USSR.

Anuj Dhar also mentions about one Mr. Ardhendu Sarkar, a post graduate in mechanical engineering from the UK, who had been to USSR in 1962, as an employee of HEC—Heavy Engineering Corporation. His senior at the Plant in Ukraine was one Zerovin, a German, who had been brought to USSR in 1947 and was sent to Siberia for indoctrination. Zerovin told Sarkar that he had met Subhash Bose in a gulag there, where some VIPs had been lodged, and had even talked to him. When Sarkar brought this to the notice of the Indian Embassy in Moscow, he was asked to keep shut, mind his own business, and forget what he had heard. Thereafter, out of fear, Sarkar, never opened his mouth till his children grew up and were settled. Breaking his long silence, Sarkar testified before the Mukherjee Commission in 2000, and detailed the whole incident in Russia.

In *India's Biggest Cover-up*, Anuj Dhar details how the requests of many countries for their missing persons had been repeatedly stonewalled by USSR, but how they finally extracted the required information through sheer persistence and diplomatic pressure. In sharp contrast, rather than USSR, it was India itself, its Congress Governments from Nehru downwards, which stonewalled even making requests to the Russians.

BELATED BHARAT RATNAS

Radhakrishnan was awarded Bharat Ratna in 1954, Rajaji in 1954, Nehru in 1955 (when he was himself the PM), Govind Ballabh Pant in 1957, B.C. Roy in 1961, Zakir Hussain in 1963, Indira Gandhi in 1971 (when she was herself the PM), V.V. Giri in 1975, Kamaraj in 1976, MGR in 1988, and Rajiv Gandhi in 1991! But, Sardar Patel, Subhash Chandra Bose and Dr. Ambedkar, being not as great as these worthies (!!), got it later! The dynasty did not like them!! It has been that personal in our feudal democracy. Of course, the only unjust thing that the dynasty did was to have left out poor Sanjay Gandhi!

Dr. Ambedkar, Sardar Patel and Subhash Chandra Bose were awarded Bharat Ratna in 1990, 1991 and 1992 respectively. And, that too because there were non-dynasty governments since December 1989—V.P. Singh, then Chandra Shekhar, followed by Narsimha Rao.

That great man from Assam, Gopinath Bordoloi, despite his achievements—far more than most of the Indian leaders, with the added uniqueness that Bordoloi helped expand India's geographical boundary to Assam and the Northeast—was not awarded Bharat Ratna by the successive Congress Governments starting from Nehru, while many, not as deserving, got that award. He had opposed Nehru—and for good reason. It was only when a non-Congress government came to power that Bordoloi, a veteran Congressman, was awarded the Bharat Ratna posthumously in 1999. That was thanks to Atal Behari Vajpayee.

Non-dynasty greats can wait, may even die, there is no hurry. Posthumously, Ambedkar got it in 1990, Sardar Patel in 1991, Netaji Subhash Bose in 1992 and Bordoloi in 1999, when all the four of them should have been the first to get it in 1954 when the award was introduced.

But, dynasty-scions, great or otherwise, can't be made to wait: two allowed themselves to be awarded Bharat Ratna when they were themselves in power—Nehru in 1955 and Indira Gandhi in 1971—while Rajiv Gandhi was awarded the same soon after his death in 1991!! When sounded for Bharat Ratna, Maulana Azad declined and told Nehru it was totally improper for those deciding on the awards to pin the medal on themselves! Azad got it posthumously.

There ought to be a provision to withdraw the awards given if it is later found that those awarded did not really deserve it.

15
Assorted FAQs and Issues on India

During talks and discussions on India, frequently topics turn to questions that are sought to be covered below, partially.

POVERTY AND PROSPERITY

Do Climate, Geography, Race,...Matter?

Are one or more of these the factors that make a country poor or prosperous: climate, geography, location, abundance of natural resources, race, history, "type of people", "character of people"?

No. None of these.

Daron Acemoglu and James Robinson in their book ***Why Nations Fail**: The Origins of Power, Prosperity and Poverty* demonstrate, inter alia, that climate, geography, location, history, race, "type" of people are not the reasons a country is rich or poor.

They take examples of neighbouring countries with identical climate, geography, location, history, race and "type" of people, where one-side is poor and the other prosperous: Mexico and the states of the US bordering it like Texas; North Korea and South Korea; Haiti and the Dominican Republic in the Caribbean region. One can add to these comparisons the Mainland China till the early eighties versus Taiwan; and Malaysia versus Singapore.

The determining factor, the authors say, are the institutions: human-made systems, rules and regulations, and how they are implemented on the ground. '*Extractive* Institutions' cause poverty and misery, while '*Inclusive* Institutions' lead to prosperity and freedom.

What are *extractive* institutions? Characteristics of *extractive economic* institutions are: lack of law and order, insecure property rights, entry barriers and regulations preventing functioning of markets and creating a non-level-playing field. Characteristics of *extractive political* institutions are: concentrating of power in the hands of a few without constraints, checks and balances or rule of law. *Extractive* institutions exist because there are powerful vested interests who stand to lose if the institutions were to become *inclusive*. *Extractive* institutions are normally the feature of monarchy, feudal system, political or military dictatorships, fascism, socialism and communism. Capitalist societies that are not fairly capitalist, or where crony capitalism prevails, may also lead to *extractive* institutions.

Inclusive institutions are the opposite of the above. Their characteristics include: encouragement of investments; harnessing the power of markets by better allocation of resources; allowing entry of more efficient firms; ease of starting businesses and provision of finance for them; and generating broader participation in the economy through education and ease of entry for new entrants. Growth under *inclusive* institutions involves both creative destruction (replacement of the old methods, technology, industries by new) and investment in technology.

Inclusive institutions are not compatible with socialism, communism and feudal societies, or with dictatorships and monarchies. Only a society with *competitive capitalism* is capable of having *inclusive* institutions.

COULD INDIA HAVE BEEN A FIRST-WORLD COUNTRY BY 1980?

Yes, certainly. Extrapolating the time it took Singapore, South Korea and Taiwan to become First-World countries by adopting competitive capitalism, and the time it took West Germany and Japan to rise from the ashes of the Second World

War by adopting capitalist economy, it seems reasonable that India would have been a prosperous, first-rate, First-World country by 1980 had it too adopted competitive capitalism and befriended the West.

Unfortunately for the crores of starving Indians and millions of others who had great hopes for themselves, their families and the nation after independence, Nehru guided India into a poverty-and-misery-perpetuating socialistic-bureaucratic black-hole. His descendents, Indira and Rajiv Gandhi, by doing much more of the same, made the situation worse. UPA-I and II, by part reverting to the Nehru-Indira disastrous ways, have reversed the Narsimha Rao-Vajpayee upward trend.

"UNLESS PEOPLE CHANGE...INDIA CAN'T PROGRESS!" ARGUMENT

"The public is like that. Unless the society improves,... Unless the society takes active interest... Politics is but a reflection of the society..." goes another argument.

However, there is little evidence to show that the prosperous countries have become prosperous thanks not to the competence of its leaders, but to its amorphous public and civil society which suddenly decided to improve itself and take active interest in the well-being of the nation. There is no evidence to show that it was not Lee Kuan Yew and his band of competent leaders, but the suddenly awakened common Singaporeans, who, by themselves, took Singapore to such heights. Yes, good leaders choose competent teams, inspire people, motivate them and take the nation ahead with their cooperation; but it is rare that general public by itself, without a competent leadership, transforms a nation. India's tragedy has been a lack of genuinely competent leadership. Our so-called great leaders were really Lilliputs.

Common man is busy earning his or her livelihood. They are working on their chosen vocations and thus contributing to the society. They have outsourced supply of water, electricity and other utilities to companies at an agreed payment. Similarly, they have outsourced development of the nation and maintenance of towns, villages, cities, provision of security, and so on to elected politicians and appointed bureaucrats and technocrats. Each of them, whether a politician or a bureaucrat or a technocrat, is getting paid by the public (indirectly through taxes) to perform its allocated work. Just as each member of the public is doing its job (as a banker or an IT professional or a factory worker, and so on), so also each of its (indirectly) appointed persons (a politician or a bureaucrat or a technocrat) ought to do his or her work. It is because these appointed or elected politicians and babus, whose cost is borne by the public, are failing to perform their tasks that the nation is going to dogs. Hence, it is illogical to blame the society or public. Of course, having elected or appointed these politicians and babus, it is the duty of the electing/appointing authority—the general public—to take them to task for non-performance and ensure they serve them and do their allocated task.

SPURIOUS REASONS FOR INDIA'S FAILURE

Why has India failed? There are any number of spurious reasons: problem of national character; people not being hard-working; lack of discipline; corruption; colonial baggage; democracy, which is "soft"—what is needed is dictatorship, preferably military dictatorship. Those who advance such pleas should be asked: "Why was the economy doing relatively much better after 1993? Had the lazy of the old days suddenly became very hard-working? Had the national character changed for the better? Were people suddenly more disciplined? Why the Indian software professionals proved themselves to be highly competent and hard-working?" The real reason for the woes had nothing to do with those spurious factors. It was a plain, bad, borrowed Nehruvian economic model of socialism that did us in. There was a brisk progress even with marginal liberalisation.

UNLESS WE HAVE "PEOPLE WITH CHARACTER", INDIA CAN'T TAKE OFF!

So goes the plea of many. Including that of the organisation devoted to "character building", and which claims monopoly on patriotism, on "what is good for India", and on prescriptions for setting the country right.

These advocates of "character building" need to be asked: "Has the Indian character changed for the good or for the worse during the last 66 years after independence? Their answer would mostly be: it has changed for the worse. If so, where is the guarantee it would improve in the future. And, what if the character continues to remain for the next 1000 years like it has remained so far? Is India then doomed for another millennium?"

Among the best cities in the world are several from Australia, which is now a first-rate, First-World country. It has no great civilisational heritage. Nor can it boast of "character" that has propelled it to where it is now. Their "character" heritage comprises murderers, rapists, dacoits, thieves, debtors, fraudsters, and the like, who were herded in ships in Britain and brought to Australia to undergo their jail terms. January 26 is celebrated as Australia Day, because in January 1788, eleven ships packed with convicts from Britain landed at Botany Bay in Sydney leading to the formation of the colony of New South Wales in Australia.

Priests, reformers and character-builders did not land in Australia to uplift the characters of the settler-convicts who made Australia their home. However, Australia dramatically progressed despite the "bad" characters and despite the absence of "character-builders". Why? How? That's what one must try to understand, and apply the lessons learnt to India, where applicable, rather than advancing silly pet theories like "requirements of character". Competitive capitalism lies at the root of their prosperity. They never touched socialism even with a long pole.

Lee Kuan Yew and his band of competent leaders were not "Character-Builders". They didn't have that luxury of time, nor did they believe in those crazy notions. They knew what mattered was forward-looking economic policies and good governance. They therefore focussed on implementing solid competitive capitalism, coupled with developing well-paid, merit-driven and competent bureaucracy.

In the process of building and enhancing competitive capitalism, and with increasing prosperity and peace both in Singapore and Australia, the "character" automatically "improved"! It is well to remember that character is also shaped by economic condition. You can't have millions in hunger and poverty and in wretched condition and with little to look forward to, and expect people to develop "good character"!

SOCIALISM/LEFTISM DEFINED

For the context of this book, we will use leftism, socialism, *scientific* socialism, communism, Marxism and socialistic state interchangeably to mean dominance of the state, pubic and state sector at the commanding heights of the economy, predominant state controls of the economy and means of production, over-regulated bureaucratic state, mai-baap Sarkar and lesser or marginal role for the private sector and individuals. We are not implying socialism or socialistic state to mean a welfare state or a state engaged in social justice and equality, because as per the actual global experience such a socialistic state as just defined by us is neither capable of ensuring general welfare nor social justice nor equality.

ISN'T "SCIENTIFIC" SOCIALISM A CONTRADICTION IN TERMS

Marxists call their socialism *scientific* socialism, as if the self-assigned, self-adulatory adjective *scientific* is sufficient to testify to it being *scientific*—correct; however preposterous it might be from a genuine scientific angle, where the litmus test is the real practical proof. Mere dialectics of self-serving arguments and logic does not result in truth! Marxism as a science or as an alternate economic thought for a nation to build on has failed—it has been proven wrong both in theory and in practice.

For anything to be scientifically correct, it has to be proved truly and convincingly in practice, without a shadow of doubt. Till the same is done, it remains merely a conjecture, a hypothesis, a theory. Has the so-called *scientific socialism* or Marxism proved successful anywhere in the world in practice? No.

Those who do not genuinely understand science or scientific-methods are taken-in by mere allusion to something as *scientific*. Many became Marxists because being so implied being *scientific*-spirited, rational, progressive, pro-poor intellectual, aligned to the *forces of history*! Rather than being aligned to the forces of history or being on the right side of it, to the dismay of the

Marxists, the unfolding history proved them to be on the wrong side; and their science ("scientific" socialism) turned out to be an alchemy!

The capitalist economic thought, the capitalist societies and the associated democratic system themselves evolved and adapted since the time of Marx in such a way that they not only brought unprecedented prosperity to the concerned nations, they also significantly uplifted the status of the masses—falsifying, in the process, many of the foundations and assumptions of Marx.

In science, society, economics and indeed all disciplines knowledge evolves, concepts change, new theories replace old ones in the light of new experiments, experiences and knowledge gained. To be scientific is to keep an open mind on things, to be willing to change, to be ready to jettison the old in the light of new evidence, and to go by actual practical results.

HAS SOCIALISM EVER MADE ANY COUNTRY PROSPEROUS?

No. Facts, figures, statistics and ground-level experiences of various countries prove that all brands of leftist politics—Communist, Socialist, Fabian, Nehruvian, and so on—are inherently incapable of delivering anything positive for any nation or for its poor. In fact, they have actually been at the root of poverty, want and stagnation.

Dismal fate of all nations that went socialist proves the point. Take USSR. It claimed to be following *scientific* socialism or Marxism. But, what were its practical results? It drew an iron-curtain so that no one got to see the disaster: the widespread poverty and famine and suppression of human rights. Had things been really good, why would USSR be so secretive about it, and not let those interested—journalists, writers, academicians, researchers, politicians, sociologists, and general public—have unrestricted access and see the state of affairs for themselves, especially when they wanted other nations to emulate them, and go communist! Ultimately, the USSR fell apart, and all its parts are still struggling to throw away the bad old days of communism.

Millions died from hunger and famine in Soviet Russia, yet the communist leadership did not have the heart to save them by seeking help from outside, lest the outside world became aware of the pathetic conditions. Same with China under Mao—about 40 million perished in famines! Country-wise unofficial estimates of the total number of persons who perished thanks to communism, through man-made famines and state-terror, as per *The Black Book of Communism* are: USSR–20 million, China–65 million, Combodia–2 million, North Korea–2 million; the world-total being around 100 million! Compare this with the estimate of Holocaust victims at about six million, and total World War II military deaths of all countries put together at about 25 million.

Take the case of East Germany: contrast it with the prosperity in West Germany. Why the Berlin Wall ultimately fell? See the fate of the East-European countries: Czechoslovakia, Yugoslavia, Poland, Bulgaria, Romania. Consider the case of Albania under its *Mao*—Enver Hoxha. What of Cuba under the "great" revolutionary, Fidel Castro: it is now desperately trying to shed its socialistic past. Note the growing economy of Vietnam after the gradual shedding of its communist policies. The terrible fate of Cambodians under the Khmer Rouge and Pol Pot—brought out so chillingly in the movie, *The Killing Fields*! Appalling conditions in North Korea: George Orwell's "1984" continuing in the 21st century!

Take the example of the relatively recent red-hot socialist showman given to mega posturing on the world stage, Hugo Chavez, the president of Venezuela for the last 14 years, who succumbed to cancer on March 5, 2013. Called *Commandante* by his followers, he implemented several populist measures—which he could afford thanks to the country's oil-wealth—to remain popular. But, what is the legacy of his 14-year socialist revolution? Decline in oil-production, a severely dented economy, dysfunctional state institutions and administration, and Caracas, its capital, turning into one of the most dangerous cities in the world. Of course, this is not to overlook the blatant exploitation of Venezuela by the West earlier—it is only to highlight that even if Chavez can be credited with fittingly rebuffing the West, socialist policies implemented by him proved to be no panacea.

There is not a single example of a country which prospered or whose poor were better off under communism or socialism.

The democratic countries like the UK which were going downhill with their socialistic policies did course correction under Thatcher and prospered. Near home, see the unfortunate and the pathetic fate of India and its poor thanks to India's socialistic policies, which are only gradually getting dismantled.

It is also worth noting that terror has always been a dominant factor in communism. Besides, like the vandals of the olden times, they destroyed precious cultural treasures. Pol Pot dismantled the Phnom Penh cathedral and allowed the jungle to take over the Angkor Wat temples. In China priceless treasures were smashed or set on fire by the Red Guards.

We know how communists wrecked West Bengal during their 34-year rule! Those who still advocate socialistic policies do so not because they are innocent about these facts, but because it suits them politically, so what if those policies actually amount to being anti-progress and anti-poor.

Marx didn't elaborate on the nature of society and organisation that would replace capitalism, and how it would be managed, except talking vaguely about the "dictatorship of the proletariat"—without allowing for the possibility of the Frankenstein monster it would unleash, and the surreal "1984" it would beget.

Socialism, Communism, Nehruvianism, Maoism have proved themselves in practice to be anti-poor, anti-worker, anti-peasant, anti-prosperity, anti-development and anti-freedom.

WHY IS NEHRUVIAN SOCIALISM THE FOUNDATION OF INDIA'S MISERY?

Post-independence, and till the early 1950s, India did command great respect and prestige around the world, and there were lots of expectations from democratic India as a beacon for other developing countries, particularly the erstwhile colonial ones, to follow. Unfortunately, Nehru's policies proved so disastrous on the ground that all hopes stood belied. Nehru's socialism delivered a monumental tragedy lacking not only in growth and poverty alleviation, but also in delivering social justice. Although one can't doubt Nehru's good intentions, one can't ignore the fact that the road to hell is paved with good intentions.

Nehru, through his anti-private-sector policies, throttled industrialisation. Not learning anything from Japan and others, who had dramatically prospered with their outward-looking, export-led growth, India under Nehru went in for inward-looking, import-substitution model, denying itself a world-class, competitive culture, incentive for production of quality products, share in the world-trade, and the consequent prosperity. Instead, India invested heavily in the inefficient public sector, over-regulated and strangulated private enterprise, shunned foreign capital, and ignored better technology. India under Nehru also neglected the two vital sectors—agriculture and education.

By 1954, Nehru made Parliament accept as the aim of economic development the "socialist pattern of society". Socialism was enshrined in 1955 as the official policy of the Congress at its Avadi session. The 1956 version of the Industrial Policy Resolution made the state even more dominant—it allowed new ventures in textiles, automobiles and defence only to the state, and vested exclusive controls to it over many other sectors. All these inaugurated an era of stifling private enterprise, grievously hurting industrialisation and development, severely limiting employment opportunities, plunging the country in chronic poverty, and promoted babudom and corruption.

Many industries were barred for the private sector. When entrepreneurs in the countries in Southeast Asia, like South Korea, were being encouraged to expand and set up industries and their government was offering them cheap credit, here in India we were doing the opposite: GD Birla was refused a license for setting up a steel plant; scores of business proposals of Tatas were rejected; Aditya Birla, looking to the hostile business environment in India, chose to set up industries outside India;...the list is endless. Krishna Menon [the right-hand man of Nehru] had reportedly snubbed offers of the Japanese corporate representatives for collaboration saying it was out of question on account of the vast differences in the policies of the two countries.

Given license-permit-quota-raj, reluctance to give licenses to the so-called "monopolies", anti-business policies and extortionist taxes—maximum slab rate being over 80%—industrialisation had to suffer. Industrialisation and industries were sought to be controlled and managed by Nehru's IAS babus who knew next to nothing on how to run an industry. Nehru and the socialists had very simplistic notions on wealth creation: Nehru thought that all it took to have economic prosperity was to invest in industrialisation, especially in heavy industries, and to put babus in charge. Market, competition, entrepreneurship, quality, top-line, bottom-line—those funny words existed in the English dictionary in total contempt of the Nehruvians. No entrepreneurship was required. Sarkar was the entrepreneur. It would decide what to produce, what not to produce, and how much to produce, and at what rate to sell—the market itself would be controlled by Sarkar.

Nehru and the socialists never understood what it really took to create wealth and banish poverty, and persisted with their sterile, copycat methods. Socialists concerned themselves more with the distribution of wealth, than with its creation. They shunned understanding the complexity of wealth creation. Nations which understood this raced ahead, created wealth and also managed to distribute it, while India failed to create the wealth itself, what to speak of distributing it: India stagnated.

Indira Gandhi did even worse. Both politically and economically, she took many negative steps. India is still suffering from those ill-thought policies of Nehru and Indira.

WHY WERE THINGS NOT WORKED OUT BEFORE INDEPENDENCE?

One finds it immensely distressing that while we succeeded in doing all the wrong or mostly wrong things after independence be it the socialistic economic policy or the external security matters or internal security; we failed to carry through any of the needed reforms or rectifications or restructuring be it babudom or police or criminal-justice system or our outdated laws or our past or contemporary history or our slavish colonial culture. What is amazing is that Nehru, and after him, his dynasty, had a field day doing as he (or they) pleased unconstrained by any policy constraints. Hence, the baffling question. Why had the freedom-fighting greats and the Congress not studied each important segment in sufficient detail and why were they not ready with a blueprint well before the actual independence.

They could have formed separate study/expert groups on policies on economy, finance, transport infra-structure like railways, airways, waterways and roads, power and energy sector, mining, environment, heavy industries, small and medium industries, village industries and handicrafts, trade and commerce, agriculture, allied-agricultural activities, literacy, education at various levels, specialisation in arts, medicine, engineering, science and other fields, research, historical research and recording of correct past and contemporary history, industrial and agricultural training and research, India's borders with neighbours and their status and steps to be taken after independence to firm up borders and ensure peace, foreign relations, defence and external security, internal security and firmer integration of all states, language policy, popularisation of Sanskrit, compulsory English for all, massive mass-campaigns across India on sanitation, hygiene, garbage-disposal, keeping environment clean, healthy and garbage-free, and mass-campaigns to root out casteism and communalism, and so on.

The study/expert groups should have visited other countries, particularly the prosperous ones like the US (unlike the conducted tours of the USSR designed to impress Nehru, and bias him into copycat Indian disaster), and studied what could be applied in the Indian context. They should have started building foreign relations with various countries, particularly the US, as part of the independence movement. It would have helped the freedom movement itself. The exercise would have thrown up many experts in diverse fields who could have steered India right after independence. It would have greatly helped mitigate the risk of letting only one person like Nehru have his way.

The list given above is long, and the scope vast. But the freedom-fighters and the Congress had all the time in the world for it. Their major agitations were only once-in-a-decade affairs: early 1920s, early 1930s and early 1940s. There were long gaps between the major agitations to do the suggested studies and to discuss and thrash out the details. Even in jails during the agitations, they had plenty of time. Some did spend time reading and writing. Some experimented with home remedies and food and fasting. The remaining passed the time in various other ways. However, no set of individuals or groups engaged themselves on any of the vital matters enumerated above. You have volumes full of Gandhi's writings, Nehru-Gandhi correspondence, and voluminous writings by others. But hardly anything worthwhile on what really mattered for the independent India! So irresponsible, and so surprising! What was the result? Post-independence, whatever Nehru fancied, he did, and we know the result!

"INCLUSIVE" GROWTH AND CAPITALISM WITH A HUMAN FACE

The Congress talks of 'inclusive growth', but doesn't care either about inclusive governance or federalism. Besides, how does 'inclusive' growth fit-in with UPA's mega-scams that are cumulatively far larger than UPA's designed-for-votes-and-corruption dole-outs like MGNREGA and FSB? Subsidies and give-aways that UPA and many State Governments indulge in does not lead to inclusive growth, it results in making beggars of all, and ultimately state and national bankruptcy.

The Congress defames Modi's development in Gujarat as "non-inclusive". An economics Nobel laureate also endorses this view! One has to know if 24-hour electricity supply to all urban and rural homes is inclusive or not. Whether drinking water supply to all is inclusive or not? Whether good roads help only the rich? Whether the higher employment on account of increased industrialisation can be considered inclusive or not? Whether annual agricultural growth of over 10% helps or does not help the farmers and the agricultural labourers, and is effectively inclusive?

A term invented by reforms-apologists and leftists-socialists is "Capitalism/Reforms with a Human Face". It is the socialism and communism which have always been inhuman. One need not enumerate the crimes against humanity in practically all communist countries. But for Nehru-Indira socialism millions would not have been condemned to biting poverty and hunger for decades—also a form of violence and a slow torture. Capitalism, liberalisation and reforms have helped remove poverty and hunger; and all countries that adopted competitive capitalism are free from it. So, capitalism is the only human-friendly system. It is not in need of a qualification like "...with a human face". If at all such qualifications are called for they would apply to socialism and communism.

SOCIALISM BENEFITS ONLY THE VESTED INTERESTS

Socialism and leftism is something which benefits large sections of vested interests, but not the intended beneficiaries. Why do poor, who can ill-afford, prefer private schools to government schools, private hospitals to government hospitals? They know that this socialist claptrap is for the babus and politicians to make money, not to help them. Communism and socialism assume the State as a kind, empathetic *mai-baap*, meant to do good for the people; when the experience and the practical reality is that very often it is the State—through its agency of politicians, babus and police—that is the biggest *exploiter* and *mafia* around.

WHY SOCIALISM REMAINS POPULAR?

It remains popular because it has very smartly been projected as pro-poor. Who popularise it to be so? Of course, the ones who have vested interest in it—the politicians, the babus and the leftist intellectuals we labelled as LIDS in an earlier chapter, who have spawned the academe, the establishment, the NGOs and the media. What has been benefitting them, they publicise it as benefitting the masses. And they succeed!

INDIA'S MISERY AND THE DYNASTY APOLOGISTS

DEDs, the unabashed Defenders and apologists of the Establishment and the Dynasty highlight the changes since 1947 to tom-tom the achievements. Well, with passage of time, things would change. The right and the honest way to evaluate India's progress since independence is not to talk of changes in a general and absolute way, but in a relative way and compared to what it could have been. We have to compare ourselves with nations who were about as good or as bad or worse off than us, around the time India got independence [like China, Japan, South Korea, Taiwan, Singapore (formed later), and so on] but are now far ahead of India. Compared to them, we cut a sorry figure, having been left far, far behind!

However, the DEDs are careful to compare India only with such nations as Pakistan, Bangladesh, Nepal, Afghanistan. Bangladesh and Nepal are better than India on a few indicators, and should they do better in future, these DEDs would have to give examples of African countries. However, they would need to be careful on that score too—on several indicators, certain African nations are ahead of India. If the ambition of these DEDs doesn't go beyond these countries, one can only pity their dreams and vision for India—unfortunately, these DEDs even include a famous lyricist, who is professionally supposed to dream!

INNOVATIVE COUNTERFACTUALS!

Not being able to come up with any solid positive arguments to defend the dynasty, the DEDs (pl. see above) come up with innovative "it could have been worse" counterfactuals: India could have fallen apart, it could have been a military dictatorship, it could have gone the way of Pakistan, and so on—and thanks to the dynasty, it is not as bad.

What if someone posed alternate counterfactual: Had India been lead by other than the dynasty after independence, like Sardar Patel and Rajagopalachari, it would have been a much more united first-rate, First-World country like Singapore and Australia by 1980!

INDIA, AN RDC : REFUSING-TO-DEVELOP-COUNTRY

As per the article "World's Only RDC" in *India Today*'s issue of 12 August 2013, Japan, which had almost the same GDP as India in the early 1950s, grew so fast that by 1980, India's GDP was a mere 17% of Japan's. Japan grew at massive 18% annually during the 15-year period starting 1965 and took its GDP from 91 billion dollars to a mammoth 1.1 trillion dollars by 1980. In 1982, India's per capita income was 39% higher than China's; but, by 2012, it had become mere 24% of China's—during the period China's per capita income grew 30 times, while

India's grew mere five times. South Korea's per capita income is currently 1400% that of India, although at the time of our independence it was on par! While India is variously terms as a Developing Country or as LDC, Less Developed Country, or as UDC, Under Developed Country, the article finds India uniquely as a RDC—*Refusing-to-Develop-Country*.

That Japan achieved what it did, and so also South Korea, Taiwan and Singapore, was because their leaders refused to follow the politically convenient and self-serving populist socialistic path to nowhere. Thanks to the wisdom that dawned upon China, it junked its socialistic past, tremendously improved its governance, and is now a superpower both economically and militarily. That India remains an RDC is thanks solely to our politicians, economists and intellectuals of the socialistic/leftist variety.

SARDAR PATEL AND HIS OPPOSITION TO SOCIALISM

Sardar Patel never believed socialism was a panacea like Nehru and many other socialists, including Jayaprakash Narayan and Rammanohar Lohia, believed. Sardar was liberal enough to even offer a deal to the socialists on these lines: "Select a province and run it on socialist principles. If they did better than others, he would gladly hand over the country to them" (quoted by Rajmohan Gandhi in *Patel—A Life*, p. 491). The offer was not taken, as J.P. and Lohia later recalled.

Even in 1930s, on account of differences between Nehru and Patel on the issue of socialism, the selection of the Congress president for the next annual session had assumed critical importance. Incidentally, Patel, Rajagopalachari and Rajendra Prasad were opposed to socialism. If only they had led India after independence, rather than Nehru, India would have been a prosperous First-World country long ago.

This is what J.R.D. Tata reportedly remarked: "While I usually came back from meeting Gandhiji elated and inspired but always a bit sceptical, and from talks with Jawaharlal fired with emotional zeal but often confused and unconvinced, meetings with Vallabhbhai were a joy from which I returned with renewed confidence in the future of our country. I have often thought that if fate had decreed that he, instead of Jawaharlal, would be younger of the two, India would have followed a very different path and would be in better economic shape than it is today."

SOCIALISM AND INDIAN PROVERB

There is an age old Indian proverb: *Raja Vyapari taya Praja Bhikhari*. That is, people become beggars when government enters into business. Nehru, not familiar with the Indian culture, did not know this.

PREDOMINANCE OF LEFTIST CLAPTRAP

It is India's tragedy that rational, bold, no-nonsense, rightist leadership and influential intellectual class that unapologetically supports competitive capitalism is absent. It is a crucial handicap in tackling poverty and in India's rise to a prosperous First-World nation.

It is high time the general voting public was educated to realise that leftism, socialism and sops would take them nowhere and would condemn them further to a life of want and misery; and that the jholawallahs, like the religious and communal fundamentalists and the casteists, belong to the past, and have no relevance for modern India.

Sadly the leftist "intellectual" brand and the leftist politics predominate in India. It's a vicious cycle. Leftist/socialist vote-catching-sops create poverty and misery. In turn, poverty and misery fuel further socialism and sops. The worse you get, the more leftist and socialist you become!

Practically, all regional parties (SP, RJD, JDU, Trinamool Congress, ...) profess to be socialists. The Congress is anyway an opportunist socialist and "electoral secular" party. Even the BJP had once professed to be a Gandhian socialist party. AAP, a young party, with many young professional faces, was expected to be different. But they plan to be more socialist that all the other parties put together!

Is it that Indian intellectuals and politicians—both young and old—lack courage, and want only to play the safe, populist way, and socialism comes in handy.

That's why when people say why does one have to hark back to Nehru-Indira, who are long dead, one has to assert that their malinfluence still prevails, and afflicts intellectuals too.

DEMOCRACY AND SOCIALISM: ARE THEY COMPATIBLE?

Many say they don't like capitalism, but they want democracy. Many talk of democratic socialism. But what is the historical origin of "democracy"? Did socialism give rise to democracy? Did communism give rise to democracy? No. Historically, all socialist and communist societies have curbed freedom, democracy being a far cry. Did a feudal system or a monarchical system or a dictatorship give rise to democracy? No.

It was the mercantile-industrial capitalism that led to democracy. Democracy and capitalism go together. Competitive capitalism needs democracy to thrive. Vice versa, democracy can thrive where competitive capitalism exists. Of course, vitiated forms of capitalism, like crony capitalism, can go along with dictatorships and oligarchies.

However, socialism and communism, where the state dominates and predominantly controls the means of production, can't have real democracy, because true democracy is unsuited to those systems. That's why when India went more socialist under Indira resulting in difficult economic conditions, she had to wind up democracy and declare Emergency.

WHAT SYSTEM TO FOLLOW: SOCIALISM, CAPITALISM, GANDHIISM... ?

Most Indian political parties profess to be socialists, and presumably want some kind of socialism. Maoists in the red-districts of India and their "intellectual" supporters want Maoism/communism. Gandhiites would like Gandhian Gram Swaraj. Some say, "neither Marx not Market", but some form of "Ram Rajya". Ultra-nationalists want something uniquely Indian. Some ignoramuses would even like to go back to the pre-independence days of the British! Then, there are the capitalists.

As many groups, as many systems. If this does not work, try that. Funnily, no group poses questions relevant to arriving at a satisfactory solution. For example, which system has triumphed in the world? Let's not be frogs-in-the-well, let's look around in the world, let's look at other countries. Let's check which countries are prosperous and rich and why? How they achieved that? Which of them also have freedom and democracy, and which don't, and why? Which countries are struggling like India and why? Which countries are poor and why are they so?

If one examines the above, one finds that socialist or communist countries are invariably poor or struggling or not so well off. China progressed very fast after it junked Maoism/communism and adopted competitive capitalist practices. Certain countries are rich on account of mineral wealth (like the Arabs) but their people have no freedom, and are ruled by kings, monarchs, dictators or oligarchies. The rich countries, whether of the West or Asia or elsewhere, like the US, the UK, France, Germany, Canada, Singapore, Taiwan, Japan, South Korea, Australia, New Zealand, have invariably both competitive capitalism and democracy. This being the case, does it not make sense for India to also adopt competitive capitalism. In fact, India has no alternative if wants to rise from its grinding poverty, become prosperous and join the first-world.

As for people advocating Gandhism or some form of "Indianism" or some other prescription, it would be good to ponder over these questions: To purchase a car, does one go for a tested model of a reputed brand of car, or does one choose a car merely by its listed features, ignoring the fact of its not having been well tested on the road? Does one take that risk? However, you don't mind crores being guinea pigs in your experiments with Gandhism or some form of "Indianism" or some other prescription! Even if it has to be given a chance, try Gandhism in a district, and monitor the results. It is another matter that if any reasonable person were to read Gandhi's economic prescriptions that he wrote in *Hind Swaraj* in 1909 and later, he would get a shock.

CAPITALISM EVOLVED ORGANICALLY. OTHERS ARE ARTIFICIAL CONSTRUCTS

It's not as if there is a menu of systems, and one can choose which to adopt. Constructivism does not work in the field of economics. A set of complex economic, mercantile, industrial, societal, survival, cultural, psychological and organisational factors have led to the evolution of free enterprise and capitalism. Free enterprise and capitalism were not something that were first theorised, then planned, and then implemented or rammed down. They evolved as a sequence of civilisational growth, were taken cognizance of, and then theorised after the fact. Facts and practice led to the theory, and then the theory enhanced the practice. Thereafter, it was a beneficial evolving cycle, each helping enhance the other. Democracy, in turn, evolved out of free enterprise and capitalism; and again there was a cyclical effect between the two, each helping enhance the other.

In comparison, there is nothing natural, organic or evolutionary about Socialism, Communism or Gandhism. They are all artificial constructs. You first theorise. Then you plan how the theory could be implemented in practice. And, when you implement you find there are just too many variables, too many unknowns, and too many practical difficulties and unforeseen human factors and frailties to contend with. Russians tried it for over 70 years, failed, reverted, and have since been struggling to implement capitalism. Same with the East European countries that went communist thanks to Russia. China wisely junked its Maoism before it was too late, and steered itself capably into a version of capitalism.

Gandhism! Nehru, Gandhi's chosen disciple, shuddered even to try it, despite Gandhi's persuasion. It is another matter that Nehru tried another bad artificial prescription—imitating the Soviets. In fact, Gandhi could not implement his own prescriptions satisfactorily even in the restricted environment of his own ashrams.

WHY "HINDU RATE OF GROWTH" IS A MISNOMER?

While the developing countries of SE-Asia, which had been far behind India in 1947, raced ahead at over 9% growth and became highly prosperous, with infrastructure rivalling Western countries, India plodded along at what was derisively referred to as the *Hindu rate of growth* of just 3%, and became a basket-case, begging aid and food from all.

However, the term "Hindu rate of growth" is highly inappropriate and unfair, besides being derogatory. Let us examine why?

One, the "Nehruvian rate of growth". The low rate of growth was thanks to Nehru-Indira-Rajiv's policies. If rather than the "Hindu rate of growth" it was called the "Nehruvian rate of growth" or "Nehruvian socialistic rate of growth" or "NIDP [Nehru-Indira-Dynasty policies] rate of growth", one would have no quarrel.

Two, the "Colonial rate of growth". The rate of growth during the pre-independence period, the colonial period, was even less! In fact, it had even turned negative during several long periods!! Why was the rate of growth then not called the "Colonial rate of growth" or the "Christian rate of growth" in a pejorative sense?

As per an estimate by Angus Maddison, a Cambridge University historian, "India's share of the world income fell from 22.6% in 1700, comparable to Europe's share of 23.3%, to a low of 3.8% in 1952."

Hindu-India had been highly prosperous in the past, thanks to its *massive* "Hindu rate of growth", which is why first the countries to the northwest of India, and then the Western countries invaded it. Until the rise of the West, India was possibly the richest country in the world, which is why it presented an irresistible target for the ravaging Mongols and their descendents, and then the West. Why then was the term "Hindu rate of growth" not used in an adulatory sense?

Three, how do you explain the recent growth rate of over 9%? The same India, after only part junking of the Nehru-Indira-Rajiv socialistic policies, reached a growth rate of over 9%! Junk more of the Nehru-Indira socialistic policies, and the growth rate will rise to double-digits.

Four, absurdity of religious-cultural connotation. Many Islamic countries prior to the world demand and discovery of oil were very poor. Was their growth rate called the "Islamic rate of growth"? The growth rate during the dark ages of Europe was static or negative, when during the same period India was immensely rich and progressive. Was it ever called the "Christian rate of growth"? Sri Lanka and Myanmar have had long periods of no growth or measly growth. Were they castigated for being under the spell of the "Buddhist rate of growth"? China's growth rate after going communist and till the end of the Mao-period was pathetic. Was it termed the "Atheistic rate of growth"? Why associate "Hindu" with a rate of economic growth unless there is an ulterior motive of deliberately showing Hinduism in bad light? Of course, many use the term unfeelingly, without being conscious of its implications.

Five, Nehru vs. Hinduism. Nehru was an agnostic, and was more English than Indian, more western than eastern, more "something else" than a Hindu, and therefore it is grossly inappropriate to name a rate of growth, which was thanks to him and his dynasty, as "Hindu".

Six, why not "Secular" rate of growth? Nehru, Nehru-dynasty and company have raved ad nauseam on "secularism", without ensuring it in practice. Why not credit the growth rate thanks to them as the "'Secular' rate of growth"?

Seven, Socialism vs. Hinduism. Hindu-India has had long tradition of free international trade and commerce, and of liberal religious and world view. Such an ethos can never accept the Big Brother denouement or the run-up to it. There is an age old Indian proverb: *Raja Vyapari taya Praja Bhikhari.* That is, people become beggars when government enters into business. A belief in self-reliance and an overweening socialistic state on the part of Jawaharlal Nehru and Indira Gandhi actually did India in, rather than something that had anything to do with Hinduism.

Eight, Socialism vs. Mahatma Gandhi and Others. Mahatma Gandhi was no socialist. Nor were the other stalwarts like Sardar Patel, Rajaji and Rajendra Prasad. All the four—Mahatma Gandhi, Sardar Patel, Rajaji and Rajendra Prasad—quite unlike Nehru, could be considered as also representing the Hindu ethos, and perhaps precisely for that reason they were against socialistic claptrap of Nehru.

Nine, a camouflage. In any case, using "Hindu" as in "Hindu rate of growth" in a pejorative sense is not only insulting, it camouflages the real reasons—socialistic claptrap was never going to give you a respectable growth rate to enable you to ameliorate the lot of the poor.

But the question arises as to why did the term "Hindu rate of growth" gain currency? Well, here are the reasons.

One. Raj Krishna. The term was reportedly coined by the economist Raj Krishna to draw attention to the embarrassing rate of growth during the Nehru-Indira period. India being predominantly populated by the Hindus, he called it the "Hindu rate of growth". But, of course, he didn't mean it to be insulting to Hinduism. He just used another term to represent India. It would have been more appropriate had he used the terms like "Nehruvian socialistic rate of growth", which would have been really representative and meaningful.

However, what is interesting is the way it was lapped up, used, and made popular by the Nehruvians themselves, the socialists, and the leftist intellectuals; and also by the India-baiters and the colonialists.

Two. Blame Hinduism rather than Socialism. Indian politicians and bureaucrats never wanted to admit that the fault lay with the socialistic apparatus. Why blame self? Especially, why blame something on which you have fattened yourselves? The leftists, socialists and communists got prized slots in the government or government-aided organisations, societies and universities, and dominated the intellectual discourse in India: professors, historians, economists, journalists, and so on. Socialism and Marxism could not be wrong—what was required was more of it! The whole band, be it politicians or bureaucrats or intellectuals, didn't mind the blame shifting to the religious-cultural heritage. Someone coined the term, the next one picked it up, and it spread.

Three. The Secularists. For certain class of intellectuals the touchstone of secularism is whether you can be abusive to Hinduism. The term "Hindu" in "Hindu rate of growth" serves that purpose. It serves for them the double purpose: camouflage the ills resulting from socialism, and be also hailed "secular" the cheap way—by casting a slur on Hinduism.

Four. The Colonialists and the India-baiters. Other groups, which received the term with glee, lapped it up, and enthusiastically promoted it to disparage India, were the colonialists or those with the colonial mind-set or the brown sahibs, or the India-baiters. Give power to the Hindus, and what you will get is the "Hindu rate of growth"! Had the British Raj continued, things would have been better!!

WHAT NEEDS TO BE DONE AND UNDONE?

Here are a few among the many things that need to be done or undone.

Junk Poverty-Perpetuating Socialism

As has been established earlier in the book, socialism guarantees permanence of poverty. High time the vote-catching gimmicks of socialism were exposed and the pro-poor competitive capitalism was given respectability and adopted.

Thanks to Sonia-NAC-socialism inflicting a deep rot in the economy, even as India's GDP growth rate has halved, inflation rate has doubled, rupee has depreciated by 20%, and CAD (Current Account Deficit) has climbed to a record level of 6.7% of GDP.

Mercilessly demolish all socialistic claptrap.

Introduce Systems to Root-out Crony Capitalism

Eliminate or reform or redesign all those Sarkari processes and systems that give rise to crony capitalism.

Eliminate/Minimise Corruption

Introduce effective preventive, detective and punitive systems to eliminate or minimise corruption.

Prevention is better than cure; and hence preventive systems are more important than the punitive systems. Preventive systems include elimination of possible avenues of corruption. That requires a number of steps. Electoral reforms. Government has no business to be in business—disinvest and sell off public sector units. Shrink the government. Formulate transparent rules. Put them up on the web. Eliminate discretion and discretionary quota. Reform and restructure the Babudom and the Criminal-Justice System.

Detective and punitive systems include an independent Lokpal and an independent investigative agency.

Electoral Reforms

There has to be complete transparency about the funding of the political parties. All sources of funds, irrespective of amounts, must be declared and also audited by an independent auditor.

While most of the other areas should be denationalised or privatised, election funding and political activity could be one area that could be nationalised by creating a Common Central Election Fund (CCEF). Corporate funding could be to CCEF, rather than to individual parties. A criteria could be devised to apportion funds to parties. Provide TV and radio time, and publicity in the print media from the national fund for the purpose. Allocate public grounds and construct platforms for election rallies. Provide funds for political activity. Create a level-playing field for the parties. There should be stricter norms for candidates, so that proper candidates come in the fray.

Judicial Reforms

Even though the Law Commission had recommended there be at least 50 judges per million population, we hardly have between six to fifteen—the correct figures are not available—which is less than even Bangladesh! Augmentation of numbers, so necessary for expeditious delivery of justice, would require massive intake of judges, and ramping up of infrastructure.

Creation of an independent *National Judicial Commission* has been gathering dust.

Governance Reforms

We are plagued by woeful, substandard governance. Selection and promotional system in the civil and other services has to be drastically overhauled. You can't have promotions predominantly on seniority. Competence and performance have to be given greater weightage.

All post-retirement assignments for IAS-IFS-IPS should be banned. It would help curb continuance of pliable officers after retirement.

IAS and the like should be banned from all top-level appointments requiring special expertise; and there are many such areas: Defence, Education, Electricity, Energy, Environment, Finance, Information Technology, Mining, Nuclear Energy, RBI, SEBI, Telecom, and so on.

Police Reforms

Police reforms have been pending for decades. They need to be expedited. The living and working conditions of the constabulary have to be drastically improved.

Open, Competitive Market Structures

To minimise crony capitalism and the opportunities for gain from bribe-driven decisions, non-discretionary rules and strong open competitive market structures are required, coupled with transparency of rules and processes.

Transparency

There has to be transparency in all processes of the government. All rules and regulations should be made simple, clear, open and accessible on the web. High time the colonial legacy of keeping things under the wraps is abolished. RTI should be made stronger. Discretionary powers have to be done away with.

No Retrospective Changes in Law

India touts its democracy and 'rule of law' as its edge over China, but when it comes to crux, its debilitating socialistic-leftist-bureaucratic mindset, the incapacitating legacy of the Nehru-Indira raj, doesn't hesitate going back retrospectively 25 years to change the law and tax a global company, Vodafone, that is one of its biggest investors. Retrospective changes in rules and laws should be banned.

Lokpal

Apart from appropriate preventive systems and change of policies to eliminate avenues of corruption, there should be an effective independent detective, investigative and punitive system in the form of a Lokpal.

Shun the Dole-out Economy

The Congress and other parties have been indulging in hand-outs, not out of any compassion for the poor, but to garner votes. Dynasties only think survival and are driven by the short-term vision of winning elections. Part indulgence in such short-cuts can be understood as a political compulsion, but to elevate it to the level of economic policy and to completely ignore the far more important task of reforming the system can only be understood if one makes due allowance for the incompetence of, and the irresponsible nature of the dynasties.

Both the rural employment scheme and the food security bill demonstrate a paternalistic, feudal, mai-baap sarkar approach. After six decades of independence all that India can promise its poorest are wages for 100 days of employment in a year—less the leakages. It does not even plan to provide 365 days of gainful employment to as many as possible. That requires too much of planning and efforts and management that dynasty-led governments are incapable off. Find an easy way out.

In MGNREGA, the create-useless-work-scheme for the poor, Sonia-NAC have already frittered away over ₹ 1,70,000 crores, of which only a fifth (₹ 34,000 crores) went as wages, while four-fifth (₹ 1,36,000 crores) went to well-off as overheads and swindle. What kind of Sonionomics is this where nation builds no productive assets, poor get meagre wages and a major amount is siphoned off.

Wrote Minhaz Merchant in his article "Rich MPs, Poor Voters" in *The Economic Times*, Mumbai of 9 June 2012: "A study by Shikha Jha of the Asian Development Bank and Bharat Ramaswami of the Indian Statistical Institute has shown that only 10% of the benefits of the public distribution system (PDS) reach the 'deserving poor'. Around 43% is siphoned off illegally, 28% goes towards administrative costs of the Food Corporation of India (FCI) and the balance 20% is misappropriated by other vested interests. Pouring more money into this leaky system without first fixing it—as the NAC, to its credit, has suggested in its detailed submission on the proposed food security Bill—will lead to the worst possible outcome: the poor remain poor even as politicians become richer."

Subsidies and give-aways that UPA and many state governments practice does not lead to inclusive growth, it results in making beggars of all, and ultimately national bankruptcy.

The Economic Times, Mumbai of 27 February 2014 reports under the heading 'Food Delivery Spend Thrice the Cost: Independent Evaluator': "The government spends ₹ 3.65 to deliver Re 1 worth of food, the Independent Evaluation Office (IEO) under the Planning Commission has pointed out. The IEO, which was formally launched on Wednesday, says despite this high cost incurred on distribution, less than 50% of the subsidised grains reach the intended beneficiaries. Over a third of the food grain is pilfered from the supply chain...".

Economists like Amartya Sen who have generally been supportive of the Congress and the Left, including the CPM, had been pushing for the UPA-II's Food Security Bill (FSB). It allows them and the political parties to project themselves visibly as pro-poor, and as doing something concrete to fight poverty. Strangely, these "pro-poor" political parties and leftist intellectuals and economists have rarely fought against the disastrous economic policies since independence that have condemned millions into poverty in the first place; nor have they campaigned for pro-growth economic policies that are the real panacea out of poverty. Anti-reform NAC-driven dole-out Sonianomics has ensured millions remain submerged in poverty, rather than emerge from it, with productive jobs that genuinely boost the country's wealth and allow them a dignified existence, rather than remaining beggars at the receiving-end of the crumbs thrown at them. Faster growth is much more effective in curbing hunger and poverty than the Food Security Bill. However, for politicians, FSB is much more visible a tool for garnering votes than the invisible growth-rate.

FDI, FII

Why the senseless socialistic-bureaucratic restrictions like 16% or 24% or 49% or 51% FDI? Why not 100% for all sectors deemed worth inviting investments for.

If foreigners want to invest in your country, which would thereby boost your economy and infrastructure and would provide jobs, should you welcome them with open arms and make it easy, smooth and red-tape-free for them to invest, or should you shun them and put up hurdles. All right-thinking countries of the world openly welcome and encourage foreign investment, including China, but here we are, the inheritors of the irrational self-damaging inward-looking socialistic legacy of Nehru-Indira, suspicious of all things that might benefit us.

Nehru, Indira and descendents see the ghost of the East India Co. in every foreign investor. As if foreign investors are free to tag along an army, like the East India Co., nurture and expand it, which in turn would help them expand their business empire, and who knows, political empire too! Are we simpletons?

Besides, many Indian capitalists have been increasingly investing abroad, finding the Indian investment climate discouraging, and corruption and red-tape a huge burden. Their investments abroad are FDI from India. Are we then saying that FDI abroad by India is fine, but FDI by foreigners in India is not so?

Why should FIIs including Vodafone, Cairn and Posco been given negative signals. But, what else could have been expected from Pranab Mukherjee as finance minister, who managed to thwart India's economy. How could a product of Nehru-Indira socialism have done justice to the requirements of India's 21st century economy. Strangely, Pranab Mukherjee, "Pranab da" as Sushma Swaraj called him, was a favourite of the BJP-Old-Guard of Advani-Sushma.

Discourage Industrialisation of Food and FDI that Promotes It

Unhealthy packaged food and industrialisation of food, like in the West, is something to be discouraged and shunned on health, taste and medical grounds, and also on account of the possible long-term damages to the land by inadvisable farming practices, and the cruelty to animals for "efficient" production of non-vegetarian food. FDI for such purposes should be banned.

We should not go the ways of the West in the area of food, whether through FDI or otherwise. Even unhealthy packaged food like potato chips and Kurkure, and soft drinks like Coke and Pepsi should be heavily taxed so as to discourage their consumption. Their advertising should be banned like for cigarettes.

However, we must build infrastructure of warehouses, cold storages, transport and supply-chain for food-items, excluding that for unhealthy packaged food.

Govt. has No Business to be in Business. Privatise PSUs

Air India and PSUs are kept under the government only so that they could be bled to make money for the politicians and the babus. Government has no business to be in business. It is incapable of managing them. It must disinvest and get out. PSUs are no family-silver or crown-jewels as the leftists-socialists like to term them, they are actually bleeding ulcers, as Arun Shourie called them.

Industry-Friendly, not Industry-Hostile

The Nehru-Indira-leftist tradition that still prevails considers it legitimate, and even 'intellectual' and empathetically pro-poor, to be abusive to capitalists and industrialists. That gives them cheap cheers from the public—like AAP is getting lately. It has not dawned upon them that it is thanks to capitalists and industrialists that jobs get created and poverty can be fought. Of course, no one is thereby defending the cosy-crony-capitalism practised between the socialist politicos and babus and the business-persons. But it is the nation's patriotic duty to encourage healthy, competitive capitalism to get us out of poverty and make India a prosperous nation. It also requires showering appreciation and according dignity and respect to entrepreneurs, capitalists and industrialists, so that more and more young professionals are motivated to become entrepreneurs rather than employees or babus.

Here is a telling example from an article "The Regulation Raj" by Jaithirth Rao in *The Indian Express* of 5 May 2012: "The irony is that in 1947 we had a decent share of the world market for textiles and the Chinese had zero market share. The rhetoric of the times cast mill owners as evil, blood-sucking capitalists (remember the Bollywood movies of that time?). The very first economic legislation of free India's government was the Textile Industries (Development and Regulation) Act. We created a czar known as the textile commissioner who told mills how much inventory they could hold, what their product mix should be, how many spindles and looms they could have and so on. We taxed the industry mercilessly. We wilfully destroyed a glorious industry. Today the Chinese textile industry is several orders of magnitude ahead of us. In 1947, we had a dominant share in the world tea market. Tea-planting in Kenya grew fast after India imposed export duties (believe it or not we had duties on exports!) on Indian tea."

Deny land, deny mining, deny electricity, deny motorable roads, deny flexible labour laws, do little for skill-development and for making skilled-labour abundantly available, put back-breaking road-blocks by stipulating plethora of permissions to be obtained and then delay or deny those permissions, unleash inspectors of all kinds looking for their pound of flesh, invent new ways of harassment, change laws adversely and retrospectively, and be as insulting, as defamatory and as abusive as you like, and yet expect Indian manufacturing to take off and compete with China!

Encourage Entrepreneurship. Make it Easy to Start Business

As per a World Bank report on ease of doing business, India ranks 166 among 189 countries. Plethora of permissions are required, besides greasing of palms. And, it takes too long to get all permissions. The whole process must be made simpler and must be put online so that it is transparent, fair, fast, and free of corruption.

Bring Back Black Money Stashed Abroad

Billions of dollars of Indian money is stashed abroad. Many countries, including the US, have aggressively gone against their country's money illegally kept abroad, have arm-twisted the Swiss and other banks, and have recovered billions.

Why not India?

Implement GST

Implement Goods & Services Tax (GST) as soon as possible.

Mining

Politicians and babus indulge in massive corruption, and when there are unsavoury disclosures, the nation simply shuts down the mining sector. That's no way to manage economy. Leftists and NGOs target principally the supply-side of the corruption—the mining barons and capitalists. They do not as much focus on the demand-side, the recipients—the politicians, the babus and the faulty laws and the discretionary powers that make corruption possible. It's not a pleasure for the industrialists to give rent. It's the corrupt system that forces them into it.

Mining is a very vital segment of the economy that can't be stopped or discouraged. Yes, environment has to be protected and the affected population has to be taken care of. But it is not as if it is a choice between the two. If sensibly managed, environment can be protected even as mining is expanded, and the consequent development can be a boon for the affected population, enhancing their income and prosperity. Also, mining is a huge employment generator.

The iron-ore deposits of Australia and Brazil are almost the same as India's, yet their iron-ore mining output is respectively six times and four times as much as India's 100 MT, when India needs increasingly more iron and steel for its infrastructural and industrial growth. In 2012, against China's steel output of 717 MT, India's was mere 77 MT—about 10th!

SAIL has said investments of $200 billion would be required to achieve the steel production target of 300 million tonnes by 2025. But, can that be done without tackling issues related to raw-materials, mining, power, land acquisition and environment, when UPA has been engaged in making all these issues tougher to resolve.

India has the world's fourth-largest deposits of coal, yet we are importing coal! Why? Because, we are unable to mine sufficient quantity to fuel our power and steel plants and other infrastructure requirements. Why? Because only Coal India Limited (CIL), a state-owned company, is allowed to mine coal. (The companies related to coal-scam were to mine coal for captive purpose only.) And, CIL is unable to mine enough. For example, against the Reliance's Rosa plant's order for delivery of 53 rakes of Coal in March 2012, CIL delivered only one rake, sending the plant into a crisis! Coal sector has to be denationalised.

India imports nearly 1,000 tonnes of gold. Needful has to be done on the gold-mining front. Setting right the mining sector would give a major boost to the economy and employment.

Energy Crisis

India has a severe power shortage, yet it allows coal-fuelled power plants to remain starved of coal, despite having fourth-largest deposits of coal in the world. Stark mismanagement! Thousands of crores of power projects worth thousands of MW of power are remaining stuck for lack of environment clearance. Why should setting up of a power plant require plethora of permissions that take five to seven years when the need of power is so urgent. Shows that netas and babus see no urgency in the urgent requirements of the nation.

In the last decade, the cumulative debt of Indian power utilities, rather than decreasing, has risen from $4 billion to $45 billion, thanks to free power to agriculture and mismanagement. Gujarat had been facing problems similar to all other states, but it has managed to tackle them. It has segregated its feeders and now provides 24x7 three-phase power supply to all its 18000 villages! Why can't other states imitate the Gujarat model?

Grains Storage

It's shocking callousness that huge quantities of grains are allowed to rot even as millions go hungry. It's shameful that the government has failed to construct sufficient number of modern warehouses to properly store grains, nor does it have schemes in place to distribute to the needy the grain it is, meanwhile, unable to store properly.

As per an ASSOCHAM study, up to 30% of food-grain harvest is wasted on account of inadequate storage capacity, unprofessional storage and deficient logistics.

Link Rivers

Linking of rivers had been proposed long back. It has tremendous positive potential for drinking water and irrigation.

Also for water-transport and related businesses. Besides, it would help tackle both the problem of flooding and of drought. The proposal needs to be revived. It would be very positive for the economy and growth, and for employment generation and poverty elimination.

Indian Railways

Look at any government-run or government-controlled organisation. Its condition would always be pathetic. Take *Indian Railways* [IR], the major undertaking, which is India's lifeline and transports millions daily. How ill-kept and dingy are majority of the railway stations and trains. While most of the countries, except countries not worth comparing with, boast of fast, smooth, comfortable trains and bullet trains, we force our millions to take risks with slow, ill-maintained, accident-prone, bone-rattling, rickety tracks and trains.

IR is in dire need of massive investment and competent, enlightened management, free from political interference. Apart from tracks that need replacement, 25% of railway bridges are over 100 years old, requiring urgent repairs/replacements. IR's *Vision 2020* document estimated the required investment at 14 lakh-crores. IR modernisation requires 5.6 lakh-crores over the next five years as per the Sam Pitroda committee report. IR's urgent safety requirements alone require one lakh-crore, as per the Kakodkar-Sreedharan committee.

China's railway network length (27,000 km) was about half that of India (53,000 km) in 1947. We have since added just 12,000 km, an increase of 22% in 65 long years since independence amounting to an average of just 185 km per year! Meanwhile, China's network length has touched a whopping 1,00,000 km.

China's indigenously built high-speed trains run at speeds up to 350 kmph, while India's fastest train runs at 150 kmph. Railway stations in China and other countries are spic-and-span like airports, while ours are mostly decrepit and dirty.

Garbage-free, Clean India

In March, 2014 there was an excellent episode of *Satyamev Jayate* on Garbage management. All-out efforts ought be made all over India for "Clean India, Garbage-Free India!" It should be taken up as a mass campaign, and all the states should be involved. Targets should be set for each district.

Open Up the Education Sector

Education sector deserved to be delivered from the clutches of the government and the babus and from the business-politicians running their educational establishments for making money.

We are in dire need of quality colleges, universities and research establishments, yet the government, rather than encouraging the private sector, remains a major road-block. Quality of graduates from engineering and management colleges is so poor many remain unemployable. Not a single Indian university or institute of higher learning, including the premier IITs, figure in the top 200 universities of the world, listed by the QS World Rankings 2012! The only ones close to the best are IIT-Delhi at 212, IIT-Mumbai at 227 and IIT-Kanpur at 278. India remains the only BRICS nation without a university in the top 200.

We need gear up our literacy campaign, and have to drastically overhaul our primary and secondary education. In literacy, India is 183 among 214 countries—below many African countries. Reports *The Economic Times* of 18 January 2013: "The Annual Status of Education Report (ASER 2012) by NGO Pratham shows that the number of Class V students who could not read a Class II level text or solve a simple arithmetic problem has increased. In 2010, 46.3% of kids in this category failed to make the cut and this shot up to 51.8% in 2011 and 53.2% in 2012...In 2010, 29.1% children in Class V could not solve a two-digit subtraction problem without seeking help. This proportion increased to 39% in 2011 and 46.5% in 2012."

Singapore and Finland recruit teachers in schools from among the brightest 10% of graduates and offer them salaries on par with engineers. And, in India?

Writing Contemporary History

Our contemporary history since independence has many gaps and the little that has been written is highly flawed. This is because the government has refused to make available relevant documents. Academics, researchers, historians, journalists, army-men, bureaucrats and others who may be interested are thus handicapped. How do you record authentic history, how do you discover and analyse your good deeds and misdeeds, and how do you ensure you rectify your shortcomings and don't make the same mistakes again, unless you have access to the original material.

All democratic countries declassify their documents after a set period as per their law, but not India. Even where the provision exists, politicians and babus find some excuse not to declassify on the pretext of "national interest". They want the official version and the wall around the lies to remain intact. The colonial Official Secrets Act of 1923 still rules. The RTI Act notwithstanding, there are many departments and organisations that are specifically exempted from disclosures. Besides, documents that could "prejudicially affect the sovereignty and integrity of India, the security, strategic, scientific or economic interests of the State, relation with foreign State or lead to incitement of an offence" are also exempted. Thousands of documents including the Henderson-Brooks-Bhagat Report on the India-China War 1962, Netaji Subhash papers, Shimla Agreement with Pakistan have therefore been kept "top secret". Nothing has been done regarding the Mitrokhin Archives.

By ensuring secrecy, the vested interests—politicians (especially, the Dynasts) and babudom—have managed to ensure they are not exposed. This must change. A healthy democracy can't permit secrecy calculated to shield the vested interests in the name of protecting the national interests.

THE CURSE OF BLOOMING BABUDOM

"B" in the Evil Triangle of DSB?

It is unfair to only target the politicians. The greater culprits are the babus, especially the upper crust comprising IAS, IFS, IRS and the like, and those at the top of the Criminal-Justice System like the IPS.

They represent the "B" in the evil triangle of DSB: "**D**" for <u>D</u>ynasts, the dynastic politicos, and the <u>D</u>ynacracy, the dynastic democracy that India has been unfortunately reduced to; "S" for poverty-perpetuating Socialistic claptrap and populism and the crony capitalism that goes with it; and "B" for the callous, incompetent, ineffective, kleptocratic Babudom—the bureaucracy and the criminal-justice system. The three nodes are interdependent and feed one another.

Isn't it strange that while political parties excoriate one another, TV and print media pans the political class, and NGOs and Civil Society groups fulminate against them, hardly anyone highlights the venality, lack of probity, incompetence and corruption of the babus, without whose complicity or negligence no scam is possible. Khemka, a capable and honest IAS officer who has been at the receiving end, had commented, "If bureaucrats did their duty, there would be no scams."

Indeed, Babudom is a strong pillar in the foundations of India's misery.

Who is Responsible for the Misgovernance Mess?

When a private company fails or does badly you blame its top-executives, who are generally made to resign. The top executives of the government are IAS-IFS-IPS-IRS combine. You have to blame them for failure of India both at the Centre and in the states. Sadly, these non-performers continue irrespective of their performance.

They sit at the top of the dung-heap, and are in many ways more powerful than the politicians, who come and go every five years, while they continue, irrespective of their performance, on account of their constitutional sinecure. ICS prospered under the British, while the nationalists suffered jails. Post independence, the top babus—not all, but an overwhelming majority—have been having a good time: making money, misusing power, contributing little, taking the country to dogs, and then blaming the politicians for all the ills, and how they are not allowed to function! The babus indeed have very low IQ—low *Integrity Quotient*.

Why have Babus been Supporters of the Socialistic Way?

Most of the babus have been supporters of socialism or significant state controls and regulations, not because they think it would do any good to India, but because it results in enhancement of their powers and importance and opens avenues for making money.

To Hell with Primary Responsibilities!

The primary duty of any government is to provide justice to all, ensure internal and external security, and build infrastructure and institutions of good governance. Nehru dynasty did the reverse. While it miserably failed to deliver on all the primary counts, it arrogantly went into business, which is none of government's business. It sought to be a trader and an industrialist—with no qualifications or expertise whatsoever. The generalist IAS babus salivated at the opportunities for power and pelf. Primary responsibilities went for a toss.

Babus and the Failure of the Criminal-justice System

Justice to all? The powerful and the rich and the well-connected can get away with murder and huge scams and corruption; while the poor—and not just the poor, anyone bereft of power and right connections—can go to dogs: the state of the police and the judicial system being what it is.

The kind of criminal-justice system the governments, predominantly run by the Nehru-Gandhi dynasty since independence, have managed to build is exemplified by this story that was reported in newspapers in May, 2013. A poor lady, Vijai Kumari, living in a village in Aligarh district was arrested and imprisoned, and later granted bail by Allahabad High Court in 1994. However, she could not fulfil the bail conditions of a personal bond and two sureties. Nobody came to her help, and she had to stay behind bars. She was pregnant when arrested. She gave birth to a son in the jail. Her son, whom she named Kanhaiya, grew up in jail and then in Children's home. Upon turning 18, he was sent to a rehabilitation centre. He had received training in garment manufacturing. With his earning he arranged for a lawyer and bail amount and finally got his mother released after 19 years! Can a state and criminal-justice system be more callous?

Babus and the Colonial Culture

Nehru and subsequent governments have done nothing to change the babudom and make it people-oriented, service-oriented and development-oriented—they continue with their feudal class consciousness and arrogant ways, ill-suited to public service. The pre-independence babu culture of living like a rajah, misusing power, exploiting people, becoming rich at their cost, and aping the British ways to look cultured, continues.

How the Babus lord it out

As per 15 October 2013 *Times of India, Mumbai* news-item '*2,600 cops serve in homes of IPS officers in state*' by Prafulla Marpakwar: "...The question now is whether [the government] will withdraw the 2,600-odd police personnel deployed at the residences of 280 IPS officers across the state [of Maharashtra]... At least seven to 10 constables are deployed at the residence of an Indian Police Service officer, a senior IPS officer said. If this number is reduced, the state will get enough policemen to fill up at least 10 to 15 police stations... [A conscientious] IPS officer said, 'I am shocked that so many constables are deployed. Occasionally I feel we are still in the British Raj...'" The report states that 5 to 9 constables, 3 orderlies, 1 cook, 2-3 telephone runners and 2 drivers are deployed at the residences of SPs/Commissioners; while 2 to 5 constables, 2-3 orderlies, 2 telephone runners and 2 drivers are deployed at the residences of other IPS officials. The report continues: "'Many officers have even more staffers, depending on their influence. In Pune, a high-ranking officer in the prisons department had 15-20 constables at his official residence,' said a senior IPS officer... What was more shocking, the officer said, was that the staff remained the same even if the officer were to be shifted to another city, and even after an officer retired, the police personnel continued to serve him for a period ranging from three months to a year."

So, while the citizens may remain insecure and crimes against women may be a growing menace, the IPS babus, like their IAS counterparts, must lord it out. Which other democratic country in the world would allow such shamelessness, brazenness, colonial luxuries, feudal lordliness, priority of services to self over services to people, and utter contempt for the general public! And, can an abysmally poor country like India where millions go hungry afford this? Only a feudal, dynastic democracy like India, where those at the help similarly lord it out in utter contempt and disregard of the people, can permit such gross insult and indifference to the public!!

Babus Care too Hoots about Their Subordinates

The way the IPS babus allow their subordinates to be treated is astounding. There are many shocking examples. Here is a sample, a report in *The Indian Express* of 11 March 2014 titled '*No beds or bathrooms at SRPF's training base in Mumbai*': "There are no beds or bathrooms, and the toilet facilities are almost unusable. About 700 personnel of the State Reserve Police Force are living in such conditions in the SRPF training base in Mumbai's Aarey Milk Colony. They sleep on dirt floors in the barracks..." Why can't IPS babus or their associations take up the cause of their subordinates? Or, are they concerned only with their own luxuries?

Why "Service" Attached to Their Names?

What has the Babudom done—especially the IAS at the top, who ought to be accountable for it—to transform the state from a callous exploiter to one that serves citizens. One wonders why that "S for Service" is attached at the end of IAS, IPS, IFS and IRS, unless it signifies only self-service or service to their masters. Do they serve the public? Or, do they get served? Has the Babudom cared to evolve a system that provides incentives and rewards for desirable behaviour for their fraternity; and penalties for undesirable behaviour? They can't just put the blame on the political class. If they can't do all this as individuals, they can surely attempt it as a group—they have their own powerful associations. What do they do?

In the mid-1930s Nehru denounced the ICS—Indian Civil Service—as "neither Indian nor civil nor a service". He further said it was "essential that the ICS and similar services disappear completely". Unfortunately, after independence, with himself in power, such pledges, like other promises, faded away. The term 'Indian Administrative Service' is a misnomer considering the criminal absence both of "administration" and of "service" to public.

Attributes of Indian Babudom

The Indian babudom is authoritarian, arrogant, callous, unfair, heartless, insensitive, ill-mannered, indifferent, incompetent, inefficient, ineffective, uninnovative, nepotistic, rude, sloppy, sluggish, self-seeking and shamelessly corrupt. Bureaucracy is now Kleptocracy. The only thing that partially saves us from the bureaucracy is its inefficiency. Even if politicians are willing, the babus are incompetent in executing anything positive or constructive, or delivering reforms on the ground—how can they, when they are unable to reform themselves?

Wrote Kuldip Nayar in *Beyond the Lines* about the Emergency: "Only a handful of civil servants stood their ground, others were too scared to lose their jobs. Some found in it an opportunity to occupy high positions on the understanding that they would carry out illegal orders. Sanjay Gandhi converted the civil servants into a servile breed; the willing tools of tyranny. They have not to this day recovered from the loss of esteem in the eyes of the public if not their own. They wield authority, not respect. Their political masters know that bureaucrats are beholden to them because they are partners in the loot in which both of them indulge without a twinge of conscience."

Are All Babus Corrupt and Incompetent?

Of course, not all babus are bad. It is only 99 percent of babus, as someone said, who give the rest a bad name! There are a few like Kiran Bedi who are fighting for better systems. Also, persons like TSR Subramaniam, the ex-Cabinet Secretary, who has written the book, *Journeys through Babudom and Netaland*. It is worth reading.

BABUDOM AND THE *METAMORPHOSIS* OF FRANZ KAFKA

Babudom reminds one of Franz Kafka's *Metamorphosis*. What if Kafka was born in India and was witness to post-independence India; and what if he wrote *Metamorphosis* in the current Indian context? Would it still have the undertone of absurdity and alienation, and of a random and chaotic universe with no governing system of order and justice? Would it still have Gregor, a travelling salesman, metamorphose into a gigantic insect? Or, would it rather have the undertone of a crass, callous, corrupt, rusted, unjust system—all man-made; with Gregor, a babu rather than a travelling salesman, metamorphose into a gigantic cockroach?

Indian Babudom Independently Evaluated

PERC (Political and Economic Risk Consultancy: www.asiarisk.com) rates Indian bureaucracy as one of the worst bureaucracies in Asia responsible for, as an article in *The Indian Express*, Mumbai of 16 October 2013 states, "bottlenecking key policies, widespread red tapism in everyday affairs, massive corruption, being uninnovative and insensitive, and harbouring generalist officers who lack expertise." A report "Corruption's Impact on the Business Environment" for 2013 for Asia-Pacific was published by PERC. It grades countries on a scale of 10, 0 being the best and 10 being the worst—most corrupt. Singapore came at the top with a score of 0.74, Japan and Australia tied at number 2 with a score of 2.35, and India came at the bottom with a score of 8.95!

What Should be Done about the Babudom Going Forward?

The India bureaucratic system is beyond reform. The only remedy is to dismantle it completely and put up a new system in its place. It is badly in need of creative destruction.

Should Babus be Employed Post-retirement?

No. Because, the carrot of post-retirement assignment makes them compromise on their pre-retirement responsibilities. Besides, why let retirees block available positions. Give those in service a chance. Make way for the young. In case the retirees are keen to serve the country, let them come on as honorary advisors, without payment or perks.

For the Nation's Doom—IAS: Indians Always in Service!

As if their normal service-period is not sufficient to ruin the country, a large number of retired babus manage a government position in some establishment or the other, and never really retire. No wonder *Indian Express* [IE] in its series of articles in July, 2012 expanded IAS as "*Indians Always in Service*". The probability of procuring a "*confirmed gravy train ticket*", as IE called it, is predominantly influenced by the extent of one's servility to the powers that be.

Although politicians are largely blamed for India's misery, the babudom is as much or perhaps more responsible. In fact, political class and babudom, mainly IAS, have co-opted each other. Politicians can't amass wealth, handout favours and perpetuate their rule and that of their dynasty without the cooperation of the top babus; and the top babus, in turn, can't keep getting plump postings, a cut in the moolah and gain indemnity for their misdeeds without the kind intervention of the politicians. Being a mutually beneficial combination, the top babus seek and the politicians facilitate their continuation even after retirement. In expectation of life-long employment and/or opportunities of making of money, most of the babus have practically sold their souls to the politicians and are free from all scruples. They serve not the nation, but the politicians, and in the process, actually serve themselves.

Why Generalist Babus for Positions Requiring Expertise?

Indian Babudom predominantly harbours generalist with expertise in nothing except in bottlenecking key policies, holding or pushing files, red-tapism and corruption. However, thanks to the prevailing system of political patronage, powerful, pliant, generalist babus have long since expanded their tentacles to capture not only governorships, but also most of the critical positions requiring specialist expertise, such as position of RBI governor, CAG, head of TRAI, CCI, NDMA, CERC, and so on. It is worth noting that almost all top positions require high-level expertise, and the generalist IAS (even if they have done some course or taken some training or gained some little experience just to corner those posts) are gross misfits, because top-level expertise demands years of focussed work in a particular field, which the IAS can never gain. IAS therefore has nothing worthwhile to contribute in those areas, and become mere file-pushers passing their time. Why shouldn't the head of TRAI be a telecom expert rather than an IAS babu? Why should the CAG be from IAS rather than from the Indian Audit and Accounts Service? Why shouldn't the RBI governor be an accomplished, experienced economist—why should he be an IAS babu? How come the USA manages to have high-level experts from the concerned fields to head the relevant positions; while in sharp contrast, we put in the IAS babus as square pegs in round holes in all top positions.

Why is it so? Actually, politicians require compliant people who would do their bidding; and IAS babus more than meet that requirement. Why take academic, judicial, social, financial, revenue, security, disaster management, law-enforcing, business, trade, management, information technology, telecom or other technical experts from outside to head those positions and run the unnecessary risk of having honest, conscientious and forthright persons? IAS babus are safe bets, more so the retired ones begging for assignments.

With the economic liberalisation post 1991 it was expected that the bureaucratic stranglehold would loosen. But, sensing the vastly enhanced scope of making the moolah with the unprecedented expansion of the economy, the politician-bureaucratic combine ensured that the plethora of new bodies, especially the regulatory ones that came into being, were hijacked by the babus. With a nod from the politicians, serving and retired babus have captured practically all important decision-making bodies. With IAS babus as heads of regulatory bodies, autonomous, independent, honest, competent and sane regulation is a chimera. Babudom, as it has existed, is incapable of delivering, as the experience of over six decades after independence bears out. There have been some babus who have tried to do good, but that's a miniscule percentage and an exception, and even they could not go very far, as they stood check-mated by the establishment, including their own colleagues.

An article, 'Revenge of the Babus' in *India Today* of 27 September 2013 states: "Of the 12 economic regulators created since liberalisation, nine are headed by retired bureaucrats. Appointments to constitutional bodies like CAG, Central Vigilance Commission or RBI inevitably come from their ranks. In 20 states, the chief information commissioner is the state's former chief secretary. They head human rights commissions, SC and ST commissions and finance commissions, and are even part of bodies like the National Disaster Management Authority (NDMA)... Two decades after liberalisation, Babu Raj is back as India's only permanent establishment... [For the] Competition Commission of India (CCI), a new regulatory body...instituted in 2003... a technocrat was apparently considered for the job but retired commerce secretary...was picked instead. The appointment was challenged in a PIL... Then chief justice V.N. Khare was quoted as saying, 'At this rate, a day would come, maybe after 20 years, when the 26 judges of the apex court would be replaced by bureaucrats.' [that's what the corrupt politicians and babus would love!] ...At the central level, there has been a near-complete dominance of IAS appointees to head regulatory bodies, a 'regulatory capture'... In the same month that Khullar [former commerce secretary] was appointed chairman of TRAI, the Federal Communications Commission in the US appointed two young commissioners, Ajit Pai and Jessica Rosenworcel. Both had extensive experience in communications law. So why aren't young domain specialists heading regulatory bodies in India? ...According to S.L. Rao, a senior economist who was appointed chairman of the first CERC in 1998, the top post was kept vacant for 10 months after his term ended in 2001 so that the incumbent power secretary, Ashok Basu, could take over the job after his retirement. ...S.L. Rao explains that part of the reason that electricity regulation hasn't taken off in the states is that bureaucrats heading the regulators refuse to take tough decisions on pricing..."

IAS and the like should be banned from all top-level appointments requiring special expertise; and there are many such areas: Defence, Education, Electricity, Energy, Environment, Finance, Information Technology, Mining, Nuclear Energy, Regulatory, RBI, SEBI, Telecom, and so on. In fact, practically all departments at the top level (not just the top-most level), except perhaps a few, require high degree of expertise which can be earned only by almost life-long work in the chosen field.

Should Outsiders/Experts be Inducted?

Yes. Top-level assignments in all categories discussed above must be of specialists taken from outside. They can be given say a one-month course to familiarise themselves with the Babugiri, that is, the government working. IAS-officers may be appointed as their PAs to take care of the nitty-gritty of administration and file-movement.

Indian Bureaucracy Needs to be as Competent as the Chinese

Most of China's bureaucrats are engineers, scientists, professionals, and experts in various fields, who have risen up the hard way—by merit and performance. Compare that with file-pushing expert-in-nothing babus in India rising up the ranks on the basis of seniority and chamchagiri. This has to change. India can't afford to carry on with its existing Babudom. It has to drastically change itself and transform into an accountable, innovative, efficient, meritocratic machine. It has to learn from the Chinese.

To take care of SARS-infected patients in 2003, China built a 1000-bed hospital in Beijing in just 7 days—excluding, of course, the time for planning, design, blue-prints and approvals. Using 500 construction machines, over 4000 construction labourers worked non-stop during April 24–30 to build the giant hospital. It was made operational within days, with 1200 medical staff procured nationwide from military hospitals. Such is the competence of Chinese managers.

At its fastest growth-period, the US was doubling its living standards every 30 years; something which China has been doing every 10 years for the last 30 years! Consequent to a mega annual meeting of Chinese leaders in Beijing on March 5, Prime Minister Li Keqiang declared the country's war on pollution, and the anti-pollution campaign commenced. Do we see such huge political-neutral initiatives in India.

What takes decades in other countries, China does in mere years. In the recent past, it extended pension coverage to an extra 240 million (!!) in the rural area in just two years. Public-pension system in the US, that took decades, covers lesser number of persons!

CORRUPTION

How Does Corruption Hurt?

Why does corruption hurt—apart from ethical considerations?

The necessity of curbing corruption goes beyond the purely ethical considerations of ensuring honesty and fair play, and beyond just monetary considerations of checking leakages.

Many critical benefits, including investments, economic growth, poverty-removal and India's demographic dividend, are dependent upon it. Corruption hurts economic growth because it allows crony capitalists get an upper hand over genuine ones. Graft discourages genuine Indian and foreign investors. Corruption affects investments, which affects growth and employment generation, which affects the millions of young coming into the labour market every year, leading to frustration and social instability. Can India afford a volatile political, economic and social environment?

Curbing of corruption would give a boost to the Indian economy: more foreign investments, more people opening new companies, ethical companies getting competitive, and so on. It would also help India realise a global leadership role.

WHAT IS THE RIGHT WAY TO TACKLE CORRUPTION?

Corruption is not an one-dimensional problem and there is no one single way to root it out. A multi-pronged strategy incorporating preventive, detective and punitive measures is required, including, among other things, liberalisation and economic reforms that have been stopped half-way, much higher level of transparency, innovative automation and online delivery of services, systemic changes, and also independent Lokpal, with investigative powers.

AAP's one-point agenda of Lokpal is a very partial solution. The major, impactful solution is change of policies, liberalisation, and economic reforms. Unfortunately, these latter don't fit-in with the backward-looking, pink-to-red, socialistic claptrap policies of AAP. Hence, AAP can never really be instrumental in removing big-time corruption. They can only talk, shout and be abusive to get votes.

How Does "Liberalisation" Reduces Corruption?

Even though all brands of *Socialist/Leftist Economics* have proved a dud both in theory and in practice, Socialists/ Leftists keep concocting rationale for their defunct economics to somehow retain their relevance. The latest being that the increase in corruption is thanks to *Liberalisation* since the nineties. That it is the *neo-liberal* policies from the times of Narsimha Rao onwards that have led to increase in corruption.

Leftists do not seem to appreciate that a moribund, minuscule economy till 1991, thanks to the disastrous socialistic policies of Nehru-Indira-Rajiv, has grown to over a trillion dollar, precisely because of post-1991 reforms. To the extent the economy has grown many-fold, the corruption has also grown, because the necessary preventive, detective, regulatory and penal systems to control the corruption have not kept pace with the change in the post-1991 economic policies, thanks to the rapacious politician-babu combine, who have retained the pre-1991 socialistic-bureaucratic setup.

It is worth remembering that there was wide-spread corruption before 1991 also—right since Nehru's time, and even before in the British-India. It became much worse with Indira and her descendents! The Congress ministries elected in the various states of the British-India in the late thirties had turned so corrupt that Gandhi had called for disbanding of Congress after Independence!!

Although Indira's and Rajiv's times were much more corrupt and Sonia-MMS times have crossed all limits, even the Nehru period had many financial scandals: the Jeep scandal, the Mudgal case, Mundra deals, Malaviya Sirajuddin scandal, Pratap Singh Kairon case—to name a few.

Those who talk of "better, less-corrupt pre-liberalisation days" of Nehru-Indira-Rajiv are suffering from amnesia. In the "good" old days of Nehru-Indira-Rajiv socialism, if you wanted to bunk the long queues extending to several years for getting a gas-connection or telephone or scooter, you had to bribe. Contrast that with the position now. Each of these things are now for the asking—the concerned companies would come to your home to do the needful. It took India 110 years to reach 5 million phones by 1991. However, thanks to liberalisation, that number grew to a whopping 300 million by 2008! In the pre-1991 days, even if you were the lucky one to have a gas-connection, you still needed to bribe periodically to get the gas-cylinder in time. Not so now. Same for telephone—if you did not want your telephone to be dead, you had to grease palms. Now the poor and the rich all have telephones, and they hardly go dead. Even items like cement and steel were on quota. If you were building your house, bribe the officials to get your quota. Same with the railway reservations—stand in long queues and try your luck, or bribe.

Those bad-old days are now gone. Thanks to the post-1991 reforms, common people have been freed from many hassles and humiliations, as many avenues of corruption have been done away with—but, not all. Much more needs to be done. What are needed are more reforms, not rollback of what has been done, more liberalisation, not going back to the command-and-control-license-permit-quota-raj economy.

In the pre-liberalisation days, if you travelled abroad, upon return, you stood as a suspect culprit in a long queue to be pounced upon by ill-mannered customs officials looking for their chance to make *moolah*. As an entrepreneur, if you wanted a license or a permission or an import licence or if you wanted to stop your competitor from getting one, you needed to bribe a set of officials—which continues even now, because reforms are incomplete. Many new firms like Infosys with no pedigree like Birlas and Tatas have sprung up in India from scratch thanks to liberalisation, and have massively contributed to GDP, exports-earnings and employment.

The current crop of mega-corruptions are not on account of liberalisation and economic-reforms, but on account of government's decision to stop halfway with reforms, massive discretion still exercised by politicians and babus, and lack of empowered, autonomous institutions to prevent, detect, and penalise corruption. What are needed are institutional reforms to eliminate or minimise corruption.

Leftists also need to note that without the massive revenues growth, thanks to liberalisation, there would have been no funds for MGNREGA, NRHM, FSB, RTE, and the like.

In a bureaucratic-socialistic culture, which still prevails, reforms being still an unfinished project, the culture is of easy money through corruption; and incentive to retain this system of graft and to run-down reforms is very high, because reforms are anti-easy money. Crony capitalism, thanks to bureaucratic-socialistic culture and half-baked reforms, has to give way to rule-based capitalism by undertaking reforms across the board. Only then would corruption be effectively curbed—not fully eliminated.

Can a Socialistic-bureaucratic Country be Ever Corruption-free?

Doubtful. More the spread and hold of the state, more areas would likely be infected with corruption. Contrary to what the socialists/leftists and the new kid on the block, AAP, say, an unreformed, non-liberalised socialistic setup is likely to be much more corrupt.

HONESTY AND COMPETENCE

Is Honesty a Qualification?

No. Honesty is a basic requirement. It is a pre-requisite for a job or assignment. That is, it is a pre-selection criteria. For persons deemed dishonest or "not of good moral character", the question of processing their application does not arise. Actual qualifications and experience and other requirements are evaluated for only those candidates who are deemed to be honest and "of good moral character".

Is Honesty a Measure of Competence?

Certainly not. Honesty is but a basic requirement. It has nothing to do with a person's competence for a job or assignment.

Would You Employ a Person Who is Honest, but Incompetent?

Certainly not. Can you employ a driver who is honest, but is rash and not quite skilled at the wheels? Can you employ a software coder who is honest, but whose coding is generally faulty and error-prone? Can you employ a teacher or a trainer who is honest, but whose speech is unintelligible and who can't really teach?

Personal Honesty is not Enough: Professional Honesty is the Real Test

It is not enough to be only personally honest. Where others report to you, and you are responsible for their performance, professional honesty demands you ensure the conduct of those under you is also honest and above board, and that they are not indulging in any malpractices and corruption. In case it is found to be otherwise, you need to take action against them. Your professional duty demands that you ensure the whole area or department or ministry or ministries under you perform their duly in an honest and professional manner. Professional honesty requires that while you yourself don't do a dishonest or unprofessional act, you also don't ignore those acts in others under you.

What is easier: personal honesty or professional honesty?

Personal honesty, of course, because it concerns only yourself. If you are not a greedy person, or if you are already a well-provided person, or if you are by nature or upbringing upright, or if you are a self-respecting, principled person, or if you are a conscientious person, it is not difficult to be personally honest. So many are. In fact, you take pride in being so. It gives you a sense of self-worth. You feel good about yourself.

However, it is not easy to be professionally honest. Because, that requires competence to manage, evaluate, judge and control those under you.

What is better? To have honest people or competent people?

You need people who are both honest and competent. It is not worth having in employment or on assignment people who are honest but incompetent, or people who are competent but dishonest.

What would you say of Man Mohan Singh (MMS)?

MMS is personally honest, but dishonest in the higher level of honesty—professional honesty. Can the supposed personal virtue of personal honesty of prime ministers exempt them from accountability for the actions and omissions of their subordinates?

What about AK Anthony, the Defence Minister?

He is personally honest, but incompetent. It is unfortunate that a few who happen to be honest are incompetent.

AAP: A DISAPPOINTMENT SO FAR

AAP and Its One-point Agenda of Corruption and Jan Lokpal

Corruption is certainly an important issue, but if it is a serious political party which wants to take India out of its depth, it can't be the only issue or even the main issue. Also, Jan Lokpal is only a punitive measure, it is not a preventive measure or a measure that would eliminate avenues of corruption. Hence, Jan Lokpal, which they have been projecting as the only solution, is actually a partial solution, and not really as effective as the other measures could be.

The foremost issues have to be the following: economic philosophy, economic vision and economic policy to lift India out of its poverty and make it a prosperous nation; ensuring good governance, which in turn requires wide-ranging administrative, police, judicial and electoral reforms and a slew of policy measures; external security; internal security, including tackling the red-corridor and the northeast.

AAP's Song and Dance on Austerity

AAP has been doing lots of song and dance about "simple living" of their leaders, their non-VIP culture and their shunning official perks and privileges. It's another matter what a little digging-in by the media revealed about Arvind Kejriwal and his ministers.

However, there are many leaders who are genuinely austere compared to the AAP show-offs, but have never publicised their life of simplicity.

Manik Sarkar. He has been CM of Tripura since 1998, and is from CPM. He is probably the poorest Chief Minister in India—with no land or vehicle or any moveable or immoveable assets and a bank balance of less than ₹ 14,000. The salary and allowances that he receives as CM he donates to the party fund. The Party, in turn, gives him ₹ 5,000 per month as subsistence allowance. His wife is an officer of the Central Social Welfare Board under the Central Government, and her salary helps run the household. Sarkar's wife also leads a simple life and prefers travelling in cycle rickshaws. If Sarkar and his wife take part in the same programme, the Chief Minister goes in his official vehicle while his wife travels in a cycle rickshaw or an auto. Sarkar inherited a small house in Agartala. He donated it to a kin.

Buddhadeb Bhattacharjee. This former CM of West Bengal resides in a rented government flat. In an affidavit submitted to the Election Commission, he had declared he neither owned a house or a vehicle and had cash in hand of only ₹ 5,000.

Manohar Parrikar. This BJP CM of Goa (alumni of IIT, Mumbai) drives himself to work in his own modest small Maruti car, doesn't use the red beacon and abjures official accommodation. He uses official Innova for safety when going to mining area. Even during his previous two tenures as CM, he lived in his ancestral house at Mapusa, 13 km away from Panaji, the capital. He uses his official residence as office to hold meetings and for visitors. He is often seen pillion riding a scooter.

The following is from *Foundations of Misery, India, 1947-64: Blunders of the Nehruvian Era*.

Wrote MO Mathai, who was Special Assistant to Nehru from 1946 to 1959, in *Reminiscences of the Nehru Age*: 'At 10 Downing Street, the British Prime Minister has only a couple of suites of rooms for his personal use. All the rest are offices and a few are public rooms...Tage Erlander, the Social Democratic Prime Minister of affluent Sweden, for twenty years lived in a three room flat. His wife was a teacher...The Swedish

Government did not provide him with a car. The PM and his wife had a small car which they drove themselves. They could not afford to keep a driver...Labour Prime Minister Joseph Chiefley of rich Australia lived in two rooms in a second class hotel near his office. His wife preferred to live on their farm... The PM was not provided with a car. He walked between his hotel and his office...'

What an irony! The non-Gandhians of the rich, Western countries were being Gandhi-like; while the "Gandhian" Congressmen of our own poor, pathetic, post-independent India were adopting the ways of rajas and maharajas, whose feudal, privileged lifestyle they, particularly Nehru, had been cursing all through!

Writes S. Nijalingappa in *My Life and Politics*: "But after becoming prime minister, he [Nehru] left 17 York Road, a fairly large building and moved to possibly the second largest official residence next to the Rashtrapati Bhavan. His reason of doing so was that official dignity required it. In contrast, I may mention the instance of Ho Chi Minh, the president, Vietnam. When I saw him during his visit to Delhi, he said he had only a few clothes and only two pairs of sandals and lived in a small house. But, in independent India, simple living became an exception. Sardar Vallabhbhai Patel, throughout his stay in Delhi, whether before or after accepting office, lived in a small house at Aurangzeb Road, only large enough for himself and his daughter."

Do Austere Persons Deliver Better?

True, Manik Sarkar and Buddhadeb Bhattacharjee, as we have seen above, lead a simple, austere life. But, did they succeed in making the life of the people of their states better and more prosperous. Were the states relatively much better under them? No. So, personal austerity is just personal. It does not necessarily translate into great or wise policies for the betterment of the people.

One would prefer people who lead non-austere life (but, of course, within the legitimate salary, perks and privileges provided by the state), but deliver non-austere, prosperous life for their people; compared to those who lead austere life and condemn their people to austerity too.

AAP: Why Does One See Red?

From what one can discern, AAP is not a forward-looking party, but a backward-looking one. Economically, it wants to be the Congress of 30 years back. Considering the further addition of pink to red-hot Maoists as its prominent members, it is bound to be a party of jholawallahs. And, jholawallah-policies can only take the nation to dogs.

Without further economic liberalisation and reforms, you can neither root out corruption, nor can you remove poverty.

AAP—Like Others?

The short-lived AAP government was quick off the block to indulge in the populist game à la Congress, SP, DMK, AIDMK and others of sheer giveaways, simply to curry favour with the electorate. What great administrative skills or management or leadership is required to make something free or to give part waiver? Ultimately what the government foregoes by way of electricity or water charges it would have to make-up elsewhere, perhaps by cutting down on the much more desirable and beneficial social or infrastructural expenditure. How then is the AAP different from the other parties? One needs to be wary of the questionable populist policies and the warped give-away economics of the AAP, which people may hail in the short-term, but which would rebound in the medium and long term.

What Does AAP's Abandonment of Delhi Demonstrate?

They are not competent to rule. They have no commitment to improve things. They can only do rabble-rousing by being in the opposition.

It doesn't take anything to announce cuts in power or water tariffs. Any irresponsible party can do it. What matters is whether you can absorb those cuts without cutting corners on the more crucial areas like education, health and infrastructure. That requires a holistic approach to the budget, revenues and expenditures, and requires commitment and competence to design and implement a good budget and carry through the policies required for it.

But, when this real challenge came, they just ran away. And, rather than being honest about it (if you call yourself non-corrupt, then that attribute includes honesty too), they grabbed on a flimsy excuse of the Jan Lokpal Bill, saying the other parties were not co-operating in its passage. The fact was that both the Congress and the BJP were more than willing to facilitate passage of the bill, provided lawful procedures were followed. If Jan Lokpal Bill was so critical for AAP, and they were indeed serious about it, they should have shown some patience, and should have found a way to pass the bill through discussions with all the stakeholders, that is, the LG, the Congress, the BJP and the Central Government. If even after that they had failed to get the Bill passed then their resignation could have been understandable. In that case, the opposition, that is, the Congress and the BJP, would have automatically stood exposed.

But, the AAP didn't take that course, fearing the Jan Lokpal Bill might indeed get passed, and then they would not be able to be abusive towards the opposition.

The other reason, indeed the main reason, was that their incompetence and muddle-headedness was getting exposed with each passing day, and if they had continued further, they might have been totally exposed. They therefore wanted to cut their losses to be able to face the Lok Sabha elections.

What are the Strengths of the AAP?

They have shown that candidates of even a new political party can win elections without the hitherto-considered-must-negatives, if they can convince people they indeed have something positive to offer. By negatives is meant money-power, muscle-power, offering of enticements like booze, and indulging in regional or casteist or communal propaganda.

They have been able to use TV and social media effectively to popularise themselves, saving in massive campaign costs.

They have skilfully exploited the public sentiment against wide-spread corruption to gain an edge.

They have managed to attract many good candidates, with excellent background and clean records, for Lok Sabha elections. They also have many dedicated, selfless supporters.

What are the Main Negatives of the AAP?

It's a populist, jholawala party fishing for populist opportunities to gain power. The party has no worth-while policies that could launch India into the first-world. They have a populist agenda à la Congress and other such parties. They are only trying to differentiate themselves by projecting themselves as non-corrupt. But, you have to be in power to become corrupt. They haven't had that opportunity so far, but for their 49-day farce in Delhi.

They are careful not to articulate their policies in detail. Because, that might expose them. They want to let everything remain vague, so that they remain free to take positions as might suit them in the times to come. That's dishonesty.

And, dishonest and liars they are. They freely engage in false or unsubstantiated allegations, and they aggressively spread misinformation. On top of it, they are crude and abusive.

Corruption—The Broad Definition and AAP

What is corruption in a broad sense? Corruption is usage of unfair means to gain an unfair advantage or to retain a position. Unfair advantage includes getting or retaining money or promotion or position of power. Unfair means include giving/taking of money, gifts, sexual favours, and so on; and maintaining "irresponsible silence"—knowingly keeping quiet at the wrong-doings of one's subordinates. Unfair means also include deliberate lying, false allegations and misinformation to damage others.

It is not true that only if a person accepts money he is corrupt. A rich person may have no interest in more money, or a person given to modest living may not attach much importance to money. However, in lieu of money, he or she may be interested in sex or in promotion or in position of power or in retention of his or her current position, which he or she might otherwise lose. He may permit wrong-doings for sake of these, rather than for money.

Viewed from this angle, "honest" Man Mohan Singh was corrupt, as he allowed wrong-doing under his watch to retain his position/power.

Similarly, Arvind Kejriwal and many other members of his party are corrupt as they have been engaging in unfair means (deliberate lying, false allegations and misinformation to damage others) to gain unfair advantage (position of power/winning elections).

Why IAC, AAP's Predecessor, Failed on Lokpal?

There are several reasons why IAC failed on Lokpal despite massive public support. It demonstrates deficiency of several vital ingredients: foresight, persistence, patience, strategy and tactics, flexibility, prudence.

Reason 1. They should have persisted further with what they had been doing: non-political, peaceful agitation and fasting. They should have been more patient. More and more people were joining the agitation with each passing day. They should not have given up.

Or, was it deliberate? Utilise the public support obtained to float a political party to gain power.

Reason 2. Why give up agitation on the pretext that even if they die from fasting, government won't do anything?

Actually, why do people have to fast to death or fast to the extent that their health is severely affected? Make it a symbolic fast, a relay fast, and not a fast to death for anyone. One group can fast for one to three days, followed by another group, followed by yet another group, and so on—stretch it till the government bends. Try and organise similar relay fasts at as many other centres as possible. Make it into an all-state-capitals, followed by all-districts, then all-cities-towns-and-villages relay-fasts. What you have to demonstrate to the powers-that-be is the extent of support for your demands? Why look forward to the sensitivity of the establishment—if they had any they wouldn't be so corrupt—and seek their intervention to save you from death due to fasting?'

Reason 3. Team Anna should have stuck only to its demand for a strong Lokpal, without bringing in additional issues like setting up SIT to probe alleged corruption charges against cabinet ministers, which vitiated the atmosphere.

Reason 4. Even on Lokpal, they should have focussed, to begin with—say, as Stage-1—only on three things: independence of investigation agency, method of selection of Lokpal members, and limited coverage—all central and state ministers and only senior babus comprising IAS, IFS, IPS, IRS, etc. No compromise on these. Coverage of others should have been left to subsequent stages. Rather than creating a behemoth from the very start that might falter and fail, get the most critical things passed first in Stage-1, and gaining from that experience, push for extended coverage.

Reason 5. They should have been flexible. They should not have insisted on all or none. Sticking to the "Stage-1" above would have been wiser.

Reason 6. Self-control. To build a favourable atmosphere to achieve the above, they should have strictly restrained their members from doing anything that could harm the achievement of that limited, basic objective, and should have demonstratively hauled up those who violated that discipline. It required being non-abusive, non-aggressive, non-accusive and non-dismissive towards elected MPs and MLAs and democratic institutions, and usage of polite and cultured language irrespective of provocations. Also, there should have been a genuine, intensive attempt to take into confidence all political parties—ruling and opposition—and as many non-political groups and NGOs as possible.

However, in sharp contrast to the above requirement, they managed to annoy almost all. One did not have to parade one's own good qualities, nor arrogantly run down others, if one had to achieve a specific objective.

MINORITIES AND WEAKER SECTIONS

Safety, a Very Basic Requirement

Among the very basics expected from any government is safety for its citizens, particularly the vulnerable sections like the minorities, dalits, women and children. This is fundamental. Other things come later. People should not feel vulnerable to communal, caste, gender or domestic violence. They should be able to breathe freely and live fearlessly—otherwise what is the point of gaining independence. Safety is what independent India should have firmly ensured within the first five to ten years of its existence. Not a difficult goal to achieve at all, given the desire and the will. The safety and social justice should have been ensured whatever it took: persuasion, education, publicity, unbiased and empathetic governance and criminal-justice system—even violence where needed.

Doing so requires desire, determination, uncompromising commitment against injustice, ideas, planning, well thought-out strategy, reforms and action. But, have things changed much in the last 66 years? No. The heartless anti-weak and anti-poor and corrupt criminal-justice-police system continues as in the colonial days. There is no reform or replacement.

What actions have been taken to ensure safety? Verbiage. More verbiage. Keep talking of secularism and protection of minorities and dalits. Let them feel insecure and vote for you in the hope that perhaps one day you might translate your promises into action.

Is It a Distinction to be Secular? Is Being Personally Secular Enough?

Strangely, being secular and non-communal is considered as something very special: "That leader was totally non-communal!...This party is thoroughly secular!!..." The fact is about 99.99% of the Indians are indeed secular and non-communal. So, it is a very common quality and a feature of the Indian society. Why then tom-tom about it? If you are not communal, so are the other 99.99%. What's the big deal? But, no. With little worthwhile practical achievements on the ground to beat the drums about, and on the self-serving presumption that "all those" are communal, I have at least one thing to show off—I am secular!

However, for a political leader, is it sufficient to be personally non-communal, but do little to ensure communal harmony? If communal riots continue to take place, if the minorities, the dalits and the weaker sections continue to be on the receiving end, what's the use of your being personally non-communal or pro-weaker sections. The real test of secularism or pro-weak for leaders is what they did to achieve communal or caste harmony on the ground, and what was the actual record of communal and caste incidents under their watch. India and its rulers since independence cut a sorry figure on this aspect. How can you hail Nehru's secularism or his being non-casteist when reportedly 243 communal riots happened between 1947 and 1964 and there were hundreds of anti-Dalit incidents; and no worthwhile robust system was put in place to ensure their non-recurrence and give confidence and a feeling of safety to the minorities and the weak. Things did not improve under subsequent secular leaders. Therefore, is it enough for a leader to be just personally secular?

Communal and Caste Harmony could have been Achieved by 1965

If universal education up to class 10 had been made compulsory after independence, if people had been specifically educated on secularism, anti-casteism and women's rights, the post-independence generation would have been different. Simultaneously, the colonial bureaucratic, police and criminal-justice system should have been thoroughly overhauled to make them empathetic and responsive to the minorities, the weak and the vulnerable. Had these steps been taken, dalits and women would have regained their dignity and the term "secularism" would have become redundant by 1960.

Take Singapore. Lee Kuan Yew managed to create a unique Singaporean identity within the umbrella of multiculturalism in just the first 15 years of his rule, despite the fact that Singapore never had a dominant culture to which locals and immigrants could assimilate. They have ensured religious and racial harmony through the decades. Singapore has consistently been ranked as the safest country in the world; and among the top five in the Global Competitiveness Report in terms of its reliability of police services.

Most Indians wish the communalism had been firmly curbed within a decade of independence, and secularism and communalism were made non-issues by 1957. Had Congress done the actual work on the ground of overhauling our criminal-justice-police system and babudom, launched vigorous educational campaign on the issue, held netas and those in administration and police accountable for disturbances and riots, punished the guilty and made examples of them, and adopted a non-compromising attitude to the issue, the curse of communalism and of ill-treatment of dalits would have vanished within a decade of independence. It was not an unachievable target. But, when you yourself allocate seats and win elections on communal, religious and caste considerations, where is the remedy? Most of the so-called secular parties have been great talkers, but, non-doers. They want to keep the secular, communal and casteism pot boiling to win votes, because, in practical terms on the ground, they are incapable of solving any real issues. Our "tryst with destiny" rather than taking us to achievable and fondly wished-for heights, sank us into a quagmire of violence and misery.

Firmly Implement "Rule of Law" and Riots/Violence would Disappear

The whole debate on parties, people and groups being secular or communal, casteist or otherwise, pro-dalit or anti-dalit, pro-women or male-chauvinists, traditionalist or modern, conservative or liberal is irrelevant to the issue of safety of vulnerable sections of the society, that is, minorities, dalits, women and children. The only relevant issue and the only possible solution is "proper governance"—competent, effective and accountable law-enforcing agency and criminal-justice system that is unbiased, well-staffed, well-equipped, well-trained, and autonomous and independent.

Who cares if people and groups and parties entertain secular or communal or casteist or patriarchal or fundamentalist ideas. If they engage in any unlawful act, let the law come down upon them firmly. Once that happens, they would dare not harm others, and cases of violence would drastically come down.

The "Rule of Law" is often not implemented thanks to the very same political parties who cry loudest on secularism and casteism. They have so weakened and compromised the instruments of governance that justice is denied to the weak and the vulnerable.

The Bizarre Secular-Communal-Casteist Drama

Is it a case that so long as there are communal or casteist or patriarchal people, groups and parties, communal riots or caste exploitation or violence against women would continue to happen? Is it a case that not until all rise above those negative characteristics, little can be done to prevent their fall-out. That's like saying the only solution for corruption is that all become honest. Since that is never going to happen, "well, what can we do?" It is basically an excuse for not doing one's job of good governance and blaming other factors. The hidden agenda of many secularists and casteists is "let there be communal or caste riots so that we can keep getting votes" and as good-governance comes in the way of that goal, to hell with it. The gross failures, like failing to implement "rule of law", have their positive aspects too—they help you retain power by scaring the minority or dalits into giving you votes!

Nehruvian Trick

Rather than making secularism-communalism-casteism a non-issue by instruments of good governance and strictly enforcing the "rule of law" within a decade or two of independence, the Nehruvians, the Congress and other hypocritical people, groups and parties, have turned it into a weapon to commend or condemn parties or people right since the Nehruvian times—they even went to the extent of casting aspersions on one of the greatest sons of India and a leader and freedom fighter head and shoulders above all others, next only to Mahatma Gandhi—Sardar Patel.

Mere words and labels should fetch them votes—work or action on the ground is unnecessary.

Communal Harmony = Function of (Functioning "Rule of Law")

Communal harmony is a function of functioning "rule of law" and is directly proportional to it. It has little relationship with people and parties professing and brandishing their secularism or communalism.

Governance Index (GI) is Reflected in Secularism Index (SI)

The real issue is "governance", which includes enforcing "rule of law". If a party claims to be secular, the touchstone of its credentials is "governance". If its "governance" is poor it is unfit to be called a "secular" party. Like one measures GDP, per-capita income, literacy, poverty, human development index (HDI), quality of living index and so on, one needs to measure GI, "Governance Index", for each of the states and for the central government. It is this GI which would actually reflect the SI—"Secularism Index". SI can't be measured by your decibel levels and your protestations. It has to be measured by your real actions on the ground—a tough call. By this yardstick, which indeed is a real genuine measure, most "secular" governments would score pathetically low on *Governance Index* (GI), and hence on *Secularism Index* (SI).

Shocking Cases about Dalits

Little has been done for the Dalits after independence. Even now the position is pathetic. It is shameful how they are still treated. It is not enough to pass laws if they are not implemented in practice. Apart from reservations, precious little has been done to eradicate untouchability and ensure at-par and dignified treatment of Dalits and Adivasis.

A news-item in *DNA, Mumbai* of 1 June 2012 is titled "*Even doctors face caste discrimination in TN*". It reports that even medical doctors in government hospitals face humiliation at the hands of their colleagues. "You are the only untouchable scheduled caste dog and we will see to it that you will be chucked out soon," one doctor told another colleague. "In Cuddalore, 150 km south of Chennai, more than 20 Dalit doctors at the General Hospital suffer silently as high caste Hindus humiliate them. 'Patients choose doctors based on their castes. Caste Hindus do not allow us to attend to them,' said a senior surgeon...Another Dalit doctor is fighting to get his annual increments which were withheld by the administrative staff. 'There are dozens of doctors with post graduate qualifications working in this hospital. But they are discriminated against because of their Dalit background,' said Vincent Raj Kathir, founder, Evidence, an organization tracking atrocities on Dalits."

Another report in *DNA, Mumbai* of 16 October 2011 titled "*Where do we take our dead and go, ask Dalits*" says: "If pain had a face, it could be Narayan Sonawane's. The 45-year-old Dalit farmer keeps scratching a shaving wound on his face till it bleeds, and makes him flinch. The pain, perhaps, momentarily takes his mind off the gruesome reality outside his hut—a seven acre plot that used to be a Dalit cremation ground until a year ago. In June 2010, it was usurped by upper caste Maratha farmer Mahadeo Khandu. And on this day, as Sonawane stands watching mutely, Khandu supervises the tilling of the land. The land where the bodies of Sonawane's parents were laid to rest. 'I buried my father here two years ago. And my mother a year before that with my own hands,' says Sonawane, fighting back tears...Such casual take-over of Dalit lands by upper castes is fairly common, not just in this district, but all over Maharashtra. According to figures compiled by the Maharashtra ministry for social justice, Dalit burial grounds have been usurped by upper castes in 72.13% of the state's 43,722 villages...It has been less than a week since violence erupted over a Dalit's attempt to bury a deceased family member in the demarcated cremation ground. Upper caste men stopped the funeral procession, brutally attacked the pall-bearers, and flung the [dead]body of 39-year-old Shevanta Pawar to the ground. The pall-bearers, including Pawar's husband, Mahesh Pawar, 42, barely escaped with their lives..."

Yet another report in *The Times of India, Mumbai* of January 26, 2013 titled "*MP dalit family ostracized for singing bhajan*" states: "...a dalit family being ostracized for singing bhajan at a function organized by members of the upper caste. The incident took place on December 15 last year, following which the upper caste people of Mathni village allegedly issued a diktat directing villagers to cut off ties with tailor Rajesh Kumar Uvnare and his family...But Uvnare contradicted the SP's claims and said no action was taken despite his written complaint in December. Uvnare said following threats from the village strongmen, villagers stopped talking to him and his family. 'We don't get milk or grains from shops. When a friend came and met me, he was fined by the village strongmen,' he said. His family members said they had to travel to the neighbouring village to get daily needs. Uvnare is also facing financial problems as residents of his village have stopped getting their clothes stitched by him."

Dalits and Capitalism

One tends to agree with what Chandra Bhan Prasad and Milind Kamble state in their article "*Manifesto to End Caste*" that appeared in the *Times of India*, Mumbai of 23 January 2013. The obliteration of caste in a major way would be when caste, that evolved from a feudal, rural setting, transforms into class through capitalism, industrialisation, professionalization, modernisation and mechanisation of agriculture, and urbanisation. Class is not hereditary, there is no stigma attached to it, and one can move up or down. They say, "Capital is the surest means to fight caste. In dalit's hands, capital becomes an anti-caste weapon... The manifesto demands that India embraces capitalism publicly as its official ideology..."

In a way, the continued plight of the Dalits is thanks to the disastrous socialistic ways down which Nehru-Indira took India. Had India adopted competitive capitalism resulting in massive growth and urbanisation, much of casteism would have disappeared.

THE NORTH-EAST

ASSAM AND MIGRATIONS

One would not obviously be talking about the North-East [NE] were it not part of India; and it would not have been part of India had it not been for the foresight, wisdom, strategy, tact, daring and efforts of Gopinath Bordoloi—a truly great leader. It is necessary to first highlight this, because the way Indian history has been written post independence and taught in schools and colleges, one does not even know of the contribution of such leaders, for it is as if the only leaders who fought for Independence and who matter were Gandhiji and Nehru.

Bordoloi was associated with the Assam Congress from its beginning in 1922, went to jail several times for anti-British agitations, won elections for the Congress in 1937, very ably handled Chief Ministership in the late 1930s, ensured Assam remained part of India, and did commendable work as the first Chief Minister of post-Independence Assam: rehabilitation of millions of Hindu refugees who had fled East Pakistan upon Partition; maintenance of communal harmony; establishment of the High Court of Assam and setting up of many educational institutions like Guwahati University, Assam Medical College and Assam Veterinary College. A gifted writer, he wrote several books while in British jails. He died in 1950.

The initial British Plan of 1946 for the Indian Independence—later superseded by the Partition Plan in 1947—included grouping of states into three categories for selecting representatives for the body for making the constitution. Assam and Bengal were clubbed together in the third group—Group C. Such an inclusion would have had the consequence of Assamese being in a minority—to be overruled into ultimately being absorbed in East-Pakistan. Sensing this ominous possibility, Bordoloi prevailed upon the Assam Pradesh Congress Committee (APCC) to oppose being clubbed into Group C, contrary to what the Indian National Congress Working Committee (INCWC) under Nehru had agreed to. With Nehru remaining not amenable, APCC started mass agitation in Assam, forcing INCWC to agree to a working formula in which ten representative from Assam would form their own constitution without joining any group and would merge with the national committee to form the Indian constitution. Gandhiji had backed Bordoloi in the matter.

Without Bordoloi there was a good probability that the North-east might have gone to East-Pakistan. Writes Sanjoy Hazarika in *Writing on the Wall*, "People often do not appreciate that one of the reasons that a state like Assam is in India today is due to the courageous stand of Gopinath Bordoloi, the first Chief Minister of Assam, who fought the Muslim League's effort to include Assam and other parts of the North-East Region (NER) in East Pakistan. The Congress Party at the national level, led by Nehru, would have acquiesced to the Muslim League had it not been for a revolt by Bordoloi, backed by the Assam unit of the Congress Party and supported by Mahatma Gandhi and the Assamese public."

Among the biggest problems of the Northeast is the problem of the migrants.

With the annexation of Assam by the British in 1826, British brought in the peasantry from the over-populated East-Bengal, now Bangladesh, for tea plantation and other purposes. The AIML, All India Muslim League, in order to improve its strength in the predominantly non-Muslim Assam, strategized back in 1906 in its conference at Dacca to increase the Muslim population in Assam, and exhorted the East-Bengal Muslims to migrate and settle in Assam. The fact of large-scale migration was also noted in the Census report of 1931.

Congress leaders Bardolai, Medhi, Chaliha and others raised this serious issue of migration, but did not get due support from the Congress leadership at the Centre. After the Congress election victory in 1937, Bordoloi, as CM, tried stopping the migrations. However, consequent to Congress High Command's decision of resignation by all Congress Provincial Governments in 1939, Bordoloi's government too had to resign—a huge blunder made by the central leadership of the Congress. Both the Congress leaders of Assam and Subhash Chandra Bose had advised exemption for Assam from the disastrous decision, but they were overruled. Thanks to that unwise step of the Congress leadership at the Centre, the Muslim League [AIML] came to power in Assam headed by Sir Saadullah. The AIML-led government allotted thousands of bighas of land in the Assam valley for the East-Bengal Muslim migrants, and opened a flood gate for them, ignoring protests by the Assam Congress. Land Settlement Policy of 1941 allowing holding of 30 bighas or more for each homestead introduced by AIML resulted in pouring of migrants from East-Bengal into Assam. Lord Wavell, the Viceroy of India, highlighted this problem. He had reportedly remarked: "...The chief political problem is the desire of Muslim Ministers of Assam to increase the immigrations into uncultivated Government lands in Assam under the slogan of 'Grow more food', but what really is to 'Grow more Muslims'." The Muslim population of Assam, thankful to AIML, aggressively supported its demand for Pakistan. Jinnah came up with the demand of the League for inclusion of Assam in the proposed Pakistan.

It is significant that many Muslim Leaguers who were ardent supporters of Pakistan not only stayed back in Assam but also joined the Congress, in which they were honourably accommodated! It is suspected they were advised to stay back by Jinnah to help East-Pakistan immigrants settle in Assam. One of these was Mainul Haq Chaudhary who was Private Secretary of Jinnah and leader of the youth wing of AIML—he was even inducted into the state cabinet. He was reportedly assured by Jinnah: "Wait for ten years, I shall present Assam on a silver plate to you."

After Independence, when the Central Government could have taken a tough stand and effectively dealt with the problem, it remained ostrich-like, and demographic invasion from East-Pakistan continued, becoming a major source of ethnic bitterness and tension. The ongoing Bodo-Bangladeshi Muslim clash is an offshoot of this bitterness.

Writes Kuldip Nayar in *Beyond the Lines*: "The state subsequently paid the price...when illegal migration from the then East Pakistan reduced the Assamese-speaking population in Assam to a minority...It was not Chaliha who initiated the issue of illegal migration but his senior in the Congress, Fakhruddin Ali Ahmad, who rose to be India's president. In fact, the entire party was guilty. Its simplistic solution was to win elections in Assam by allowing would-be settlers from across the border into the state thus creating a vote bank...[Gobind Ballabh]Pant [the then Home Minister in Nehru's cabinet] knew that large number of people were coming across the border. After all, his party had connived at the migration since independence..."

Congress Government of Assam under Chaliha, alarmed by the cultural and the demographic crisis of Assam, launched an aggressive campaign to flush out illegal Muslim migrants in the early sixties. Nehru, however, wanted Chaliha not to do so. Later, the Chaliha government brought in the *Prevention of Infiltration from Pakistan (PIP) Act 1964*, but on account of its opposition by the Muslim MLAs, who threatened to topple his ministry, he dropped it.

Congress came to be dubbed pro-Bangladeshi by the opposition; and the continued infiltration was condemned as a vote-bank politics of the Congress even by BK Nehru, a cousin of Jawaharlal Nehru and Assam's Governor during 1968-1973 when Indira Gandhi was the prime minister. It was the Bangladeshi infiltration that sparked the *All Assam Students Union* (AASU) agitation.

Lt Gen. (Retd) SK Sinha, the then Governor of Assam, in his report to the President of India in 1998 called the infiltration a "national threat", and warned that "if the present trends are not arrested, the indigenous people of Assam would be reduced to a minority and there may, in course of time, be a demand for the merger of Muslim dominated bordering districts with Bangladesh." Although precise figures are not available, as per an estimate, about 20 million Bangladeshi nationals are staying in India.

Of the 4000 km long border between India and Bangladesh, only about 1600 km is fenced. Thanks to indifference and neglect, the settlers—Bangladeshi Muslims, whose Indian citizenship is contested—have become the dominant group in about 11 of the 27 districts of Assam. The Bodo uprising is an upshot of their marginalisation and loss, and their exasperation at the failure of the state to protect their land and living in the face of illegal migrations. In fact, the protracted demographic invasion from erstwhile East-Bengal to Assam since its annexation by the British in 1826 has been a major source of conflict; and the ongoing Bodo-Muslim clashes are offshoots of that tension and ethnic bitterness.

NORTH-EAST: GEOGRAPHICAL AND ECONOMIC OVERVIEW

The North-east was ruled as a part of Bengal Province during the British times. The state of Assam came into existence in 1874. At the time of Independence, the whole of North-east was known as Assam, although apart from the state of Assam, there were two princely states of Manipur and Tripura. Four additional states were created subsequently: Arunachal Pradesh, Meghalaya, Mizoram and Nagaland. Thus, there are a total of 7 states in the North-east.

Sikkim merged with India in 1975, and though it is to the NE of India, but being not contiguous to Assam, it is not including in this coverage of the Northeast region.

The total population and geographical area of the NE is about 40 m [million] and 3,24,000 km^2 [square kilometres] respectively; and the same for each of the seven states are: Arunachal Pradesh–1.1 m, 84,000 km^2; Assam–26.7 m, 78,000 km^2, Manipur–2.2 m, 22,000 km^2; Meghalaya–2.3 m, 22,000 km^2; Mizoram–0.9 m, 21,000 km^2; Nagaland–2.0 m, 17,000 km^2; and Tripura–3.2 m, 10,000 km^2. Two-thirds of the population lives on plains, that form one-third of the land; and one-third of the population lives on hilly area that forms two-thirds of the total area of the NE.

There are over 220 ethnic groups in the states that comprise the NE, and about 160 languages.

Almost 90% of the people in Meghalaya, Mizoram, hilly-areas of Manipur and Nagaland are Christians.

The region has about 4500 km of international border. Four countries abut on the region: Bangladesh, Bhutan, China and Myanmar. 96% of the region's borders are with these four foreign countries, and only 4% are with the Indian mainland. The only land connection with India is a narrow corridor, called the Chicken's neck—it is the Siliguri Corridor in West Bengal, with a width of 21–40 km. Arunachal Pradesh is what was NEFA earlier, bordering Tibet and China. Its northern border follows the McMahon Line.

The NE is potentially one of the richest regions. A third of India's water-resources are in the NE, with tremendous potential for irrigation and generation of hydroelectric power. Its major river is Brahmaputra, known as Tsang-po in Tibet and Siang in Arunachal Pradesh, into which many rivers flow in: 33 major ones in the NE, 22 in Tibet, and 3 in Bangladesh, including Ganga. India has a total of about 16,000 km of river-embankments, of which about 5,000 km are in the NE.

The NE has oil and gas, and also coal and uranium. It is rich in forests and is known for its biodiversity. About 60% of its area is under forest cover, as against 20% for the rest of the country. It has about 50 forest-types, 6 vegetation-types out of a total of 9 in India, and over 15,000 varieties of flowering plants. It has a huge potential for horticulture and floriculture, blessed as it is with hundreds of varieties of orchids, flowers, bamboos. It is gifted by nature and has tremendous potential for tourism.

NORTH-EAST: DIVISION, MISGOVERNANCE AND CORRUPTION

Despite its massive potential for being one of the richest areas in India, North-east is poor and under-developed—basically on account of wrong policies, endemic corruption, migrations and insurgency.

The insurgency and the political demand that initially started in Nagaland soon spread to many other regions of the North-east. They were helped also by the international forces inimical to India. An appropriate foreign policy could have helped minimise their effect.

Egged on by Verrier Elwin, Nehru's advisor on tribal matters and a British missionary and anthropologist, Nehru's broad policy was to treat Nagas and the like as "anthropological specimen". This came in the way of development and integration of the North-east.

Nehru's policy of division of Assam into a number of smaller states to satisfy certain ethnic groups has actually been counter-productive. *One*, because there are so many different ethnicities. There are over 220 ethnic groups. To what extent can one keep dividing? *Two*, it started divisive identity politics. Others too have raised their demand for separation. *Three*, such small states are not economically viable.

The states are unable to take care of either their development or their expenses. All the states have been categorised as Special Category States: they get 90% of the funds as grants from the Centre, and have to only generate the remaining 10%. In other words, all are totally dependent upon the Centre for their expenditure for salaries of government employees, maintenance, and development.

North-east is devastated by floods every year, causing misery to the displaced millions, yet no proper solution has been found in the over six decades after Independence.

Infrastructure is pathetic. Even national highways are in a poor condition. This region with largest water resources and highest hydroelectric potential is abysmally short of both. Health services are very poor. Educational system is in shambles.

There has been abject failure of governance all through—it has practically collapsed in a number of states, with the citizens at the receiving end from both the security forces and the insurgents. And, not only that. They are at the receiving end from the corrupt government machinery too. In many regions, the government has simply abdicated its responsibility to provide normal life to citizens. The state institutions neither provide security, nor essential services, nor development. Poor governance is responsible for insurgency, rather than the other way round. There is a dearth of private investments on account of the poor security environment.

The "freedom" fighters and insurgents of yesteryears are now extortionists of today. They extort from all: businessmen, traders, professionals, contractors, and also from politicians and employees. There has long since been an unholy nexus among politicians, bureaucrats, contractors and insurgents. Contractors get rich by executing either paper-projects—everything happens on paper, nothing on ground—or by executing sub-standard work, or work at highly inflated prices. Politicians and bureaucrats get rich by taking their cut from the contractors. Insurgents, in turn, extort from all the three, or directly take a cut on the contracts. In some regions, the insurgents levy taxes on employees too.

The PCB nexus ("P" for politicians, "C" for contractors, and "B" for businessmen and bureaucrats), and in many regions the PCBI nexus (PCB plus "I" for insurgents) takes care of major portion of the funds. Without ensuring proper end-use of funds, the Central Government keeps announcing special economic packages for the region, most of which go to line the pockets of the PCBI. Continued militancy, and need for development to tackle it, provide a convenient pretext to get more and more funds to loot.

Poverty in the region is more on account of defalcation of funds by the PCBI than on account of any paucity of funds. Despite pumping the highest per capita development funds, the region continues to be underdeveloped. Although corruption is not unique to the NE, it touches a new high there.

Writes Ved Marwah, who had been Governor in the region, in *India in Turmoil*: "There are projects where the entire funds have been misappropriated. During President's rule in 2001, I decided to visit some of the projects. What I saw and found was unbelievable! In more than one project the entire funds had been misappropriated. During a visit to one such multi-crore project not very far from the state secretariat we saw an amazing sight. It was still barren agricultural land and not a brick had been laid, though on paper the project had been going for a few years. The officers concerned were suspended and an inquiry ordered, but that too had only a temporary impact. The suspended officers knew very well that they had nothing to fear. They were right, as the new government after the end of President's rule promptly reinstated them. The roots of corruption are deep and all-pervasive. The suspended officers not only got their full arrears but also prize postings for their proven ability in looting public funds...While the people are deprived of even the most basic services, the corrupt are prospering and living a life of luxury... Things are much worse in the interiors. One gets the impression that time has stood still."

Elsewhere in the book, Ved Marwah gives another example: "Even the so-called mainstream political parties are guilty of playing partisan politics that has serious consequences in the state...I was told by more than one state leader that adding another state to their tally of state governments ruled by their state is not the only reason. They make open allegations about the payment of 'levy' to their high commands in Delhi...I had some experience of this phenomenon during my tenure as the governor of Manipur. Manipur was under President's rule in 2001-2. The Online Lottery contract case during this period tells the story of this sordid state of affairs. The 'Lottery King'

M.N. Subbah, a Congress MP from the Northeast has allegedly made his money in such lottery deals, which is a highly lucrative business. As the lottery is floated in the name of the state, it is considered fair and honest by ordinary buyers of lottery tickets outside the state. The gullible people get easily duped by the confidence trick played by the unscrupulous lottery managers, the corrupt politicians and civil servants...One of the first delegations that met me...led by the BJP...demanded cancellation of the [Lottery] contract...After detailed discussions with all concerned officials, I endorsed their recommendation for the cancellation of the contract. But what followed was unbelievable! There was a spate of calls from Delhi, including from some bigwigs, as to why I had cancelled this contract...The fact that it was the state BJP that had spearheaded the agitation against the contract did not mitigate the annoyance in New Delhi [where the Central Government was headed by BJP] against my action...Overnight I became a persona non grata in the corridors of power in Delhi... After the end of the President's rule, the new Congress chief minister became an equally strong supporter of the deal...one of the first acts that the new elected Congress government did was to reopen the case and once again sign the Online Lottery contract with the same business house..."

Basically, the problems of the Northeast have their roots in the Nehruvian era on account of faulty understanding of the issues, distorted world view, defective grasp of national security interests, and the flawed policies and remedies that flowed from them. Subsequently, the legacy continued. Nehru, thanks to his foreign policies and policies on internal security and administration, managed to make all our international borders and the regions in the border areas sensitive and insecure, costing us a fortune to maintain them. Nehru could have and should have put in place a reliable and robust mechanism to plug the migrations from East-Pakistan after Independence; but he remained casual and indifferent.

Looking to the fact of scores of ethnic groups and languages in the Northeast, Nehru should have understood that sub-dividing the region into multiple states would be an endless process that would give rise to further divisiveness, without doing any good for the people at large, each new state being economically unviable. What would have won the hearts of the people and brought them into the mainstream would have been not a State for each group, for that benefits only the elites; but solid, good, empathetic governance, effective criminal-justice system, assurance of security to people, delivery of various services, education, health-care, providing connectivity and communications, putting in place adequate infrastructure, and economic development.

The problems that took roots during the Nehru era—migrations from East-Pakistan, divisive tendencies, corruption, misgovernance and mismanagement—have continued. We have not learnt from the past.

16

Mental Slavery: Carry Over from the Nehruvian Era

FIRANG NAMES, FACES, CULTURE AND SYMBOLS

You come across building names like Blooming Heights, Delphi, Glen Gate, Kensington, Ocean, Olympia, Sigma, Somerset, Spectra; street names like Central Avenue, Cliff Avenue, Forest Street, High Street, Lake Boulevard Road, Orchard Avenue, Ridge Street, South Avenue, and so on, and wonder if you are in India or in the UK or the US or Australia or Canada. If you observe the advertisements in property pull-out pages of newspapers and periodicals you would rarely fail to see firang faces aplenty cheerfully gazing out of flats and bungalows or squatting on lawns or having a swim!

What's happening? Have we run out of Indian names and faces? Or, are Indian names and faces not hip? They don't convey quality and class. For that you require a Firang touch.

How we Indians excel at demeaning ourselves and our heritage? Haven't you noticed actors, directors and sundries of Hindi movies, rather than talking in Hindi about their Hindi films, always make it a point to converse only in their atrocious English. No Hindi in Hindi-movie award functions! Only English—broken or otherwise. Even the titles of Hindi movies are mostly in English: A Wednesday, Blood Money, Dirty Picture, Don2, Housefull, No one killed Jessica, Players, Ra-One, Ready, Wanted... Also the titles, credits and castings at the beginning and at the end of Hindi movies generally happen to be in English.

Take another area. A hill station. Say, Matheran. What are the names of the various points? King George Point, Alexander Point, Coronation Point, Lord Point, Louisa Point, Hart Point, Mount Barry, Malet Road, and so on. Can understand the name Malet Road—that guy Malet, the then collector, indeed contributed to bringing up Matheran. But why Coronation Point? Why should one be commemorating ascendency of King Edward VII!

Strangely, there are no points or roads or markets or train-stations after the names of persons who made Matheran a popular hill-station in the first place—by constructing a railway line on such a difficult, steep, hilly terrain and running a toy train on it, all with their own investment! Why? Because, those persons happened to be Indians—Adamjee Peerbhoy and his son, Abdul Hussain. What a shame!

But, of course, one has to be thankful the dynasty for having spared the places in Matheran from their names. Imagine getting up early morning at Matheran to watch sunrise at Sanjay Gandhi Point, rather than Garbut Point; making it to Jawahar Lake, instead of Charlotte Lake, in the afternoon; going down the Jawaharlal Nehru Marg through the Indira market in the evening, turning left from the Indira Chowk, bypassing Kamla Nehru Udyan on the right, going further to Motilal Nehru Spring, taking a right turn and reaching Rajiv Gandhi Point, instead of the Porcupine Point, to watch the sunset! Whole holiday fun would have been wrecked!

But, why get disturbed about these names in the relatively lesser known place like Matheran, when right at the heart of New Delhi, at India Gate, staring at all the passersby—including freedom fighters, bureaucrats, politicians, ministers—stood the statue of King George V for two decades after independence!

It was only when Bulganin and Khrushchev of the USSR visited India in late 1955 that India changed the names Kingsway to Rajpath and Queensway to Janpath in New Delhi, lest the guests feel shocked at our slavishness! However, Khrushchev did not fail to notice the statue of King George V opposite India Gate when driving down Rajpath, and wondered why the relic still stood. Strangely, it was only in 1968 that the statue was removed, and that too upon public outcry! Such is the record of the Nehrus!!

That many had become cultural slaves thanks to the British was obvious; and that Gandhiji had done much to counter it is also well-known; but, what is strange is that little was done in the post-independence period under Nehru to carry forward Gandhiji's legacy, and rid Indians of their mental slavery. If anything, it increased—in no small measure to the examples set by Nehru himself, and the policies that flourished under him.

Durga Das quotes in *India from Curzon to Nehru & After* what Gandhi told him personally: "Jawahar wants Englishmen to go but Angreziat to stay. I want Angreziat to go but Englishmen to remain as our friends." Knowing this, why Gandhi chose Nehru as PM is a mystery. Gandhi used to say that even though Nehru used to fight with him on many issues, ultimately he used to agree with him [Gandhi], little knowing that it was not because Nehru agreed with him, but because Nehru knew that to continue to differ from Gandhi might cost him his position—like it happened with Netaji—and his goal of becoming the PM. Gandhiji had also said that after he would be no more, Nehru would speak his [Gandhi's] language. If Gandhi had watched from heaven, he would have known that Nehru had buried Gandhism along with Gandhi's death. Incidentally, this last thing was told by a Nehru loyalist (Rafi Ahmed Kidwai) himself, as quoted by Durga Das in his book: "*Jawaharlal has performed the last rites not only of Gandhi but of Gandhism as well.*"

There is nothing wrong in adopting good things from other cultures—in fact, one must do so. But to be blindly follow the firangs is being slavish. Also, to criticise all things Indian, and admire all things foreign—that's being silly.

We managed to break the shackles of economic and political slavery. But mental slavery—that we have willingly adopted!

THE BROWN SAHIBS AND THE COLONIAL MINDSET

There was already a tribe of brown sahibs prior to independence, but with the departure of the whites, this tribe entrenched itself. Nehru set an example for them, and they multiplied. Nehru was reported to have said about himself that,

"*I am the last Englishman to rule India*!" We had such great swadeshi nationalists!

In his book, *Jawaharlal Nehru, a Biography*, Sankar Ghose writes: "Malcolm Muggeridge, after seeing Nehru shortly before his death, characterized him as *'a man of echoes and mimicry, the last viceroy rather than the first leader of a liberated India'*, and regretted that Nehru was much too British in his approach to have been able to bring about significant or radical changes in India."

Wrote Durga Das in *India from Curzon to Nehru & After*: "Mrs. [Vijayalaxmi] Pandit [Nehru's sister] told me: 'I never travel without Ahmed (her liveried peon). The common people know me to be a Minister because Ahmed is with me. They salaam Ahmed's livery.' Nehru himself realised this well enough when he became the Prime minister and had a retinue of peons and security staff—several times the size any Viceroy had had—when he moved among people."

Slavishly imitating the West, and adopting their mores was "forward-looking" and being "advanced", while being Gandhi-like was being native and backward. Without being jingoistic, one must adopt good things, even if foreign. But, there is a big difference between being rational, scientific, liberal, forward-looking, yet self-respecting; and being slavish show-offs and imitators. You can't start rubbishing your history, language, religion, culture, music, eating habits, medicinal practices, and so on to appear modern. To imitate is the cheap way of appearing forward-looking.

The ridiculous extent Motilal Nehru went to denigrate his own culture and be more English than the Englishmen was astonishing. You would notice a sharp contrast between the "*Motilal-tribe*" and the "*Rao-tribe*"? *Motilal-tribe*, that is, the Motilal Nehru dynasty, the ICS tribe and the like. *Rao-tribe*, that is, the current young generation of information technologists, finance professionals, management consultants and the like, who have come up thanks to reversal of Nehru Dynasty's economic policies by Narasimha Rao. Those of the Motilal-tribe were imitators, who regarded knowing English and being anglicised as enough qualities for gaining positions and privileges, and they bent over backwards to please the English and westerners. The Rao-tribe youngsters, on the other hand, are confident professionals meeting all—English, Americans, Europeans, Australians, Canadians, Japanese, Chinese, Singaporeans—on equal terms, never considering it necessary to know Queen's English—SMS English or Working English being sufficient—or to imitate them. In fact, if this Jeans generation gets to know of the Motilal-tribe and what they did, they would be disgusted and aghast.

You had characters like Nirad Chaudhuri—you can club all these in the Motilal-tribe—who would laboriously mug up histories of various wines so that they could narrate them in conversations, and impress the listener on how knowledgeable were they in things English! Listeners belonging to the Motilal-tribe would lap it up, and write glowingly of the encyclopaedic knowledge of Nirad Chaudhuri. In contrast, a member of the young generation—the *Rao-tribe*—would consider such nonsense fantastic. He or she has many better things to master, and get forward in life, than to please the whites.

Like Khushwant Singh mentions about the Indian High Commissioner in Canada, who was a member of ICS, and uncle of his wife, in his autobiography, *Truth, Love and a Little Malice,* "...for the Maliks culture meant being well-dressed, knowing European table manners and having a familiarity with exotic drinks like Old Fashioned, Manhattan, ..."

Take the example of an article, India's "silent" prime minister becomes a tragic figure, in *The Washington Post* about Manmohan Singh in September 2012, to which strong exception was taken by the PMO and the Congress—going to the extent of seeking an apology from the paper. This is what Tavleen Singh commented about the incident in her article, 'An embarrassing fuss', in *The Indian Express* of September 9, 2012: "...Could it be because the Prime Minister is more worried about his international image than about how he is perceived in his own country? I think it is. It is an old Indian tradition that must have something to do with being ruled by white colonialists for centuries. My career as a journalist began when Indira Gandhi was prime minister and I remember being constantly puzzled about why she gave most of her interviews to western journalists. She cared so much for western opinion that when she ended the Emergency, there were those who said she did it to restore her image in the western world. For the opinion of us domestic hacks, she had such contempt that she almost never gave an interview to an Indian..."

ADMIRE WHO HUMILIATE

Bengal Club in Kolkata did not allow Indians till a decade after Independence! Breach Candy Club in Mumbai continued with its sign "*Dogs and Indians not allowed*" well after Independence!! British openly insulted and humiliated Indians by having such signage in various clubs, train bogies, and other places. Yet, you have many shameless, ignorant Indians still behaving dog-like and praising and admiring the British rule.

Khushwant Singh wrote that he was turned away from Madras Club because he was wearing sandals. In another context he wrote that their group was invited to Delhi Gymkhana for a cocktail only to check whether they were properly anglicised and fitted-in!

Our TV and print media keeps referring to the area of Raisina Hill, Rajpath, and so on as Lutyens' Delhi, after the British architect, Edwin Lutyens, and there have even been grand receptions for his descendents in Delhi; little realising that Lutyens had utter contempt for India and the Indians—his writings were full of ridicule and hatred for India! Writes Pavan Varma in his book *Becoming Indian–The Unfinished Revolution of Culture and Identity*: "In 1985, ...Collins...brought out a book, *The Letters of Edwin Lutyens to his Wife Lady Emily*...provides incontrovertible evidence of the views of this man... Nothing about India impressed Lutyens...The 'natives' were 'blacks' and quite clearly beyond redemption... At Daly College at Indore he asked to meet the students, and described them as 'dear little nigger chaps'...About the people of Madras he wrote: 'But oh the people—the scallywags. Awful faces, to me degenerate, very dark, very naked, and awful habits of hair dressings. The bulk of the faces merely loony...' ...Condescendingly he accepts that India could in some way be amusing 'but the low intellect of the natives spoils much and I do not think it possible for the Indians and whites to mix freely and naturally...' Annoyed by what one of his minions had done, he fumes: 'They ought to be reduced to slavery and not given the rights of man and beaten like brute beasts and shot like man eaters...' ...his comments were dismissive of almost all the architectural landmarks in India..."

And, what do we Indians do when Edwin Lutyens descendents visit Delhi? Give them grand receptions from the President down...! Such is our shamelessness and ignorance that we honour and eulogise those who humiliate us!!

Indians, who do not think it necessary to revisit their past, especially the great damage done by the English, keep quoting Churchill, who had also said, "*I hate Indians. They are a beastly people with a beastly religion.*" Churchill was responsible for the death of three million Indians in 1943 in the Bengal Famine. Motivated both by the racial hatred and to avenge "Quit India" movement, he ensured that the reliefs did not reach Bengal, and the food there was diverted for War efforts. In terms of the net results of numbers who died, how then was Churchill different from Hitler. Of course, Churchill rightly deserves kudos for his contribution in winning World War II, and for his courage in the face of adversity.

You hear educated people talk appreciatively of the author Rudyard Kipling. But, what that character, without any conscience, had done? Claiming that Dyer (of Jallianwala massacre) was the man who had saved India, he had started a benefit fund for Dyer, raising over £26,000! A class of Indians is so shameless, slavish, insensitive and lacking in self-respect that it wanted to convert the house where Kipling lived in India into a museum!

BROWN INFERIORORISTS

Practically all educated, unbiased, knowledgeable Europeans and Americans and the British themselves are well aware that colonialism was a cruel, merciless exploitation and extraction project; and that if it left some useful legacy like railways (which natives could anyway have built themselves with less than a millionth of the sum looted from them), that was an incidental collateral actually meant for more efficient exploitation and extraction or for the comfort of the exploiters, and not as an intended benefit for the natives.

Of course, there is a minority of influential whites, including writers and academics, who skilfully highlight the concocted positives, the gains to the natives (which the natives would have anyway had if they were left alone and not colonised), while skimming over or suppressing or remaining silent on the horrible dark side, and the monstrously huge illegal riches the whites expropriated.

Whites indulging in the above, even if in minority, is understandable: if they don't defend themselves, who would? They know their ancestors were guilty of gross wrong-doing, but they somehow want to airbrush it and defend their terrible legacy. Some even paint their frightful, revolting colonial period as a charitable, beneficent and benign undertaking—"a white man's burden" as that obnoxious Rudyard Kipling—who collected funds for the butcher of Jallianwala Bagh, Reginald Dyer—called it.

However, what takes the cake are the **CB-NSR-SA-EII:** *Colonially-Brainwashed Non-Self-Respecting Self-Abusive Educated Indian Ignoramuses.* It is amazing and baffling that even in the 21st century there exists this class of Indians, young included, who despite their claims to being educated and knowledgeable, unhesitatingly and unabashedly diagnose the "misery that is India" not on the Nehruvian socialistic poverty-perpetuating policies, not on the disastrous Dynasty-driven Congress rule for most of the period since independence, not on the abysmally poor political leadership, but on "Indian-ness; Indian characteristics"—a bizarre self-flagellating racist self-attack, à la Nirad Chaudhuri. And like the British-licker Nirad Chaudhuri, this tribe has much to admire in the British and the British colonial rule in India. Dictionary definition of a racist is "a person with a prejudiced belief that one race is superior to others". You have the racists like the "White Supremacists". But, what do you call these "reverse racists" who believe "their race is inferior to others"—"brown *inferior*orists"!

One can understand British colonialists engaging in theft, dacoity and loot, and perpetrating grave crimes to achieve their nefarious designs—well, they were heartless, greedy savages. But aware of their misdeeds, do thieves also act conceited and arrogant? Do dacoits also humiliate and insult their victims? Do looters pretend they are doing a good turn to the victims? Do savages tell victims, with over seven millennium of civilisation behind him, they have come to "civilise" them. So queer and bizarre—the sheer hypocrisy bolds you. But what you have to give them credit for is that they managed to brainwash a section of the victims and their descendents that they [the British] indeed came not as their tormentors, but as their saviours!

These brown *inferior*orists do not realise that India would have been a prosperous, first-rate, first-world country by 1980 had it adopted competitive capitalism and free-market economy after independence. That is a reasonable estimate extrapolating the time it took Singapore, South Korea and Taiwan to become first-world countries and the time it took West Germany and Japan to rise from the ashes of the Second World War by adopting competitive capitalism. Had India been moving fast towards being a first-world country after independence and had it indeed become so by 1980, the brown *inferior*orists and the CB-NSR-SA-EII would not have had grounds to exist. It's thanks to the Nehruvians and the policies of the Dynasty-driven Congress that they exist. However, hopefully, with Narendra Modi in the saddle, this class should gradually become extinct.

But, one thing that the brown *inferior*orists and the CB-NSR-SA-EII must reflect upon is that when they slam India and the Indians, they are actually slamming themselves. By definition, they themselves become third-rate people. That's not the case with the rest of the Indians as they don't subscribe to their theories.

BUT THEY BUILT THE RAILWAYS!

CB-NSR-SA-EII's and Brown-*Inferior*orist's typical arguments run like this: "But look, their contribution at modernisation is so major—they brought in railways! Where would India have been otherwise?" One can only pity the intelligence and analytical power of such characters. Does a country have to be colonised to get railways? China has railway—now the fastest in the world—but it was not colonised. Japan has the best railway, but it was never colonised. If your economy is good, if you have the money, can you not invite foreign companies to setup railway, if you can't do it yourself? For airways—aeroplanes and airports—did India have to be colonised by the US? India did not have computers to start with. Did it ask the US to come, colonise it, so that it can have them! There are countries that lack software skills. Should they request India to come and colonise them so that they may have software to run their businesses! For Indians to use iPAD and iPhones, does it have to be colonised by the USA?

With even one-millionth the money looted by the British colonialists from India, India would have had the resources to build railways thousand times more dense, and of better quality! Incidentally, Matheran Hill Railway on such a difficult terrain was financed and built by Indians during the British times. It was built between 1901 and 1907 by Abdul Hussein Adamjee Peerbhoy.

Amitav Ghosh, the famous Indian author (*The Circle of Reason*, *The Glass Palace*, *Sea of Poppies*,...), making fun of the claim that the British gave India the railways, commented: "Thailand has railways and the British never colonized the country. In 1885, when the British invaded Burma, the Burmese king was already building railways and telegraphs. These are things Indians could have done themselves."

Railways were built more for transport of goods to facilitate efficient exploitation of and extraction from India and for travel-comfort of the British, and not as an intended benefit for the natives. While the British travelled in luxury, the Indian passengers were treated like dirt in the railways. For details, one can read the booklet "Third Class in Indian Railways" by Mahatma Gandhi written in 1918—available for free on the web.

Wrote Jabez Sunderland: "British treat the Hindus as strangers and foreigners in India, in a manner quite as unsympathetic, harsh and abusive as was ever seen among the Georgia and Louisiana planters in the old days of American slavery.... There have been cases in which British soldiers forcibly ejected from railway compartments educated Brahmins and courtly rajahs who had tickets for this space."

BRITISH "JUSTICE"

Britain gave India a great judicial system, it is said, and that they treated people fairly. However, these are what the discerning Englishmen themselves commented: "We, the English, ignorantly assumed that the ancient, long civilized people of India, were a race of barbarians who had never known what justice was until we came among them...The people of India possess an instinctive capacity for local self-government. It is by the reason of the British administration, only, that the popular authority of the village headman has been sapped, and the judicial power of the Panchayat, or Committee of Five has been subverted."

These are extracts from the reports of the various daily newspapers of the British times: "No man in this [India] country can knock an Englishman down without promptly being arrested and sent to jail. But an Englishman may knock a dozen Indians down and go scot-free... An Englishman kicks a sweeper, rupturing his spleen, which results in his death, and is ordered to pay a fine of 50 rupees with no imprisonment. Yet in another case, an Indian is sentenced to 20 years imprisonment for attempting to rape an Englishwoman, while in the same province an Englishman who gags and rapes a Hindu girl of 18 is acquitted, with no punishment at all... In November 1923, some British soldiers who had been out fox-hunting near the village of Lohagaon, in the vicinity of Poona, fell into an altercation with the villagers, when one of the villagers was shot dead by a soldier named Walker. The soldier was tried by the Sessions Court before European jurors and British judges and acquitted."

Another extract on the web says: "Mr. K.C. Kelkar, President of the Poona City Municipality commented, 'Such farces of trials of Europeans accused of crimes against Indians are not new among us. They date back to the times of Warren Hastings. The thing to be most regretted is that with such things taking place before their very eyes, there are persons who keep singing the praise of British justice."

What did the "famed" British judicial system do to Reginald Edward Harry Dyer, the *butcher of Amritsar,* who massacred over a thousand and injured many more at Jallianwala Bagh in 1919, and who gave a "crawling order" whereby all Indians using a certain prominent street in Amritsar had to crawl 200 yards on all fours, lying flat on their bellies. Nothing. He was tried by the Hunter Commission, but got away without any punishment—he was only censured. As if that was not enough, upon his return to Britain he was presented a sword of honour and a purse for being "the saviour of Punjab"! In the film *Gandhi* of David Attenborough, which was lapped up by the Indians and the Indian government, the director shows the trial of Dyer to impress the audience the world over the grandness of the British judicial system; without revealing that *Dyer received no punishment, and was rewarded back home*! Sometimes one wonders if Indians have any self-respect.

Warren Hastings was the Governor General of Bengal between 1774 and 1785. Edmund Burke (1729-1797) was a famous British statesman, parliamentary orator and political thinker. During the trial of Hastings in 1787, Burke charged him not only with promoting the economic rape of India but also with the literal rape of Indian women. Burke accused Hastings of not only using sexual violence as a strategy of control by his colonial subordinates but that he had also personally "undone women of the first rank" in India, noting especially his humiliation of the Princesses of Oude.

The following extracts are from the speech of Edmund Burke in the House of Commons that vividly catalogued the barbaric treatment meted out to the Indians at the hands of Hastings and his men:

"...My lords, I am here obliged to offer some apology for the horrid scenes I am about to open... I would rather wish to draw a veil over them, than shock your feelings by a detail. But it is necessary for the substantial ends of justice and humanity, and for the honour of government, that they should be exposed, that they should be recorded, and handed down to after ages...

"My lords, when the people [Indian peasants] had been stripped of everything, it was, in some cases suspected, and justly, that they had hid some share of the grain. Their bodies were then applied to the fiercest mode of torture, which was this : they began with winding cords about their fingers, till the flesh on each hand clung and was actually incorporated. Then they hammered wedges of wood and iron between those fingers, until they crushed and maimed those poor, honest, and laborious hands, which were never lifted up to their mouths but with a scanty supply of provision. My lords, these acts of unparalleled cruelty, began with the poor ryots; but if they began there, there they did not stop. The heads of the villages, the leading yeomen of the country, respectable for their virtues, respectable for their age, were tied together, two and two, the unoffending and helpless, thrown across a bar, upon which they were hung with their feet uppermost, and there beat with bamboo canes on the soles of those feet, until the nails started from their toes, and then with the cudgels of their blind fury these poor wretches were afterwards beat about the head, until the blood gushed out at their mouth, nose, and ears.

"My lords, they did not stop here. Bamboos, wangees, rattans, canes, common whips, and scourges were not sufficient. They found a tree in the country which bears strong and sharp thorns not satisfied with those other cruelties, they scourged them with these. Not satisfied with this, but searching everything through the deepest parts of nature, where she seems to have forgot her usual benevolence, they found a poisonous plant, a deadly caustic, that inflames the part that is bruised, and often occasions death. This they applied to those wounds. My lords, we know that there are men (for so we are made) whom bodily pains cannot subdue.

"The mind of some men strengthens in proportion as the body suffers. But people who can bear up against their own tortures, cannot bear up against those of their children and their friends. To add, therefore, to their sufferings, the innocent children were brought forth, and cruelly scourged before the faces of their parents. They frequently bound the father and the son, face to face, arm to arm, body to body, and then flogged till the skin was torn from the flesh : and thus they had the devilish satisfaction of knowing, that every blow must wound the body or the mind; for if one escaped the son, his sensibility was wounded by the knowledge he had that the blow had fallen upon his father; the same torture was felt by the father, when he knew that every blow that missed him had fallen upon his unfortunate son.

"My lords, this was not, this was not all! The treatment of the females cannot be described. Virgins that were kept from the sight of the sun, were dragged into the public court that court which was intended to be a refuge against all oppression and there, in the presence of day, their delicacies were offended, and their persons cruelly violated, by the basest of mankind. It did not end there : the wives of the men of the country only suffered less by this : they lost their honour in the bottom of the most cruel dungeons, in which they were confined.

"They were then dragged out naked, and in that situation exposed to public view, and scourged before all the people. My lords, here is my authority for otherwise you will not believe it possible. My lords, what will you feel when I tell you, that they put the nipples of the women into the cleft notches of sharp bamboos, and tore them from their bodies. What modesty in all nations most carefully conceals, these monsters revealed to view, and consumed by burning tortures, and cruel slow fires ! My lords, I am ashamed to open it horrid to tell ! These infernal fiends,..."

[Here Mr. Burke dropped his head upon his hands, unable to proceed, so greatly was he oppressed by the horror which he felt at this relation. The effect of it was visible through the whole auditory... Several women in the gallery fainted.]

Incidentally, Warren Hastings, despite the above horrible, unpardonable offences in India, was ultimately acquitted by the British "Justice" System in 1795, after a trial that lasted seven years. So much for the great British Judicial System!!

MAN BOOKER

Among the books short-listed for Man Booker for 2008 were *Sea of Poppies* by Amitav Ghosh and *The White Tiger* by Arvind Adiga. Although *The Glass Palace* about Burma and the Burmese king, Thibaw, and *Dancing in Cambodia*, comprising excellent reportage and essays, are among the excellent works of Amitav Ghosh, *Sea of Poppies* is perhaps his best yet. Between *Sea of Poppies* and *The White Tiger* there is no comparison. The focus of each book is different. But, if one has to choose between the two, *Sea of Poppies* is head and shoulders, and also trunk and legs and toes above *White Tiger*.

Yet, *White Tiger* beat *Sea of Poppies* to the Man Booker. Why? Well, the book did not beat, but the panel which decides Man Booker did indeed beat the other. For all their pretence of being fair, the British would never give an award to Amitav Ghosh for his highly truthful and excellent anti-colonial writings. And they would certainly reward a guy who manages to show India in poor light. Hence, *White Tiger* and not *Sea of Poppies*.

It's like *Slumdog Millionaire* getting the Oscars. An ordinary movie—its theme copied from an old Hindi movie—with ordinary music and ordinary lyrics. Rahman has given far better music in other movies, and Gulzar has written far better lyrics, but they got awarded for their mediocre contribution, because the movie chose to show India in bad light. And there were quite a number of Indian writers and journalists who freely exposed themselves by waxing eloquent about that ordinary movie.

Reminds one of how the British propped up Nirad Chaudhuri who excelled in being abusive at things Indian to endear himself to the English, and how the other anglophiles and journalists wrote eulogistically about Nirad.

NEGLECT OF INDIAN LANGUAGES, HISTORY AND CULTURE

With the ascendency of the Brown Sahibs and the obsequious academics in the academe in the Nehru era, genuine work in Indian languages and history suffered a huge setback. No worthwhile books on Indian history have come from the Indian academe. The major source continues to be foreign books and foreign writers.

No importance has been accorded to the study of history, languages, arts, archaeology and such subjects. There is no incentive or encouragement for students to take up those subjects.

Overwhelming majority therefore go in for graduation in engineering, medicine, law, finance, management and commerce. If incentives were provided and brilliant students took these subjects and did research the scene could change.

Take the condition of Sanskrit—unarguably the greatest and the most scientific language. It is becoming extinct. And unless you have mastery in Sanskrit and other older languages you can't do effective research in past Indian history. Wrote Will Durant, American historian and philosopher: "India was the motherland of our race, and Sanskrit the mother of Europe's languages: she was the mother of our philosophy; mother, through the Arabs, of much of our mathematics; mother, through the Buddha, of the ideals embodied in Christianity; mother, through the village community, of self-government and democracy. Mother India is in many ways the mother of us all."

Reportedly, those who have genuine interest in working on the Indian past now go to certain reputed universities in the US, who not only have a rich collection of relevant books, but also have faculty proficient in Sanskrit! So, to research India, go abroad!! This is what India has been reduced to, thanks to the ill-informed policies of Nehru-Indira Dynasty.

In the connection, the comments of Gurcharan Das are worth noting:

> "...an Indian who seriously wants to study the classics of Sanskrit or ancient regional languages will have to go abroad. 'If Indian education and scholarship continue along their current trajectory,' writes Sheldon Pollock, the brilliant professor of Sanskrit at Columbia University, 'the number of citizens capable of reading and understanding the texts and documents of the classical era will very soon approach a statistical zero. India is about to become the only major world culture whose literary patrimony, and indeed history, are in the hands of scholars outside the country.' This is extraordinary in a country with dozens of Sanskrit departments in all major Indian universities..."

"The ugly truth is that the quality of teaching in these institutions is so poor that not a single graduate is able to think seriously about the past and critically examine ancient texts... Where is India's soft power when there are fewer and fewer Indians capable of interrogating the texts of Kalidasa or the edicts of Ashoka?... To be worthy of being Indian does not mean to stop speaking in English. It means to be able to have an organic connection with our many rich linguistic pasts... What separates man from beast is memory and if we lose historical memory then we surrender it to those who those who will abuse it."

In sharp contrast to India, it is admirable what Israel did. Upon formation of Israel in 1948, many Jews scattered all over the world came over. They spoke different languages. To ensure a unifying language, many linguists, backed by the State, set about reviving Hebrew, Israel's ancient language, which had fallen in decrepitude. Now, all Israelis speaks Hebrew. It has given them an identity, and has greatly helped unify Israel. Most also know English, as it is taught from the primary school itself.

Sanskrit, the most scientific language, and the mother of many Indian and European languages, could have been simplified and modernized, and taught in all schools, in addition to English. It would have revitalized Indian, and helped unify it.

THE ENGLISH LANGUAGE ARISTOCRACY

The Brown sahibs managed to create an "English Language Aristocracy" after independence. How to corner good positions, jobs and privileges? Make them conditional upon knowledge of English. Restrict English to chosen schools and colleges, and restrict access to those institutions to only the privileged.

Nehru wanted to carry on with the language he was comfortable in. One doubts if he cared for things Indian and Indian languages or culture. Writes Nirad Chaudhuri in his Autobiography of an Unknown Indian, Part-II: "Nehru was completely out of touch with the Indian life even of his time, except with the life of the self-segregating Anglicised set of upper India who lived in the so-called Civil Lines." Chaudhury says that Nehru had little understanding of the actual India life or culture or of Hinduism; and was a snob, contemptuous of those who spoke English with an Indian accent.

Back in the fifties and early sixties, there were dozens of primary, middle and higher secondary schools run by Bhilai Steel Plant [BSP] authorities, where children of BSP employees studied. Out of those dozens of schools, only a few were EMS (English Medium Schools), the rest being HMS (Hindi Medium Schools). By and large, children of BSP officials in higher grades studied in EMS, and the others in HMS. EMS were accorded more importance and were given better facilities. The culture had become such that the students of EMS were regarded by others, and regarded themselves, as superior, and there was clear favouritism shown to them. You could even notice principals and teachers being partial and indulgent towards those in EMS.

So the special status and injustice began at the root itself—in schools! And, the concept, the class-consciousness and segregation into EMTs (English Medium Types) and HMTs (Hindi Medium Types) started from the primary school itself. Now, one is certainly not against English. Rather, Nehru and his team should have made English compulsory for all, and should have pumped in money to ensure that there were facilities available in all schools to teach English. With all children knowing English, the "English Language Aristocracy" would have been dead.

VIP AND VVIP : THAT STRANGE INDIAN ANIMAL

A foreigner visiting a government office asked, "Are there three sexes in your country?" His Indian companion looked at him baffled, wondering what to make of it. The foreigner helpfully added, "I notice three toilets: Men, Women and VIPs!" In a discussion on TV, a senior IAS lady was heard justifying separate, special toilets for "officers": people don't know how to use toilets, they make them so dirty! Just goes to show the extent to which the politicians and bureaucrats have managed to keep India and Indians they are expected to serve so pathetic, like the British before them did, that they, like the British, need segregation to carry on. Even taking that silly, bloated IAS lady at her face value, what about the many who have clean toilet habits but are not "officers"? And, what about the officers who have dirty toilet habits? We are still afflicted with a colonial mindset; and given the predominance of officers like that lady IAS, India is not likely to see better days.

The Indian Government under Nehru represented in many respects a continuation of British attitudes, both in form and in substance. Indians, even after the British left, were confronted with the same civil servants, and the same policemen who treated them with the same scorn, arrogance and brutality, and the same master-slave attitude, as under British rule.

Rather than his master's simplicity, Nehru adopted ostentatious Viceroy-like trappings. After Independence, Gandhiji had suggested that the Governor-General of free India should stay in a modest accommodation, rather than in the huge and imposing Viceroy palace (later named as *Rashtrapati Bhavan*) which should be converted into a public hospital. Mountbatten had also not disagreed, and Gandhi appreciated that. But Nehru advised that an alternate suitable accommodation was not available! The place next in stateliness and grandeur to the Viceroy palace was the residence of the British Commander-in-Chief, then called Flagstaff House. Leaving his York Road residence, Nehru occupied this magnificent house, which was later renamed as Teen Murti Bhavan. Others followed Nehru's example, occupying huge, spacious bungalows. British had deliberately designed these palaces and bungalows to intimidate the natives, appear remote, and command respect. What was the logic of the leaders of free India to follow in their footsteps?

Here is an example of the Nehru-Indira times from Bhilai Steel Plant [BSP]—a public sector. There were many hospitals in Bhilai run by BSP, and also a main hospital with all facilities. The hospital timings were at 8 am onwards. Patients would try to be there as early as possible so that their turn could come early—especially the employees who had to go to office in the general shift by 10 am or 11 am; and the students who had to attend schools. If you reached there at 8 am, there would already be a long queue, and your turn might come at noon or beyond. So, most tried to be there as early as possible. However, employees belonging to higher grades and their spouses, sons and daughters had a preferential treatment: the first half-hour to one hour after 8 am was reserved for them. They had a separate queue, which was always small, as they belonged to a smaller, upper echelon. So, even if they arrived at 8.30 am they could see the doctor in the next 15 to 30 minutes. The others, even if they came at 6 am, would sometimes wait till 1 pm to see the doctor, if the queue was long, which was often the case. This patently unfair and unjust system went on for decades, and may still be prevalent! Mind you, such practices started in the fifties during the Nehru period, and continued through the Indira period. What does it tell about the "socialism" of Nehru and the pro-poor propaganda of Indira and her descendents.

VIP-area, VIP-security, VIP-red-beacon lights on vehicles to let VIP car pass even as hundreds are inconvenienced, VIP passes and VIP queues even in temples to let VIPs have darshan while thousands patiently wait: what does this all represent? A gross insult to the public at large. A slap on the face of common man. A feudal culture. Why should public, on whose money these politicians and bureaucrats have been fattening themselves, suffer and get humiliated by these servants-turned-masters? After independence, and after displacing the British and over 500 rajas and maharajas from their princely states, we have not become democratic, we have become even more feudal. It's a Nehru-Indira Dynasty culture of snootiness.

Like against corruption, there ought to be a widespread civil-society agitation to abolish this obnoxious and humiliating VIP culture.

Writes Inder Malhotra in his article, "Very Indian Phenomenon" [VIP], in *The Indian Express* of 21 July 2012: "... the 'common person' [in USA] doesn't give a damn about VIPs. Here, of course, the situation is hugely different. The VIP status is flaunted in the face of countless millions every day, round the clock and round the calendar. You don't have to spell out the word; everyone knows what it means. In sharp contrast to what prevails in the US, the super-wealthy in India don't need to proclaim themselves VIPs. They get whatever they want without saying a word. The whole system seems geared to their needs and wishes. The odd tycoon who gets caught on the wrong side of the law lives in jail in greater luxury than five-star hotels can provide. It is the political class, the army of bureaucrats...that form the bedrock of the VIP cult and the perks and privileges that go with it. Like much else, the VIP is a legacy of the British

Raj. Independent India has not only embraced it with gusto but also expanded it vastly...English class system and India's deathless caste system must have rubbed off on each other to produce the wonder that is the Indian VIP...Indian scene had added to the woes of the helpless non-VIPs in direct proportion to the burgeoning privileges and pampering of those more equal than the rest...."

DISTORTIONS OF HISTORY

There has been little genuine work in Indian history after independence. No worthwhile books on Indian history come from the Indian academe. Those that have been authored by the so-called "reputed" or "eminent" Indian historians are generally insipid, superficial, wanting in serious research and lacking in insight. Going by the contents of their works, the use of the adjectives "great" or "outstanding" or "eminent" for them is highly inappropriate. The major source therefore continues to be foreign books and foreign writers—so sad!

Things have been so manipulated over the last two centuries that anything Indian has been shown in bad light, and anything English as something superior. And it has been so skilfully done that foreigners or English do not have to do it anymore, it is the Indians themselves who have become self-abusive, and appreciators of all things English or Western.

Part of the reason is that the economy did so badly under the Nehru-Gandhis and India became so pathetic that people felt there was something intrinsically deficient about India and the Indians. Rather than realising that the Indian misery was thanks to Nehru-Indira-Dynasty misgovernance and their poverty-perpetuating-but-vote-getting socialistic-claptrap, people began to blame India and the Indians themselves. Had India done well after independence, the impression would have been diametrically opposite.

If you have to exploit nations and subjugate its people on a long-term basis—for decades and centuries—you can't do it by brute force alone. You have to shake the confidence of people in themselves. You have to make them feel they are nothing—and that they were nothing—before the aggressors. To this end you have to rewrite and reinterpret their history, religion and culture to show how worthless it is in comparison to that of the exploiter. This is what the British politicians, bureaucrats, army-men, writers and historians did.

You say what you read, and are taught and told. Many books were written by the English and other foreigners like Max Mueller, a German, parts of which were either incorrect, on account of limited or deficient research, or deliberately biased and false to serve the imperial or the religious interest. In the absence of books depicting correct position, these books came to be read widely, and some of them became text-books too. You have been taught and told what the English and the Christians desired and manufactured to serve their interests. You came to believe it. So did others—people abroad in other countries also read these books. Down the generations all started believing the lies as truth.

Many Indian writers too based much of their contents on these books written by foreigners, rather than on new research. So, the writings of the Indian authors also started suffering from the same deficiencies.

After independence, one of the tasks should have been to provide all possible academic encouragement, financial help, incentives, ample opportunities, and rewarding career for collection and compilation of all available source materials, engaging in intensive research, and writing of history and social and economic life of India through the ages in as unbiased a manner as possible, pointing out of flaws and gaps and errors in the existing historical works, and supplementing them; and making available the new researched material and the corrected works in various forms: detailed, academic work, for further research; textbooks for schools and colleges; books for general reading in an interesting form; and illustrated books for children. Historical fiction too should have been encouraged: we need quality books like that from Amitav Ghosh.

Rather than doing the above, the concerned establishments came to be dominated by the leftists, Nehruvians and self-seekers who vitiated all research and writings; and by babus, who bureaucratised the academics and ensured emasculation of the direction to what suited the ideas and the convenience of the Establishment. ICHR, NCERT and other government agencies supported and promoted only those who toed the ill-conceived official line, even if they were substandard as scholars. As a result, what we have been having are political hangers-on rather than capable scholars. They have made no significant contributions, yet they have survived because of their monopoly hold over the establishment. Several have engaged in even creative rewriting of history!

If the British came across something remarkable, which showed India far ahead of the West in the past, they "discovered" its link with the West. If there was something very distinguished about the Aryans, well, they came from the West—India was subject to Aryan invasion and so on. There have been many research-findings and writings to the contrary since, and yet that false impression is allowed to continue in India even today. Apart from further archaeological revelations, an inter-continental research in cellular molecular biology has debunked the Aryan invasion theory. Of course, there is no last word on such things, but there are good reasons to believe that both the so-called Aryans and the Dravidians belonged to India only, and did not come from outside. When that racist theory was propagated, there were many takers for it among the educated Indians themselves, for they felt it enhanced their status—they were not the wretched "natives", their ancestors came from the West! Such was the level of inferiority complex, thanks to successful British propaganda!

Even Mahatma Gandhi, during his South African days, pleaded with the British authorities there that the Indians be treated on par with the British, and not like the native South Africans, for Indians too after all belonged to the superior race, the Aryans—from the West!

See the cunning of the British. They then propounded the theory of Aryans vs. the local Dravidians. Why? Several self-serving reasons. It helped create divisions—North vs. South—among Indians, vestiges of which are still there. It helped them show that if there was something superior about the Aryans, it was because they came from the West. It also helped them show that India had been ruled by different groups who came from the West. First, the Aryans, then the Muslims, and then the British. If British were foreigners then so too were Muslims and Aryans. So why crib about foreign rule, that is, their rule—especially, when they had come only to "civilise" the natives and do good for the country!

One can understand the purpose and the motivation of the British and other foreigners; but for Indians to talk like them—that's grossly illiterate, slavish and strange!

"DISCOVERY OF INDIA" THANKS TO BRITISH

It is pointed out that look, Indians were so backward they didn't maintain any history or records. Whatever has been "discovered" about India, it is thanks to the British!

If indeed that was so, how come Nalanda library reportedly burned for six months after it was set ablaze by the Turkic Muslim invaders under Bakhtiyar Khilji in 1193—what burned there were thousands of precious books. The invaders destroyed India's inheritance and books. A few books that remained were what individuals could preserve with them.

If indeed people have an iota of analytical ability and rationality they would appreciate that India remained a conquered nation and a hostage to foreign aggressors for about a millennium, and that slavery ended only about six decades back with the departure of the British. During that millennium not only was India's wealth looted, its economy shattered, its people impoverished, its cultural and religious symbols and temples destroyed, but its wealth of knowledge and its books were also destroyed.

Old historical records could not have been protected and preserved, and new ones during the last millennium could not have been written and maintained, because Indians were not in control. It requires finance, peace and independence to do the job—none of which was there.

To understand this, take Sri Lanka. It has one of the longest documented histories of over 3000 years, thanks to the Buddhists who recorded it in Mahavansa and Dipavamsa. Buddhists went to Sri Lanka from India only. You think they would not have maintained all the records in India? Only, it got destroyed with the burning of Nalanda and other places by the aggressors. And, Buddhists emerged from the Hindu stock, who too maintained records and wrote great books.

It is just that using the power they wielded and the large finance that they had at their command—looted from India only—that the British "researchers" could command services of the many knowledgeable Indians and appropriate all the credit for the "discoveries"—as if what they "discovered" was not known to many Indians.

Here is what Patrick French wrote in his review of Charles Allen's book, in the *Hindustan Times* of 21 April 2012: "From the middle of the 18th century, the East India Company controlled most of the subcontinent—by force... Early Buddhist statues were thrown into a river to make a breakwater, pillars were pulverised by military engineers, carved stone slabs burnt for lime and ancient inscriptions cracked out by glory-hunting, hammer-wielding colonial officers. A handful of Europeans preferred to study these objects rather than destroy them. Although Indians were central to the process of discovery, they were excluded from even the most basic recognition... When the British first came to India, countless indigenous priests and scholars read Sanskrit. Along comes 'amiable, gentlemanly and well connected Dr Wilson'—and our author labels him 'the leading Sanskritist of the age'. If a European collects old scriptures, he is judged to be pursuing 'a quite breathtaking range of intellectual pursuits'. When an Indian academic is mentioned, he is dismissed as a 'native clerk'... Since important positions were open only to Europeans, the 'clerks' would often find newly-arrived white men in their 20s taking credit for many years of their own research... The colonial Orientalists were often monomaniacs, obsessed with trying to prove links between Indian culture and ancient Greece—stemming from the assumption that anything important in the subcontinent must have come from the West rather than from the East. As they gradually pieced together a more accurate historical account, they depended on finding documents that had never really gone missing: it was rather that the sources had never been made available in translation in an accessible language."

While Nehruvian revisionists keep painting their distorted picture, here is what a foreigner, Peter Watson, writes in *Ideas: A History from Fire to Freud*: "In the year AD 499 the Hindu mathematician Aryabhata calculated pi as 3.1416 and the length of the solar year as 365.358 days. At much the same time he conceived the idea that the earth was a sphere spinning on its own axis and revolving around the sun. He thought that the shadows of the earth falling on the moon caused eclipses. One wonders what all the fuss was about when Copernicus 'discovered' some of the above nearly a thousand years later. Indian thought in the Middle Ages was in several areas far ahead of European ideas. Buddhist monasteries in the India of the time were so well endowed that they acted as banks, investing surplus funds in commercial enterprises. Such details as these explain why historians refer to the reunification of north India under the Guptas (c. 320-550) as a golden era. Their dynasty, combined with that of Harsha Vardhana (606-47), comprises what is now regarded as India's classical age. Besides the advancement of mathematics, it saw the emergence of Sanskrit literature..."

GLIMPSES OF DISTORTIONS OF HISTORY

There have been distortions of Indian history across the board—starting from "The Aryan Invasion" and ending with the British Rule; and even in the history of the independence movement. Post-independence too!

For a glimpse, let's look at distortions related to the history of Somnath Temple. It is on the shore of the Arabian sea in the coastal town of Somnath at *Prabhaspatan* near Veraval in Junagadh district in Kathiawar in the Saurashtra region of Gujarat. It is 6 km from Veraval, and 80 km from Junagadh. It is the most sacred of the twelve *Aadi Jyotirlings*. Somnath means "The Protector of Moon God". A legend in Skandpurana describes how this Jyotirlinga emerged. Somraj built the temple and dedicated it to Someshwara—another name of Shiv, with moon on his head. The temple is said to have been first built sometime before the common era—BCE.

It was rebuilt each of the six times it was destroyed and looted: by Junayad, the Arab governor of Sind, in 725 CE; by Mahmud of Ghazni in 1024 CE; by Sultan Allauddin Khilji in 1296 CE; by Muzaffar Shah I, the Sultan of Gujarat, in 1375 CE; by Mahmud Begda, the Sultan of Gujarat in 1451 CE; and by Aurangzeb in 1701 CE.

Mahmud of Ghazni destroyed the temple in 1024 CE in his sixteenth of the seventeen raids into India over a period of about 30 years, and carried away camel-loads of jewels and gold. It is said that Mahmud personally hammered the temple's gilded idol to pieces and carted it to Ghazni where they were incorporated into the steps of the city's new Jamiah Masjid [Friday mosque]. Thousands of defenders were massacred, including one Ghogha Rana, who had challenged Mahmud at the ripe old age of 90.

Wrote Zakariya al-Qazwini, a 13th-century Arab geographer: "Somnath: celebrated city of India, situated on the shore of the sea, and washed by its waves. Among the wonders of that place was the temple in which was placed the idol called Somnath. This idol was in the middle of the temple without anything to support it from below, or to suspend it from above. It was held in the highest honour among the Hindus, and whoever beheld it floating in the air was struck with amazement, whether he was a Musulman or an infidel. The Hindus used to go on pilgrimage to it whenever there was an eclipse of the moon, and would then assemble there to the number of more than a hundred thousand... When the Sultan Yaminu-d Daula Mahmud Bin Subuktigin [Mahmud of Ghazni, who was son of Subuktigin] went to wage religious war against India, he made great efforts to capture and destroy Somnath, in the hope that the Hindus would then become Muhammadans. As a result thousands of Hindus were converted to Islam. He arrived there in the middle of Zi-l k'ada, 416 A.H. [December, 1025 CE]... The king looked upon the idol with wonder, and gave orders for the seizing of the spoil, and the appropriation of the treasures. There were many idols of gold and silver and vessels set with jewels..."

However, our own historian Nehru writes in *The Discovery of India* in Chapter 6: "New Problems" under sub-section "Mahmud of Ghazni and the Afghans": "He met with...on his way back from Somnath in Kathiawar." That's all. There is nothing more on Somnath! But, of course, what the "historian" totally omitted in his *Discovery of India*, he did mention partially in his other book which he wrote ten years earlier in 1935—*Glimses of World History*. In Chapter 51: "From Harsha to Mahmud in North India", he wrote, "But it was in Somnath that he got the most treasure..." He further wrote, "He is looked upon as a great leader of Islam who came to spread Islam in India. Most Muslims adore him; most Hindus hate him. As a matter of fact, he was hardly a religious man. He was a Mohammedan, of course, but that was by the way. Above everything he was soldier, and a brilliant soldier. He came to India to conquer and loot, as soldiers unfortunately do, and he would have done so to whatever religion he might have belonged... We must therefore not fall into the common error of considering Mahmud as anything more than a successful soldier."

However, the writings of Mahmud's period themselves, which are obviously more authentic, belie Nehru's concoction. As per them, when Mahmud of Ghazni was carrying away the Shiva idol of gold from the Somnath temple, many rich traders came together and offered him even more wealth if he returned the idol. Mahmud's retort was: "I am an idol-breaker, not an idol-seller!"

Nehru further wrote in *The Discovery of India*: "Mahmud [of Ghazni] was far more a warrior than a man of faith..." Then about Mathura, he wrote, "Mahmud was anxious to make his own city of Ghazni rival the great cities of central and western Asia and he carried off from India large number of artisans and master builders. Building interested him and he was much impressed by the city of Mathura near Delhi. About this Mahmud wrote: 'There are here a thousand edifices as firm as the faith of the faithful; nor is it likely that this city has attained its present condition but at the expense of many millions of dinars, nor could such another be constructed under a period of 200 years.'"

What is interesting is that nowhere there is any mention by Nehru of how that Mahmud, the lover of buildings as he called him, mercilessly destroyed Mathura and Somnath! Wrote Al Utbi, an aide and secretary of Mahmud of Ghazni, in *Tarikh-e* Yamini: "The Sultan gave orders that all the temples should be burnt with naphtha and fire and levelled with the ground." Utbi wrote that Mahmud first wanted to go to Sijistan, but subsequently changed his mind for "a holy war against Hind", and details how Sultan "purified Hind from idolatry and raised mosques". He also states that the "Musulmans paid no regard to the booty till they had satiated themselves with the slaughter of the infidels and worshippers of the sun and fire."

In Tabakat-I Nasiri, Minhaju-s Siraj hails Mahmud for "converting as many as a thousand idol-temples into mosques", and calls him "one of the greatest champions of Islam". It is not for nothing that Pakistani name their missiles Ghazni and Ghori.

Nehru wrote: "Of the Indians, Alberuni says that they 'are haughty, foolishly vain, self-contained, and stolid,'... Probably a correct enough description of the temper of the people." Nehru is fine with anything negative about Indians, but has little negative to comment on the massive destruction wrought, and the wrecker. Nehru further quotes Alberuni writing about the havoc caused by Mahmud, "The Hindus became like the atoms of dust scattered in all directions and like a tale of old in the mouths of people. Their scattered remains cherish of course the most inveterate aversion towards all Muslims." Nehru then comments, "This poetic description gives us an idea..." So, Nehru found this description of Indian misfortune poetic!

Incidentally, Alberuni had travelled to India with Mahmud of Ghazni during the first half of the eleventh century CE. The book *Alberuni's India* is Alberuni's written work on India, translated by Dr Edward C. Sachau. In it, Alberuni writes: "This prince [Sabuktagin] chose the holy war as his calling, and therefore called himself Al-ghazi (i.e. warring on the road of Allah)... afterwards his son Yamin-addaula Mahmud marched into India during a period of thirty years or more. God be merciful to both father and son! Mahmud [of Ghazni] utterly ruined the prosperity of the country [India], and performed there wonderful exploits, by which the Hindus became like atoms of dust scattered in all directions, and like a tale of old in the mouth of the people..."

If you re-read what Nehru quoted from Alberuni (given above earlier), and what is quoted above from Alberuni's book itself, you would find it interesting what Nehru chooses to quote and what he chooses to ignore. Said Samuel Butler, "[Even] God cannot alter the past, but historians can!"

To resume, after the temple was destroyed by Aurangzeb in 1701 CE, it was rebuilt, not at the original site, which was converted to a mosque, but at an adjacent site in 1783 CE by a group comprising Peshwa of Pune, Bhonsle of Nagpur, Chhatrapati Bhonsle of Kolhapur, Ahilyabai Holkar of Indore and Shrimant Patilbuwa Shinde of Gwalior.

The temple was last rebuilt soon after independence at the instance of Sardar Patel and others, notably KM Munshi. Gandhiji had blessed the move, and as per his advice, the reconstruction was funded, not by the state, but by collections from the public. The ruins were pulled down in 1950 and the mosque present at that site was shifted a few miles away. Dr Rajendra Prasad, the first President of India, installed the Jyotirling in it in 1951. It was finally completed in 1995 by Shree Somnath Trust. Nehru had opposed the move to reconstruct the temple. For him, it was Hindu revivalism! But, he could not do anything about it, because it was rebuilt without taking funds from the government.

~~~

Talking about distortions in writing of Indian history, it is unwise to try and mould history to suit one's ideological bend or bias, or for political or religious or social or cultural purposes. Truth should not be fiddled with. People should not be taken for granted or taken for fools—like Nehru thought, or Nehruvian-leftist-Marxist historians or the rightists or the fundamentalists think—that they would believe the junk written. There has to be professionalism in writing of history. If history is painful or unpalatable, so be it. It is better to know the truth, whether it is good or bad, palatable or obnoxious. People must learn to face the truth, and learn from history.
~~~

It is actually a misunderstanding of what the history-writing is all about, and silly, immature notions of "what is good for the people", and an arrogance that "I know better what people should know" that leads to writing of creative history. It is actually a socialistic-communistic-authoritarian trait, a characteristic chillingly depicted in "1984".

For example, Mahmud of Ghazni did what he did thinking he was doing a good religious act. Whether you now think it otherwise, being an atheist or agnostic or liberal or of other religion, is irrelevant. At the time Mahmud did it, he and his people indeed thought he was engaging in a holy, religious Islamic act. Even the Islamic writers of that time credited him so: Alberuni, for example. Who are we to hide that fact now, thinking it is unpalatable, and give a twist to it, like (Nehru did) "however bad, it was just the act of a soldier—totally non-religious." By doing so, we are actually trying to establish that Mahmud was just a greedy invader out to enrich himself; when he himself and people of his times thought he was doing a good act—that he was on a holy, religious mission! Evidently, Mahmud was not interested in booty and killing alone.

What happened centuries ago is no reflection on people now. Notions have changed. You insult people by twisting the facts. If Hindu kings did something atrocious in the past, does it mean it should be swept under the carpet, lest it should hurt the Hindus. Christians engaged in terrible atrocities during their campaigns of conversion, inquisitions and colonisation. Do they now sweep it under the carpet? No. There have been mountains of books from the West detailing the atrocities committed. Germans teach their children on Nazi atrocities. Truth must be known. Then only can one come to terms with the reality and ensure the mistakes are not repeated in the future.

You had *The Truth and Reconciliation Commission (TRC)* in South Africa after the abolition of apartheid to let the truth out and allow for reconciliation and healing.

Would we erase the facts of anti-Sikh attacks of 1984, communal flare ups, Godhra train burning, post-Godhra riots, happenings in Assam and the Northeast, and so on, driven by the philosophy of allowing only "proper" history!

Here in India, you distort or partially erase the ancient, the medieval, the modern, and also the recent history for various reasons—silly, ideological or political. You won't let historians, journalists, researchers and those interested have access to all the documents related to the mystery of the disappearance of Subhas Bose, or the India-China War, or the Shimla Agreement of 1972 with Pakistan, and so on, and yet expect a correct history to be written.

THE ORIGIN OF CORRUPTION

With no proper historical education imparted, thanks to our deficient writing of history textbooks, there are ignoramuses who, lamenting the current corruption in India, talk of how things have degenerated after the British left!

They are not aware that it were the British who imported large-scale corruption into India. The British East India Company [EIC], their employees, bureaucrats, army-men, ICS personnel did not come to India for charity. From their angle, it was a relatively difficult environment, with hot weather conditions. They came here to make as much money in as short a time as possible, and then live happily thereafter back in Britain. They lost no opportunity to make money. They also acted very cruelly. EIC, and later the British Government, wanted to extract as much revenue from India as possible. The main occupation of the people being agriculture, that was the main source of revenue. They levied back-breaking revenues and extracted it even during famines by any means possible. That's what they were getting paid for. Which is why the ICS guys were called collectors—collectors of revenue, rather extractors of revenue. In pursuit of higher and higher revenues, they changed the established systems and wrecked te Indian agriculture and the Indian economy.

Yet, thanks to misinformation, not rectified even by independent India, the rogues are recalled with respect and admiration.

Robert Clive's salary when he came to India in 1744 was £5 per year, and an additional allowance of £3 per year, a total of £8 per year. However, he returned to England in 1760 with a huge fortune: £2,34,000 plus £27,000 per year for life from rental income from what was called Clive's Jagir, a piece of land in Calcutta. If we assume modest living for Clive at the start of his career in India, he must be getting at least ₹ 20,000 per month by today's standards, that is, ₹ 2,40,000 a year. That means, the £8 a year that he was getting was at least equivalent to ₹ 2,40,000 a year now. He, therefore, returned to England with a fortune of £ 2,34,000, that is, (£2,34,000/£8)*₹ 2,40,000, which is ₹ 7,020,000,000, that is ₹ 7.02 billion, that is, ₹ 702 crores! Plus ₹ 81 crores as annual rental per year!! He was again in India between 1764 and 1767. Upon his return, corruption charges were brought against him. Defending himself, he actually pleaded to the effect as to how much less he had looted compared to the opportunities he had: "...I walked through vaults which were thrown open to me alone, piled on either hand with gold and jewels! By God, Mr. Chairman, at this moment I stand astonished at my own moderation!" Clive is a shining example for our corrupt politicians and bureaucrats of today.

Warren Hastings, the Governor-General of India between 1788 and 1795 was impeached for mismanagement and personal corruption. Edmund Burke, author, statesman, political theorist and philosopher, said this about him: "...Unbelievable, it is a horrid sight to see one of my own kind to treat other human beings as insignificant. The East India Company located in India controlled by Warren Hastings is a place so horrid that even I doubt my own two eyes. Warren Hasting has committed high crimes and misdemeanours in India. He has taken advantage as his position of governor to extort bribes from native rulers, abuse judicial authority, despotism, and arbitrary rule..."

THE WRECKERS OF INDIAN ECONOMY

It is said and even believed that it was thanks to the British that India prospered. One has even heard people saying that the things were better during the English times. People are not even aware what was the economic status of India before the English came, and what became of it later.

Why did English, or French, or Portuguese came to India in the first place? Writes Alex Von Tunzelmann about the 17th-century India in the first paragraph of the first chapter of her book *Indian Summer: The Secret History of the End of an Empire*: "In the beginning, there were two nations. One was a vast, mighty and magnificent empire, brilliantly organized and culturally unified, which dominated a massive swathe of earth. The other was an undeveloped, semi-feudal realm, riven by religious factionalism and barely able to feed its illiterate, diseased and stinking masses. The first was India. The second was England." *That is, England was miserable compared to India*!

Francois Bernier (1625-88) was a French physician and traveller in the seventeenth century. He travelled in Bengal extensively. In his book *Travels in the Mogul Empire*, he writes:

"[Bengal] produces rice in such abundance that its supplies not only the neighbouring but remote states. It is carried up the Ganges as far as Patna, and exported by sea to Masulipatam and many other ports on the coast of Coromonclel. It is also sent to foreign kingdoms, principally to the island of Ceylon and the Maldives. Bengal abounds likewise in sugar with which it supplies the kingdoms of Golconda and the Carnatic, Arabia and Mesopotamia, through the towns of Mokha and Bassora, and even Persia, by way of Bender-Abbassy...

"Bengal, it is true, yields not so much wheat as Egypt; but if this be a defect, it is attributable to the inhabitants, who live a great deal more upon rice than the Egyptians, and seldom taste bread. Nevertheless, wheat is cultivated in sufficient quantity for the consumption of the country, and for the making of excellent and cheap sea biscuits, with which the crews of European ships, English, Dutch and Portuguese, are supplied. The three or four sorts of vegetables which, together with rice and butter, form the chief aliment of the common people, are purchased for the merest trifle, and for a single rupee twenty or more good fowls may be bought. Geese and ducks are proportion ably cheap. There are also goats and sheep in abundance; and pigs are obtained at so low a price that the Portuguese, settled in the country, live almost entirely upon pork. This meat is salted at a cheap rate by the Dutch and English, for the supply of their respective vessels. Fish of every species, whether fresh or salt, is in the same profusion.

"In a word, Bengal abounds with every necessary of life; and it is this abundance that has induced so many Portuguese, half-casts, and other Christians, driven from their different settlements by the Dutch, to seek an asylum in this fertile kingdom.

"...the rich exuberance of the country, together with the beauty and amiable disposition of the native women, has given rise to a proverb in common among the Portuguese, English and Dutch—the Kingdom of Bengale has a hundred gates to open for entrance, but not one for departure".

That is, outsiders were keen to come in, but having come, none ever wanted to depart, so prosperous was India!

Writes Madhusree Mukerjee in *Churchill's Secret War : The British Empire and the Ravaging of India during World War II*: "...But before 1757, when General Robert Clive founded the British Empire by conquering Bengal, it was one of the richest parts of the world: 'the paradise of the earth,' as Clive himself described it..."

However, the British so wrecked the economy and engaged in loot that within mere 13 years of the their rule, Bengal faced famine of 1770—something which had never occurred earlier! Not until the famine broke out did people in Britain realise the reason of the extraordinary profits of East India Co.

Clive had become one of the richest persons in UK, thanks to his Indian plunder. He was later booked for corruption, and ultimately committed suicide in 1774.

Later, Warren Hastings came as the first Governor-General of India. To make up for the lost revenues of Bengal, he subjugated the nearby prosperous kingdom of Oudh, and began extracting punishing revenues from there. Thanks to the British, like it happened in Bengal in 1770, Oudh then faced famine in 1784! And people talk of prosperity under the British!!

In fact, the famines started with the British! That was because they wrecked the rural economy through unwarranted changes for extracting maximum revenue.

As per an estimate by Angus Maddison, a Cambridge University historian, "India's share of the world income fell from 22.6% in 1700, comparable to Europe's share of 23.3%, to a low of 3.8% in 1952."

So, this is how India was before the English came. Just imagine how much better it must have been before even the north and the west Asians came in the wake of Mahmud Ghaznavi in the 11th century and carried out large-scale destruction. India had been subject to a millennium of loot and subjugation.

Wrote Arvind Kumar in *DNA* of August 13, 2012 in his article, "How British socialism created poverty and caste inequality": "The role of British policies in the destruction of India's economy was well known in the nineteenth century, but this angle has been ignored in recent times. These policies caused widespread poverty and created caste inequality in the country. The castes were similar to the economic guilds of medieval Europe and thrived until their occupations were destroyed by the British. The Banias formed the trading guilds and suffered when trading activities were taken over by the British. The Shudras who formed the manufacturing guilds suffered when the British systematically destroyed the manufacturing sector. Kshatriyas lost their livelihoods when they were disarmed. Only the Brahmins could get measly clerical posts as their traditional focus on education was made the prerequisite for such jobs."

Warren Hastings was impeached in UK, and was accused, among other things, of venality and brutality in forcible collection of revenues by Edmund Burke. It was the British policy of capturing all the trade, destroying the indigenous industry, and extracting as much as possible, from as many as possible, and in as short a time as possible, to make maximum gains that India went from one of the most prosperous countries to a basket case.

And look at the venality and cunningness of the British. Rather than laying the blame on their own disastrous policies, they started painting India as a country which had always been poor and gone case—the reason being that its people were lazy, divided, illiterate, and had a backward religion. That English had come not to exploit, but to uplift Indians.

This lie was propagated so well through books, newspapers, "research", teachings in school and colleges through the decades that even many Indians began to believe it.

British never did any industrialisation worth the name. Even the licenses that they gave for setting up of steel plant by Tata or textile mills by private Indian entrepreneurs, they did most reluctantly.

Little was done by Nehru and little has been done since to educate the people on these important aspects of our history.

BRITISH GIFT TO INDIA : A SERIES OF FAMINES

British Record : Effectively Far Worse than the Nazis

Thanks to the British plunder, callousness, indifference and cruelty, and their gross misgovernance and mismanagement, India. which had been a land of abundance and had not known famines, began to suffer huge recurring famines. The (1) Great Bengal Famine of 1769-70 affecting Bihar and Bengal; (2) the famine of 1782-84 in Madras, Mysore, Delhi and Punjab; (3) the famine of 1791-92 in Hyderabad, Southern Maratha country, Deccan, Gujarat, and Marwar; (4) the Agra famine of 1837-38; (5) the Orissa famine of 1866; (6) the Rajputana famine of 1869; (7) the Great Famine of 1876-78 in Madras and Bombay regions; (8) the Bengal famine of 1943 caused deaths totalling respectively 10, 11, 11, 0.80, 1, 1.50, 5.25 and 3 million.

That's a mind-boggling figure of 43.55 million deaths in famines. Compare this with the estimate of Holocaust victims at about six million, and total World War II military deaths of all countries put together at about 25 million. When you consider this six million Holocaust victims with over seven times as many famine victims of the British cruelty, and the fact that the death through slow starvation is far more prolonged and painful than through gas-champers, you realise that the *British were effectively far, far worse than the Nazis*.

Writes Francois Gautier: "According to British records, one million Indians died of famine between 1800 and 1825, 4 million between 1825-1850, 5 million between 1850-1875 and 15 million between 1875-1900. Thus 25 million Indians died in 100 years! The British must be proud of their bloody record. It is probably more honourable and straightforward to kill in the name of Allah, than in the guise of petty commercial interests and total disregard for the ways of a 5000 year civilization.

Thus, by the beginning of the 20th century, India was bled dry and there were no resources left."

One British historian noted in 1901: "Time was, not more distant than a century and a half ago, when Bengal was much more wealthy than was Britain."

The Bengal Famine of 1943-44 was totally man-made, rather British-made, in which 3.5 million Indians perished. It exposed the callousness, total disregard for Indian life, cruelty beyond compare, and lamentable administrative incompetence of the British. Even as people were dying, food was exported from India abroad to feed the army engaged in World War II. When appraised of the Bengal Famine crisis, Prime Minister Winston Churchill cruelly commented that as far as he was concerned "the starvation of anyhow underfed Bengalis is less serious than..." and that Indians would anyway "breed like rabbits". In response to the telegraphic request from India for food shipment for famine, Churchill had heartlessly enquired if Gandhi still alive!

APOLOGY, REPARATIONS AND RETURN OF THE LOOTED ARTEFACTS

The US and Canada have apologised to the Red Indians. Australia did so to its aborigines. Deep remorse was expressed by the former Japanese PM Junichiro Koizumi for the conduct of the Japanese army in World War II in China and Korea. The Italian PM apologised to Libya in 2008 for the damage inflicted by Italy during the colonial era. France acknowledged the massacre of Algerians at Sétif in May 1945. German Government apologised for the massacre of ethnic Herero people of Namibia by German soldiers. Late Pope John Paul II expressed contrition about the Church's denunciation of Galileo, the Inquisition, the Religious Wars, Jews, women, and Blacks. President Bill Clinton apologised for the failure to act during the 1994 genocide in Rwanda. Danish PM apologised for the forced relocation of Inuit people in 1953.

In 1997, Tony Blair regretted British inaction during the Irish Potato Famine in the mid-nineteenth century. What about not one, but over a dozen severe famines in India under the British and their callous disregard for them?

One important thing that India needed to do post independence should have been to assess, document and put a financial estimate to the damages done by the British; quantify the loot of two centuries, convert them at 1947 prices, and then claim reparation from Britain, along with written and oral apology. Additionally, a detailed list of all the artefacts, archaeological pieces, precious stones such as Kohinoor and other items stolen from India should have been prepared and reclaimed from the British. However, with anglophiles in the saddle, nothing of the sort was done.

At the minimum, the Britain ought to compensate India with USD 2 trillion, that is, USD 2000 billion, at 10 billion USD for each year of the 200 years of torment.